Treating Couples in Crisis

Treating Couples in Crisis

Fundamentals and Practice in Marital Therapy

Robert L. Barker

THE FREE PRESS
A Division of Macmillan, Inc.
NEW YORK

Collier Macmillan Publishers
LONDON

The Free Press
A Division of Macmillan, Inc.
866 Third Avenue, New York, N. Y. 10022

Collier Macmillan Canada, Inc.

Printed in the United States of America

printing number

2 3 4 5 6 7 8 9 10

Library of Congress Cataloging in Publication Data

Barker, Robert L.
  Treating couples in crisis.

  Bibliography: p.
  Includes index.
  1. Marital psychotherapy.   I. Title.
RC488.5.B34   1984   616.89′156   83-25346
ISBN 0-02-901790-4

For Maggie

Contents

Preface and
Acknowledgments

Treating Couples in Crisis is intended as a primary textbook for students who plan to enter one of the psychotherapy or counseling fields and to include marital therapy among their skills. It is also intended for more experienced professionals who plan to add marital therapy to their repertoire of practice services. The book is essentially interdisciplinary since marital therapy, a field practiced by many professions, owes much of its richness to the involvement of so many different types of practitioners. It can be equally relevant to students and practitioners in the specialties of psychiatry, psychology, social work, the clergy, guidance and counseling, nursing, the law, education, and the social sciences. The reader is presumed to be familiar with the basic theoretical orientations and techniques generally used to counsel and treat individuals, but there is no presumption of experience in or knowledge about the field of marital therapy itself. As its subtitle suggests, the book emphasizes the fundamentals of the field rather than its more arcane and peripheral concerns. Its goal is to help provide a conceptual foundation upon which the reader can later build a more specialized and personal approach to the practice of marital therapy.

While my own theoretical orientation is psychosocial, with an emphasis on structural–functional social theory, I don't believe any of the newly emerging, increasingly contentious "schools" of marital therapy have a monopoly on "truth" or on the most effective techniques for helping troubled couples. I have considerable respect for the conceptualizations of the systems thinkers and for the techniques of the behaviorally oriented therapists, as well as for those of psychodynamic orientation. But the goal of this work is not to proselytize toward any one of these schools or orientations; it is to provide a comparative analysis of the various orientations and to show how therapists have used each of them. Toward that end, I have tried to offer an objective and balanced comparison of the variety of ways marital therapists practice and perceive their craft.

Just as I don't believe any one theoretical school has the only answer for marital therapists, I don't believe any one discipline is best suited to the demands of the field. My own professional identity is with social work, but I have always been impressed with the way marital therapy is enhanced by its input from so many professions. Marriage and its treatment are too complex, too encompassing of knowledge from the diversity of cultural, social, religious, legal, economic, biological, behavioral, and intrapsychic disciplines, to become the province of only one profession.

Members of many professions have been influential in the development of this book. They include my teachers at Columbia University, particularly Nathan Ackerman, Margaret Mead, Robert K. Merton, Florence Hollis, and Alfred J. Kahn. They also include writers and conceptualizers, especially Talcott Parsons, Robert F. Bales, David Olson, Salvador Minuchin, Carl Whitaker, and Virginia Satir. More directly, they include my longtime private practice partner, Karl D. Hawver, and my colleagues at Catholic University, especially Professors Sylvia Lee, Eleanor Krimmel, Stephen Preister, Dorothy Trevino, Mary Flynn, and Dean Joan Mullaney. They were generous with their ideas, research findings, critiques, helpful suggestions, and wisdom. Providing valuable editorial and word processing assistance were Susan Fago, Barbara Nickens, Rose Queen, and Janet Young. My editor at The Free Press, Joyce Seltzer, was the most influential of all. She helped conceive this project and design its format and focus, and provided considerable enthusiasm and encouragement. Also very helpful and supportive at The Free Press was George Rowland, who saw to it that the book was readable and coherent.

A final expression of gratitude goes to Margaret York, for providing a comfortable environment during the work on this book as well as insight, constructive suggestion, and editorial help. Most important, however, were her love, patience, and support, which were always there to remind me that marriage—like the effort to help it survive—is a worthwhile objective.

Treating Couples in Crisis

Chapter One

Whatever Happened to Marriage Counseling?

The role and function of the marital therapist are often ambiguous to couples in crisis. This is illustrated by the following dialogue:

"Hello. Marital Therapy Center. Dr. Jones speaking."

"Uhh . . . I need a marriage counselor. Fast. Is that what you are?"

"Yes, ma'am, I'm a marriage and family therapist. May I help you?"

"My husband and I need counseling. I think we're about to get a divorce. So we thought we'd shop around to see about getting help. But we don't want to go to, umh, just anyone. You really have to be careful nowadays."

"Yes, ma'am. That's always a good idea."

"I'm glad you don't feel offended, sir. I'd like to find out a few things about you before going any further. Okay?"

"Why yes, of course. That's very sensible. What would you like to ask?"

"Well, basically we want to know how good you are at marriage counseling. We have a lot at stake and we want the best possible help available. So could you tell me what your success rate is?"

"My success rate? I'm not sure I understand what . . ."

"Oh, you know, how many people stay married after they have seen you, and how many divorce? You know, your success rate . . . like your batting average."

"That's really a difficult question—success can be so many different things. Sometimes people stay married only because they are too insecure to part; even though they are unhappy in their marriages. When they are helped in marital therapy, they might gain the confidence to make the break. So if they divorce, that could be considered a success in marital therapy. Others might decide to remain married—not because they have come to feel happy in their relationship, but only because they remained too afraid to part; their therapy would be considered a failure. So you see, it's very difficult to give you a success rating. It depends on how you look at success."

"Hmm. That's confusing. If that's true, then how can we or anyone else decide who the good marriage counselors are and who the lousy ones are?"

"That's a good question, ma'am. I am considered very competent. I have a doctorate from a good school, and I've attended many seminars in techniques and theories about helping couples. I've practiced for over ten years, and most people seem happy with the results."

"Are you saying that the way to tell who the best marriage counselors are is by where they went to school, or by how long they have been in practice?"

"Well, no—I suppose that's not always accurate. It's more than that. Some marriage counselors have to pass tests, too."

"Oh, you mean licensing exams like lawyers, M.D.s, and other professionals take? Do you have a license?"

"Well, actually, marriage counselors don't take tests in this state since the state doesn't have licensing for them yet. But we are working toward it. Most other states don't have licensing yet, either."

"Now I'm really confused. You can't give me a success rate, and you don't have to be licensed. Then how do we decide who we should see?"

"You could go to several different therapists and compare them."

"But sir, that would be very expensive for us. By the way, why is there so much difference in the fees? Some marriage counselors charge over $100 an hour and others are free."

"Well, ma'am, there aren't many whose services are free. If you are a member of a church, you might get free counseling there. Otherwise, if the fees are low, it's because most marriage counselors work in agencies which are subsidized by tax dollars or private contributions like the United Fund. Their fees are based on the client's ability to pay. The higher-priced counselors are usually in private practice."

"Are they the best counselors? Is that why their fees are so high?"

"No, not necessarily. Many of the best counselors work in agencies and churches. But many good ones are in private practice, too."

"Here we go again. You say 'good ones,' but how do you know who is good?"

"Ma'am, it's not an easy question. As I said, it depends on many things."

"Well, Doctor, I don't know about that. I talked with a marriage counselor on the phone just before I called you, and she didn't have any trouble. She said she had an 80 percent success rate."

"Ma'am, does that mean 80 percent of all people who go to her stay married, or what?"

"Why yes, Doctor, of course. She gave me a straight answer. I still don't understand why you can't."

Role Confusion in Marriage Counseling

The preceding dialogue is apocryphal, but every experienced marital therapist has encountered some version of it. Unfortunately for consumers of the service, and fortunately for some providers of it, most clients are not so careful or persistent. Most of them don't question the way competence is determined—they aren't certain what they want from the therapist, and are even less sure about what they will be getting. So when they ask, "What's your success rate?", they often are just asking for reassurance that they are entrusting their problems, their marriages, and their hopes for the future to someone who is capable. The therapist usually recognizes this as the implicit motive for the question about qualifications and replies with this in mind—then often quickly continues with concerned questions about the problem. The client is thus diverted from further inquiry about the therapist's abilities or the function of therapy, and the therapist has avoided a most troublesome issue: the role of marriage counseling and the capability of the practitioner.

Couples in marital crisis generally do not know what to expect from marriage counseling or therapy. Many people merely believe that when their marriages are troubled they might benefit from this type of help; too often they don't think beyond that notion. But how *does* counseling benefit troubled marriages? Is its goal only to save the marriage? Is it to make the spouse improve so that living together is once again tolerable? Is it to help the couple ease out of marriage without feeling guilt? Or is it to help them understand why they married each other so they won't repeat the same mistake after the divorce? Whatever they think counseling might do for them, they are also uncertain about how the counselor does it. How does the counselor help achieve the clients' goals? Or *do* they help achieve goals? What if the counselor considers the goals to be unhealthy, or sinful, or unreachable? Does the counselor then try to dissuade the clients from the goals concerned and seek to replace them with others? Do counselors manipulate clients into staying married? Do they ever encourage them to separate?

It would be less confusing if the goal of the marriage counselor were strictly to save marriages. Then clients could compare "success rates" and decide who is best; counselors would be able to decide what techniques are most effective and what theories are most relevant; educators and state licensing boards could better ascertain what to teach and what to test in order to determine a counselor's ability; and the counselor's supervisors could judge which personality characteristics are best suited to achieving the desired result. If saving marriages were the single goal of marriage counseling—as is perceived by most Americans—then there would be little role confusion. But few counselors or therapists would say unequivocally that this is its goal.

Why then does the public generally continue to believe that marriage saving is the function of the marriage counselor? If the public had one voice, it might reply: "Why else would anyone go to a marriage counselor? If we were crazy, we'd see a shrink. If we suffered modern day angst, or existential despair, we'd see our clergymen or bartenders. If it is merely a rueful countenance which repels our spouses from further exposure to us, we'd seek the services of a Madison Avenue image maker, or at least an attendant in a red-doored beauty salon. What else is there for marriage counselors to do, if not to save marriages?"

Most marital therapists believe they have a broader goal and function. They think of themselves as "enablers" and "helpers" who don't impose their own views or values on their clients. Rather, they purport to help clients better understand their own goals and values, help them eliminate emotional and behavioral obstacles to personal and marital fulfillment, help them to communicate and empathize more effectively with the marital partners, and help them be more effective in relating to people inside or outside the marriage. In fact, there is virtually no end to the goals and methods which some marriage counselors and therapists say are appropriate for their field. And herein lies the problem: If the appropriate role is so extensive, it may also be too diffuse to have much meaning.

The ambiguity of the marriage counselor's role has caused serious negative consequences for both the field of marital counseling and its consumers. The prestige of marital therapy is currently lower than that

of most of the other helping professions. Public regulation of its practice is very inconsistent from state to state (Sporakowski, 1980). Some
jurisdictions permit anyone to hang out a shingle; there is such a sign in
our nation's capital, which is one jurisdiction where anyone can legally
practice marriage counseling, regardless of training, background, or
motivation. The sign, located within ten blocks of the White House
for years, describes its owner as the "best tarot card reader and marriage counselor in Washington, D.C."

Marriage counseling is not a single profession or unified field. It is
practiced by clergymen, social workers, psychologists, psychiatrists, educators, fortune tellers, charlatans, and many others. Some of the disciplines have little in common and, while offering the potential for valuable cross-fertilization, have actually yielded multidisciplinary
antagonisms. Training for it ranges from years of highly specialized
post-graduate school to nothing more than having vague impressions
about how marriages should be (Liddle, 1978). Until recent years there
was virtually no underlying conceptual framework upon which to sys-
tematize its efforts; it was called a "technique in search of a theory"
(Manus, 1966). Most modern disciplines such as psychoanalysis started
as a theory which was then operationalized into a practice. Marriage
counseling started without a theory base. Its raison d'être was to fill a
practical need; its technique was primarily based on trial and error experiential observations and unsubstantiated philosophies. Marriage
counseling will never reach its potential until it achieves clarity in defining its role.

Origins of Marriage Counseling

Why is there so much confusion about the role of the marital counselor? The usual answer is that it is a very young field, still finding itself.
But this is only partly true. Actually, most of the ideas, techniques, and
goals now used in marriage counseling are as ancient as the concept of
marriage itself. History's oldest surviving literature is filled with
thoughtful advice about how people should more effectively deal with
their spouses. Written remnants from early civilizations, particularly
Babylonia, Egypt, and Judea, reveal ample concern for the preservation
of marriage and family relationships (Durant, 1935). For example, the
ancient Code of Hamurabi contained a sizeable section about the rules
for marriages. Of course, marriage in these cultures was little more than
an institution by which to subjugate women. For the most part, a

woman was property, possessed first by her father, then her husband, and finally by her son. The husband often acquired the wife through purchase, capture, or contract when she was an economic asset. When she was not, her father essentially sold her to a man through a dowry. Only the husband was permitted to divorce in these cultures, and his only obligation in doing so was to repay any dowry he initially received. In such an atmosphere there was little need for systematic marriage counseling. Still, it seems probable that wives consulted other wives, their mothers, or village elders for guidance on how to more successfully please their husbands. Husbands, too, must have sought advice about their wives, at least to determine how to get more work or babies out of them. Ancient writings reveal that the advice given to both husbands and wives was not so different from that which still constitutes the bulk of marriage counseling: listen and understand what your spouse is really saying; do this or that to improve your sexual relations; look at the situation from your mate's point of view; and use more effective strategy to get your own way.

Ancient Rome was among the first of the early civilizations to permit relative equality between the sexes. Not coincidentally, Rome also had a very high rate of divorce. It is not that equality causes the breakdown of marriage, but that it affords greater opportunity for women to leave undesirable or intolerable relationships (Humphrey, 1975). In the earlier civilizations women had no economic or social independence; but in Rome, among the upper classes at least, women were free to come and go. They were permitted to maintain their own households with or without husbands, and they could choose to remain with their spouses or to separate with ease.

The results were disastrous for Rome. The Empire fell, in large part because of its decaying family life, the foundation upon which all modern civilizations rest. Greater sexual equality and relative freedom in marital roles was accompanied by the high divorce rate and almost nonexistent family structure. This meant that fewer children were born or allowed to survive once conceived. Many of the Roman children who did survive were raised by slaves and did not learn to value the security of the family. Finally, Caesar Augustus recognized the consequences of these freedoms and attempted to reverse the trend. He instituted the "Julian Laws" which many historians consider the most important social and family legislation of antiquity. Adultery, which had been acceptable in Roman society, was outlawed. Celibacy and childlessness, formerly encouraged, were now penalized through heavy taxation. Divorce, which was once granted with ease, was now made difficult to obtain.

But the Julian Laws were in vain; the Romans were inclined to let their hedonistic interests prevail over their willingness to conform to Augustus' new rules. The people easily found ways to circumvent the laws, and Augustus was never able to legislate an end to the rampant licentiousness and marital instability of the Roman culture. Even his own daughter and granddaughter were so blatantly involved in sex scandals and disregard for the moral laws of the land that they were banished from Rome.

A close friend of Augustus' granddaughter was the Roman poet, Ovid, who could be considered the first author of a marital therapy text. Ovid's moral conduct and writings also resulted in his banishment from Rome, but during his exile he composed his infamous *Ars amatoria, The Art of Love*. This long, lighthearted poem described in detail—shocking even for the jaded Romans—methods to attract, seduce, and leave members of the opposite sex. It had little to do with marriage, but the moral leaders of the Empire were afraid that its popularity would further erode the family structure. So Ovid wrote a sequel, the *Remedia amores—Remedies for Love—*to pacify his critics. It facetiously instructed the reader who had achieved success with *The Art of Love* to know how to manage its ultimate consequences. It was filled with suggestions, "case histories," and examples about how to comfortably end affairs, how to return to one's spouse, and how to successfully be a lover in the marriage relationship. Though it was written satirically as an apology for *The Art of Love*, many of its ideas would fit comfortably in modern guides to marriage and marital therapy.

The *Remedia amores* was only the first of many documents written during Rome's decline to describe the dangers of family instability and provide suggestions for improvement (Haywood, 1958). But none had much influence. Only when the ancient Christian Church achieved control over marriage and family relationships was the trend reversed (Goodsell, 1934). Divorce and marital unhappiness became moot when marriage became a religious, rather than a legal, institution.

The status of women paralleled the decline of Roman hegemony. Rome's fall brought economic uncertainty, war, mass population movements, and changing values throughout the western world. In such upheaval, women were often considered more a hindrance than an asset. They weren't considered capable of fighting or defending themselves, and their assigned status as "homemaker" diminished their relative importance in migratory circumstances. Furthermore, the Church wanted to prevent a recurrence of the loose morals of Roman society. Women had to lose their autonomy so that society might live up to what were considered Christian values. They lost their freedom to leave marriages, their power to initiate extramarital sex, and their opportunity to live outside of marriage or convents. Medieval Christian clergymen convinced people that if they wanted sex they had to be married, and that God created all marriages. The Roman practice of divorce and easy-come, easy-go relationships no longer existed. Henceforth, God was in charge of marriage, the Church revealed, and He would tolerate no interference. Obviously there was no need to counsel people in ways to achieve marital compatibility in such an atmosphere. It was irrelevant if people felt unhappily married or unfulfilled, because they were not expected to achieve fulfillment on earth anyway. That could wait until reaching heaven, where an eternity of closeness with God and one's spouse would provide all the happiness one would need.

Medieval Guidance in Love

It was not until the twelfth century, almost a thousand years later, that the established norms about love and marriage could be questioned. It happened in the principality of Poitiers, and its protagonist was one of the most spirited and knowledgeable women of history: Eleanor of Aquitane. As a young girl she inherited several of France's most important provinces, which inevitably resulted in her arranged marriage to Louis Capet, the King of France. Louis was a dull, dour, serious, preoccupied young man, while Eleanor was intellectually curious and outgoing. She was only fifteen when she married, but she asserted herself immediately. She filled the royal palaces with poets, scholars, musicians, and scientists and kept them busy trying to answer her incessant questions and satiate her myriad intellectual interests. But her marriage was empty, except as a political expediency. This was typical for the times, but not acceptable to Eleanor. Seeking more closeness in the relationship, she insisted on accompanying her husband on the Second Crusade to the Holy Land. There, and in nearby Turkey and Syria, Eleanor was exposed to lifestyles unheard of in Europe. She saw more freedom, more openness in love and marriage, acceptance of sexuality, and an appreciation of romantic love. She enthusiastically embraced these alien standards, having affairs with and falling in love with a veritable army of European noblemen and soldiers and Byzantine rulers.

Returning to Paris, Eleanor advocated similar liberalization for the French court. King Louis could countenance such heresy no longer, and neither could the Church. The marriage was terminated and Eleanor was sent back to her family home in Aquitane.

Not one to remain idle, Eleanor took only two months to find a new husband. He was Louis's bitterest enemy, Henry II, soon to become King of England and Normandy. But her new marriage was even less satisfactory. Eleanor repeated her lifestyle in Henry's domain and introduced new fashions and revolutionary ideas about human relationships into the English court. Henry and Eleanor grew to hate each other; both openly flaunted their respective sexual affairs and intrigues. After 15 years and eight children together, they finally separated. Eleanor, only 47 years old at that time, returned once again to her ancestral castle at Poitiers. Almost immediately she gathered Europe's leading scholars and artists under her roof and engaged them in discussions about the meaning of life and the secrets of civilization. Out of these discussions emerged what historians call the "Court of Love," which explicated many ideas which are now the foundation of marital therapy.

The "Court of Love" existed to teach and study the meaning of social and sexual relationships. Knowledge-hungry young lords and ladies traveled from all over the continent to become educated in Eleanor's instruction. The court used a "case study" method of teaching; it included discussions between men and women about the intricacies of lovemaking, knight-errantry, social etiquette, philosophy, and chivalry. But most popular and influential were the mock-legal proceedings in which relationship problems were presented to a jury for a decision. Sometimes actors portrayed those with the problems, and sometimes the troubled individuals would portray their own difficulties. Eleanor often served on the jury, which could consist of 50 to 60 men and women; she was a dominant voice in giving counsel about these problems. The decisions had no legal sanction, but the nobility so respected the court that the findings were hard to ignore.

The decisions and conclusions about how to resolve relationship problems were refined, codified, and promulgated throughout Europe by the court's chaplain, Andreas Capellanus. He wrote the *Tractatus de Amore et de Amoris remedio* (*The Treatise of Love and Its Remedy*). Andreas considered his writing an updating of Ovid's work. It summarized the case examples and conclusions of Eleanor's court and spelled out some of its more revolutionary ideas: that men and women have equal responsibilities and obligations to each other; that promises about love must be kept; that women can be the predator as well as the prey in engineering relationships; that it is wrong to test a lover's love by adultery; that love is more desirable when one considers the other's desires as well as one's own. The *Tractatus de Amore* emphasized 31 rules of love which were the basis of the decisions regulating relationships. They included such precepts as "That which a lover takes against the will of his beloved has no relish; A true lover does not desire to embrace in love anyone except his beloved; A true lover considers nothing good except what he thinks will please his beloved."

The Court at Poitiers was abruptly ended after its fourth year. Eleanor's ever irate husband, threatened by her continued independence, radical ideas, and incessant political meddling, marched his army into her land. She tried to escape by disguising herself as a man, but was captured and imprisoned for the next 15 years, until Henry's death. While she was confined, her daughter Marie and Andreas Capellanus moved to the provinces of Champagne and reestablished the court; its influence was too great to ever again be completely contained (Hunt, 1959). The underlying theories, techniques, methods of teaching, and the fundamental values inherent in the art of marriage counseling might owe as much to Eleanor's "Court of Love" as to any other of the influences in its long history.

Modern Origins of Marriage Counseling

If we consider all the ideas, values, and techniques which have been used in marriage counseling, we can trace its geneology through antiquity. But if our concern is limited to direct lineage, to the evolution of those who have called themelves marriage counselors, we needn't look far into the past. The term was rarely used before the twentieth century. It was a few clergymen who first started calling themselves marriage counselors in the 1890s. Clergymen had been the primary providers of guidance in marriage and human relationships for centuries, but this function had always been of secondary importance to them. They could devote such a small percentage of their time to it that they rarely gave the activity a name or a systematic methodology.

In the early 1900s social work became the first profession to engage in marriage counseling as a full-time endeavor. This new field largely grew out of church-sponsored philanthropy and thus originally shared the clergy's religious motivation to help troubled relationships. Early social workers were primarily concerned with helping the disadvantaged get needed financial help and information about how to meet subsequent needs. Their effort to help troubled marriages came from the then prevailing belief that healthier family relationships would resolve people's economic woes (Woodroofe, 1962). Social workers were originally volunteers but, as demand for their services grew, they became trained full-time employees in social agencies (Lubove, 1968). By 1910, many agencies with full-time, trained social work staffs started to specialize in marriage and family treatment. In 1911 many of these agencies formed the alliance now known as the Family Service Associations of America (Hollis, 1949). There are over 350 FSA agencies nationwide; they still provide much of the nonreligious marriage counseling and family treatment in America.

Clergymen and social workers were the major providers of marriage counseling through the 1920s, but their dominance declined thereafter because of their very practical, rather than systematic, orientation. They told clients how to make their marriages work better. They educated couples as to their legal and social obligations and they extolled the values inherent in family life. But their suggestions were then based less on available theory or knowledge of human psychology or sociology than on impressions and untested notions. Conceptualizing was left to other disciplines which started entering the field in the 1930s. First anthropologists, then sociologists, psychologists and finally physicians studied the nature of marital relationships and methods for its improvement. While they initially contributed much to systematic inquiry and theory, they had little direct contact with troubled couples. It was necessary for the different disciplines to work together to supplement what they individually lacked.

Since the concerns of marriage cut across so many fields of inquiry, it was inevitable that there would be a marriage of disciplines to study and treat the marriage of couples. Unfortunately, it is a rocky union so far, with arguments, power struggles, threats of separation, and occasional bickering sometimes impeding the relationship. Nevertheless, there are many offspring: a variety of new marriage counseling techniques, theories, and agencies have been born. No single discipline has been able to, or perhaps even wanted to, claim exclusive domain or parentage over the practice of marital therapy. This accounts for rich and variegated approaches to the field—and for its lack of unifying identity and clarity about its role and function.

Multidisciplinary marital counseling centers emerged in the 1930s. Two physicians, Drs. Hannah and Abraham Stone, founded their center in New York City in 1929. It was an immediate success; its rapidly expanding staff included physicians, psychologists, psychiatrists, social workers, and clergymen. The different disciplines were unified by the thinking and writing of the Stones, whose immensely influential book, *A Marriage Manual*, was published in 1935. The book used a question and answer format written in the form of a hypothetical consultation between a couple and a counselor or physician. It provided considerable detail about the biological aspects of marriage as well as the emotional factors relevant to marital well-being (Stone and Stone, 1935). Other marriage counseling centers similar to the Stones' facility grew during the 1930s. Largest and most influential of these included Emily Mudd's Marriage Council of Philadelphia and Paul Popenoe's American Institute of Family Relations in Los Angeles.

Other than the Stones' book, little had been written about the theory and practice of marriage counseling during these years. Few papers appeared in the professional literature of the 1930s, and these were mostly anecdotal descriptions of some of the marital counseling techniques then in use (Bridgeman, 1932; Benjamin, 1935; Foster, 1937). The first book devoted exclusively to marriage counseling did not appear until 1943; it was a manual published by the Family Service Agencies to guide their workers in helping couples. This book was filled with practical and theoretical approaches to counseling, rich in ideas and technique, and it drew heavily on psychoanalytic and sociological theories. It is, however, largely forgotten today, probably due to its unfortunate title: *Report of FSAA Committee on Marriage Counseling* (Report, 1943).

The end of World War II marked another milestone in the development of marriage counseling. Thousands of impulsively made wartime marriages were going through the unimpulsive process of adjustment and extrication. More counseling centers appeared, and private marriage counselors from many disciplines hung out their shingles. The American Association of Marriage Counselors, founded in 1942, grew rapidly. Textbooks explicitly devoted to marriage counseling were being written and read (e.g., Goldstein, 1945; Mace, 1948; Cuber, 1948).

Marriage counseling has never had greater notoriety than in the 1950s, that surrealistic decade also known as the "age of togetherness." It was during this time that Americans saw marriage as the ultimate, if not only, way to achieve security and contentment. It was a time when love was to conquer all problems, when divorce was a catastrophe, and when the rose-covered white picket fences of suburbia represented the prototype of what life was supposed to be all about. Marriage was so important that anything claiming to save or improve it was accorded considerable approbation. Many marriage advice columns, such as Paul Popenoe's "Can This Marriage Be Saved?" series were very popular. Rarely did anyone ask, "*Should* this marriage be saved?"

The Emergence of Family Therapy

Family therapy was a minor adjunct to marriage counseling until the mid-1960s. It was given scant attention by counselors, unless children were seen as creating problems in the parents' relationship. But rarely were children treated with parents. Marriage counselors often referred troubled (or troubling) children to child psychoanalysts or therapists while work with the parents continued. Child psychiatrists often referred the parents of their young clients to marriage counselors. The rationale for the separation was that children would not feel free to explore their inner conflicts in the parental presence, and parents would be too inhibited to discuss the intimate details of their own relationship before their children. While this rationale is valid for some families, it seems too simplistic for others.

Seeing a member of the family alone or only spouses together, to the exclusion of the children, ignored an important fact: people who live together, who are as intimate and mutually influential as are primary families, can cause problems and provide solutions for one another. The family is a system, a whole made up of interacting parts. It is an entity which is in constant fluctuation, altering its entire substance with every change that occurs in any of its components. To try to understand or modify one of those parts without considering the effect by or on the other parts, or on the whole, is unacceptably limiting. This is the fundamental premise of family therapy.

Family therapy blossomed in the 1970s and is now perhaps the most innovative of the psychotherapies (Hoffman, 1981). It started with a strong theory base, and its work has been subjected to intense scientific scrutiny and systematic analysis. It is well grounded in its various theories and major "schools," but has a strong dedication to getting out of the ivory tower and into direct work with families. Family therapy training facilities are proliferating; there is general excitement and interest in participating in the inception of a new discipline (Simon, 1981).

The emergence of family therapy has had a strong impact on the fields of marriage counseling and marital therapy. Many marriage counselors have adopted the ideas and techniques developed by family therapy and have enthusiastically entered the new field. Family therapy, which largely grew out of marriage counseling, is now preeminent, and marital therapy is more a subspecialty within it. Following this switch, the professional association which originated as the American Association of Marriage Counselors changed its name and orientation in 1978; it is now known as the American Association of Marriage and Family Therapists.

Marital Therapy and Marriage Counseling

Heretofore, the terms marriage counseling and marital therapy have been used interchangably. Given the fact that the theories, goals, and methods of those who have worked with troubled marriage are still so ill defined, it is misleading to imply or state that there is much difference. But many of those who identify themselves as marital therapists claim there are considerable differences. Marriage counseling, they say, has to do with advice giving and professional guidance. They say it is a process of providing information, opinions, admonishments, and recommendations. It primarily helps the client recognize available alternatives and spells out the consequences and benefits of those choices. But those who retain their "marriage counselor" identity say they do these things and more; they supposedly enter the "deeper" realm of treating dysfunctional relationships and do everything that marital therapists do.

Some marital therapists claim their activity is more comprehensive. They say that they include the aforementioned counseling activities in their repertoire of intervention strategies, but are also devoted to changing underlying personality and behavioral patterns. Marital therapy purports to help couples understand themselves and the behaviors which consciously or unconsciously affect their partners, and to change those personality or behavioral characteristics which interfere with healthy individual and marital functioning. But there is little evidence, either empirical or inferential, which suggests much difference between the two. Therefore, the viewpoint implicit throughout this book is that the terms "marriage counseling" and "marital therapy" are not yet precise enough to justify thinking of them as different modalities.

It is somewhat easier to distinguish between family therapy and marital therapy. Since work with marriages is now generally a family therapy specialization, it uses many of the same goals, methods, and skills. But the focus of marital therapy is, of course, on the couple and not the children. Family therapy would be the treatment of choice between the two except when any one of five circumstances occur. Marital therapy would be used when the couple has no children, when the children are too young to participate (usually under age six or so), when the children are grown and out of the home, when the problem which needs attention does not directly involve the children, and when the problem is considered too threatening for the children or parents to confront. For example, sex therapy is more appropriate in work with the marital dyad than with the entire family. Dysfunctional sexuality certainly affects the children, but its treatment requires freedom from as many distractions and intervening variables as possible. There are many other instances in which couple therapy, without the children, is preferable. It often is used when the parents have problems with sexual fidelity, spouse abuse, incestuous tendencies, or other activities which they might find too discomforting for their children to experience directly. Many marital therapists who recognize how such troubles influence the children will go from couple therapy to family therapy, bringing the children into the treatment program after the more threatening material is reconciled.

Marital therapy or marriage counseling takes many forms, uses one of several theories as its unifying conceptual scheme, and uses a variety of techniques to achieve its goals. A discussion of these ideas is the substance of this book; but they must be seen in a context. So before considering these theories and methods, we need to consider the institution of marriage itself and the goals and values of those who treat couples in crisis. Without such a consideration, we would be merely perpetuating the role confusion which has played such havoc within the field since the beginning of its long history.

Epilogue

"Hello, Marital Therapy Center. Dr. Jones speaking."

"I'm looking for a marriage counselor."

"What kind of difficulties are you having?"

"Well, my wife and I are fighting all the time. We thought if we talked to a marriage counselor we could work things out. We want to make an appointment to see you but need to know a few things first. Can you tell me how many of the people who come to you get over these problems?"

"Someone just asked me that a little while ago, and I'm afraid I didn't give her a very good answer. Most couples who have worked with me have decided to stay married. I try to help people understand why they aren't getting what they need and want out of their marriages. Then I try to help them learn to communicate better with one another so they can say what they need. But some people find that their needs and wants are just too different. I don't try to talk them into doing anything that isn't in their best interests, and only you can say what those interests are. Am I answering your question?"

"I think so, Doc. But how can I tell you're the best counselor for us?"

"Well, that's a good question, sir—and it's one I really can't answer. I don't think any other marital therapist can either. Our profession just doesn't have good measurements for it yet. I can't tell you I'm better than anyone else among my colleagues. All I can say is I will respect your values and be honest with you when I do. My professional association watches over me to make sure I remain ethical, and I promise I will do my best. Would you like an appointment?"

"Uhh . . . I'm not sure yet. Can you tell me what your success rate is?"

Chapter Two

Marriage, Divorce, and Love

Marriage is a process. It is a dynamic entity, always changing, and rarely holding still long enough for analysis. No two marriages are identical and no marriage is the same from one moment to the next. The conditions which make for a successful marriage at one time can be devastating to it at another. The qualities one seeks in a marital partner continually change as one's needs, interests, and values are perpetually modifying through life. The expectations people make of it can rarely be met, yet it continues to be perceived as the major avenue to happiness and security.

Complete security and freedom from problems, which people often hope to derive from marriage, come at a high price; they occur only when relationships and the society in which they exist are static and unyielding. Security only occurs when people don't have the opportunity to learn or grow or change, when the culture only permits rigid adherence to its rules. Such conditions might have typified the marriages of medieval and ancient times, when the social controls were so encompassing that there was little opportunity to change. But modern marriage, centered in ever fluctuating circumstances, provides such security only sometimes, only in bits and pieces. Whatever else it is, it keeps changing—and thus should never be expected to assure complete security and stability.

For this reason, adaptability is among the most important components of healthy marriages in modern America. Marital satisfaction comes with the acceptance of and preparation for change. Marital dissatisfaction is likely for those who abhor change and whose expectations of marriage are based solely on romantic idealism. At least this is true in dynamic societies. In those societies which permit little cultural mobility, the need for adaptability in marriage may not be so important. Where a nation does not sanction divorce, where a culture forbids its members to be economically viable outside its marriage institution, there is less need for adaptability. If the society has no opportunity to deviate from prevailing customs, its citizens are perhaps as comfortable and happy as anywhere else; marital dissolution occurs only where there are opportunities to consider alternatives. This is why there are more divorces in dynamic societies and why marital therapists have so little work to do in rigid ones.

Americans tend to berate themselves for their appalling divorce statistics. Many moral and political leaders say divorce is symptomatic of our decaying values and bankrupt morality. Conversely, they imply that the way to uplift our values and morality is to prevent or discourage divorce. They believe there are many ways to reduce the divorce rate. We could make our divorce laws more difficult; we could require everyone who wants to divorce to pay excessive fees to lawyers so many would avoid their services; we could require all candidates for separation to consult with professional marital therapists; or we could suppress the movement for greater equality between the sexes. If women would return to their homes and not compete with men, says this view, and if they return to their natural function as child-bearer and -raiser, then there wouldn't be so much divorce (Decter, 1972). The solution to the high divorce rate, purports this view, is to eliminate the choice and the opportunity. It is like saying, "The way to end high truancy rates is to lock children in the schools."

The American divorce rate is surely discomforting, and efforts to improve it are welcome. But viewed in historical context, everything about these statistics is not unpleasant. Divorce may reflect decaying values, but it may also reveal the dynamism of the culture, the freedom, the opportunity, the relative equality between the sexes, and the tolerance for deviation. It is a logical extension of a pluralistic culture, a price we pay to have an open society.

Trends in Marriage and Divorce

High divorce rates notwithstanding, marriage in America is more popular than ever. More than 94 percent of the American people marry at some time in their lives (United Nations, 1983). Since almost four percent of the population can't marry because of physical handicaps, disability, religious orientation, or uneven geographical and age–sex distribution (Schoen, 1983), it suggests that almost everyone who can marry does, at least once (Carter and Glick, 1976). Even those who have gone through the wrenching experience of divorce retain their fundamental approbation for marriage. Four out of five divorced people remarry, and half of them do so within a year of their divorces (NCHS, 1982). Divorced people are as likely to remarry as people who have remained single, a clear example of how hope still prevails over previous disappointment. The average age of divorcing men is 33.1 years of age, and of women, 29.8. Of those who divorce, the average length of their first marriage is seven years. Of those who divorced again, the second marriage endures an average of five years (U.S. Bureau of the Census, 1979).

Actually, marriage and divorce statistics may not be completely reliable. The principal source is the census data, which is obtained by asking respondents about their past marital history. But many people choose not to disclose such personal information to census interviewers. The inadequacy of this method has been long recognized, and in 1957 the federal government attempted to improve the situation. The Office of Vital Statistics established an agency to examine the actual marriage and divorce records kept in county courthouses. The program is voluntary, however, and only about half the states participate. As a result, there has always been some controversy about how many people are actually divorcing and how to interpret the data which exists. For example, Scanzoni (1972) has disputed the predilection of some to sensationalize the statistics and to imply that divorce is getting out of hand. He pointed out that the increase in divorces has actually been rather steady. In the 30-year period from 1910 to 1940, the annual rate per 1,000 population went from one to two divorces. From 1940 to 1970, except for a short spurt after World War II, the annual rate increased from two to three divorces per 1,000 people. In other words, he points out, the increase was no greater in the 30 years after the war than in the same amount of time before. By 1970 the divorce rates in several nations, including the Soviet Union and Egypt, equaled or surpassed that of the United States. But first place apparently returned to the United States by 1975, when a divorce upsurge moved our annual rate to more than four per 1,000 (Glick, 1975).

Statistics don't reveal the people who end marriages unofficially. Thousands desert or abandon their families each year but never divorce. Even greater numbers of couples agree to separate but never divorce. And of course, the statistics don't reveal the most hidden marriage pattern: those marriages which appear healthy to outsiders because the partners remain together, but which are in fact dissolved physically and spiritually. There is no way of knowing or even accurately estimating the number of couples who live in these "empty shell marriages." Statistics only hint at the extent of the disillusionment which many American marriages experience daily.

Estimation of the extent of marital dissatisfaction occurs through inference. We assume that if problems associated with dissatisfaction, such as spouse abuse, adultery, and acknowledged discontent are great, so too is the extent of unhappy but intact marriages. Between 26 and 30 million spouses are abused annually; up to 50% of all American wives have been hit or beaten by their husbands (Goodstein, 1981; Brisson, 1982). At least 41 percent of the married men and 20 percent of married women of America have had sexual relationships outside their marriages. The incidence among only the younger men and women is much higher, reaching almost 50 percent for both sexes (Hunt, 1974). Lederer and Jackson (1968) concluded in their influential book, *The Mirages of Marriage*, that 80 percent of American couples have at one time in their marriages seriously considered divorce.

Divorces don't occur randomly in society; they afflict some groups more than others. The highest divorce rates are among those who marry in their teens, the lowest among those who marry after reaching age 40. Whites are less likely to divorce than nonwhites, and the affluent less likely than the poor. The divorce rates among nonwhites and the poor might be higher but for the fact that financial and social pressures lead a higher proportion of them to desert rather than divorce. Childless couples are still more likely to divorce than are couples with children. Nevertheless, children are much less a deterrent to those who seek to leave the marriages. Over 40 percent of all divorces are between couples with children. During the past decade, seven million children under age 18 lived in one-parent homes. The number of children who are raised in happily married households has been decreasing substantially and steadily. And, ominously, those who were raised in broken or unhappy homes are far more likely to divorce when they reach adulthood; the momentum toward divorce increases as succeeding generations model their parents.

The Consequences of Marital Breakdown

What happens to people who end their marriages? For some it might only mean making minor adjustments to a somewhat changed lifestyle. Divorcing and remarrying for them may be no more difficult than changing jobs or moving to a different city. It is inconvenient at first and possibly anxiety provoking, but not a catastrophe. However, this group is minuscule compared to the number of those who experience intense emotional, physical, economic, and social disturbance as a consequence of their marital dissolution.

The health of divorced people is much worse than that of comparably aged marrieds (NCHS, 1982). Divorced people make more annual visits to their doctors, go to hospitals more often, stay there longer, and take more time off from work because of illness. They die sooner, too. They are 50 percent more likely to die from coronary disease than are nondivorced people, and 30 percent more prone to cancer of the digestive organs. They rate even worse in violent deaths. They are 150 percent more likely to die in automobile accidents. Among homicide victims, three married and 10.65 divorced women per 100,000 are killed, and 8.6. married and 39.2 divorced men per 100,000 are killed. The disparity among suicide victims is most dramatic of all: for every 100,000 people, 5.5 married women and 18.4 divorced or separated women kill themselves; 18.0 married men and 69.4 divorced men commit suicide. Breaking up marriages is unhealthy.

It is even more unhealthy to one's emotional well-being. The proportion of divorcees receiving psychotherapy is far greater than that of marrieds. Various studies (Briscoe and Smith, 1974) show a significantly higher rate of mental disorders among divorced and separated people. Admission rates to mental hospitals is 20 times higher for divorced than married men, and seven times higher for divorced women (Redick and Johnson, 1970). Reports from some mental hospitals have shown that functional psychosis is seven times greater among divorced than married men and three times greater among divorced women (Bloom, 1975). Presumably, many of those afflicted had their problems before marriage; but no researchers have suggested that everyone who had problems before marriage had exactly the same ones after divorce.

The economic consequences of marital dissolution is also severe. Census Bureau statistics (1981) show that married men have significantly higher incomes than do divorced men. Men who divorce have an average 33 percent income loss while women lose 16.5 percent of their income after the marriage ends. Support and alimony payments account for some of the income shifts, but other factors include employment problems, taking more time off from work, lost promotion opportunities, and employment disruptions, all of which were associated with marital problems. Such figures do not include the staggering sums people pay lawyers, courts, private detectives, summons servers, moving and storage companies, health professionals, and marital therapists, simply to get through the legal process and its aftermath. Divorce is financially debilitating for so many in our culture that a poor person is now more likely to be divorced than to belong to a minority group.

Men seem to have a more difficult time being divorced than do women. More of them have problems with their health, jobs, financial situation, emotional stability, and personal comfort than do women. They are more likely to bemoan the tribulations of marriage but they remarry more frequently and sooner than do women. Despite all the myths to the contrary, men are probably less well equipped for singleness than are women (Hunt, 1966).

Why might this be so? Sociologist Jesse Bernard (1972) suggests it is because marriage is more consistently rewarding for men than for women, so its cessation is a greater loss for them. In traditional marriages, she says, women lose confidence in themselves after they have been married a few years, while men's self-confidence grows. Men's personal growth in education, social awareness, and opportunity increases after a few years of marriage—while women experience declines in each of these attributes with each year of their marriages. Married women become more submissive as they grow older and they conform more to their husband's expectations, whereas men become more dominant and conform less to their wife's expectations. Bernard says that women dwindle into the role of wife while their spouses enlarge into the husband role. Traditional marriages, she says, literally make housewives sick.

If traditional marriages are better for men and worse for women, the desire to reduce the high rate of divorce might be seen as another reflection of the efforts of men to retain their predominance. It might be said that marital therapists, moral leaders, or anyone else who works to preserve marital relationships as they are presently constituted might be implicitly performing a social control function, preserving the current well-being of men, even if it comes at the expense of women's welfare.

The consequences of divorce on children are also discomforting. Children of divorced parents have a much more difficult time than do the children of intact families. Their incidence of physical and emotional health problems mirrors the same patterns of their divorced parents. They get sicker, more often and for longer periods of time, both physically and emotionally. They are more likely to deviate from the prevailing social norms of conduct. Delinquency, substance abuse, truancy, lower grades, and much greater frequency of running away are all well-known correlates of divorce. In some ways children of divorce face more obstacles than do their divorcing parents; they suffer the same social, psychological, and economic problems as their divorced parents, and they usually face the added burden of being powerless to alter their circumstances. Not being the protagonists of the marital disturbance, they can do little about its resolution. They are often confronted with contradictory rules and expectations from their parents. Frequently one parent will use the children to form a coalition against the other parent. All too often children have to deal with rules which are contradictory, inconsistently enforced, and often not even clearly stated. This also happens in homes which remain intact, of course, but it is more frequent among children of divorce (Wallerstein, 1983).

It is an oversimplification to say that divorce causes problems of this type or that parents should remain together for the sake of their children. Researchers who study the effects of divorce on children have some conflicting conclusions, but their prevailing view is that it is not divorce per se which causes the problems, but the accompanying inconsistency and conflict between the parents (Gardner, 1977). What is clear is that parents who have a paramount concern for their children's well-being, regardless of their mutual differences, must act together in developing consistent, compatible rules and expectations. Almost one third of the children born in the 1970s will live in divorced homes before they are 18; the magnitude of the difficulty they will face largely depends on the efforts of their parents to minimize these factors, whether or not they stay together (Bane, 1976).

However unpleasant the present consequences of divorce, it was probably much worse in times past (Mead, 1970). Two generations ago, when it was still unusual to encounter a divorced person, divorcees were somehow not quite respectable or acceptable in the eyes of most. To divorce then was to be a virtual pariah in some circles. It meant the person somehow lacked strength of character, ability to make sound judgements, and even moral decency. It often brought shame to one's parents, pity for one's associates, and distrust from one's still married friends. Politicians were thrown out of office when they divorced—and, of course, no one could consider running for the U.S. Presidency after going through one. To be divorced meant encountering a court-room adversary system in public view, where only specific conditions such as adultery, cruelty, incompatibility, and desertion were acceptable justification for the decision. Going through the legal process meant there had to be a plaintiff and a defendant, someone considered innocent and someone guilty.

Improvements in the divorce system have been made. Divorced people are no longer considered disreputable, and only a minority of people still think of them as failures. Divorced people are more acceptable, in large part, because there are so few Americans who remain untouched by divorce. Almost everyone except hermits regularly encounters them. We have elected a divorced man as president of our nation for the first time in history—and it was not even a campaign issue. Other politicians don't believe divorce will harm their aspirations for public office. The legal system is changing, too. There is less inclination in many states toward the adversary system of terminating marriages. Divorces without explicitly stated grounds, i.e., no-fault decisions, are becoming commonplace. Legal grounds for divorce could never encompass the subtleties, the intricacies, and interconnected problems which compel a couple to end their relationship. Grounds are society's "pretense to understanding the mechanics of marriage, and as such they are crude to the point of ineptness," says Joseph Epstein in his beautifully written book, *Divorced in America* (1974). He adds, "Marriages founder in trickier waters than any court of law is either willing or able to navigate."

But while it is not so difficult to become or to be divorced these days, everyone still wants to avoid it whenever possible. It is usually inconvenient and anxiety provoking at best, and emotionally chaotic and life threatening at worst. People want to avoid it—and this is their primary reason for seeking the services of a marital therapist. When marital therapists do not see this as their primary function, there is a serious discrepancy in role perception. People seek marital therapy because they want to avoid the pain, or as much of it as possible, that they probably will face in dissolving their marriages. Of course, the problem could have been more easily solved if they had remained single in the first place. But no one seems to like that solution; no one thinks it will happen to them.

Why People Marry

Despite its high risks and potentially serious consequences, there is something very compelling about marriage. Social theorists say people marry because of socialization, history, education, biological drives, conformity to expectations, and the belief that it enhances one's emotional well-being. But these are not the usual explanations given by those who marry; most say they do so for love. A 1974 Roper poll revealed that 83 percent of the women and 77 percent of the men sampled said love was their primary motivation. Pietropinto and Simenauer (1979) asked more than 3800 representative subjects why they married and again love was the most popular answer; 48 percent of the respondents gave this as their principal reason. The other motives were "having a home life" (26 percent), and "having a companion" (25 percent). Much lower on the list was having children, having regular sex, pressure from the partner, pressure from the family, pregnancy, and emotional support.

Using "love" as the major criterion for marriage seems reasonable to Americans. We tend to be faintly amused, if not appalled, by the custom of other cultures to base marriage on family arrangements, economic convenience, unwanted pregnancy, or any reason other than "love." We are taught that love is the raison d'être of marriage, that they go together like a horse and carriage, that you can't have one without the other. If the criterion for marriage is love, then the criterion for divorce must be the absence of love. We expect that love is the answer, that it makes the world go around, and that if it doesn't exist, we are somehow deficient.

This is a lot of baggage to be carried around by one elusive concept. But what does the word or concept really mean? The word is a virtual Rorschach test, acting as a catalyst to stimulate thoughts which are unique to each person. It does not have one meaning, but many. English-speaking people have always had semantic problems with it. Falling in love means something quite different from "making love." The love one has for money, security, fame, humanity, mother, that sexy movie star, or one's spouse are all distinct entities. The "love" we feel for a spouse who has just made us angry is different from the "love" we feel for that spouse when our libidos have been running rampant without resolution for a week. Clearly the feeling called love which a honeymooner experiences is different from the feeling called love which an aged person feels for a spouse after 50 years. Both are equally entitled to be called love, but surely they are not the same. Yet all these meanings have equal claim to the use of the word.

Just as we envision one type of relationship when we conjure an idea of marriage—when it could mean many different things depending on one's perspective, the cultural heritage, and the prevailing norms in which we live—so too is it with love. It needs to be defined better. Actually, many philosophers, semanticists, anthropologists, and marital therapists believe that the word should be replaced by several dozen totally different ones, each to describe one of the concepts now encompassed by the single word. Many have made suggestions. Psychologist Dorothy Tennov (1979) coined the term "limerence" to apply to the passionate, zealous emotion most often thought about by poets and soap opera writers. "Limerence" is the violin music, the fluttering heartstrings, the passionate zeal, the sexual desire, and the libidinous tension experienced by those who have "fallen in love." Many others have offered their own names for the feeling. In Walt Disney's 1941 movie classic *Bambi*, the wise old owl explains this emotion to the young animals at the start of spring; he calls it being "twitterpated."

Twitterpated, limerence—none of the other words ever seems to catch on. The song writers would never to able to find enough terms to rhyme with them. It would be difficult for our culture to discard a word it has extolled with such fervor for so many years. But, if people continue to think of love as one entity rather than as many different emotions which are constantly in fluctuation, they need to be more precise. If people believe love exists only when passionate zeal is present, they are going to be disappointed. If they believe that marriage is the be-all and end-all, they will believe they failed if it doesn't maintain this exalted paragon. George Bernard Shaw described a couple's getting married for this kind of love as a time when "under the influence of the most violent, most insane, most delusive, and most transient of passions, they are required to swear that they will remain in that excited, abnormal, and exhausting condition continuously until death do them part" (Shaw, 1908).

Another reason people marry is for companionship. In the 1979 Pietropinto and Simenauer survey of reasons for marriage, 25 percent of the 3800 subjects cited this as their motivation, just over half as many as said love was the reason. The researchers concluded, however, that companionship was even more important than "love" to most people sampled. Companionship, they said, is the genuine regard couples have for one another as friends and equals. To achieve it takes time, not hormones. Romantic love was the most highly valued among the younger marrieds in the survey, but as time progresses companionship becomes more important; it was the primary consideration given by older people in the survey. What we call love is sometimes bound up with intense physical attraction for a member of the opposite sex, biological urges, something which can happen within a very short time and vanish just as quickly.

Companionship and love are still not sufficient explanations for why people marry. One need not marry to have access to sex or companionship. We can feel "love" for someone, no matter how we are using the word, without wanting to live with them. Most people in our culture love their parents but want separate residences upon reaching adulthood. Most people have friends, and companionship needs are met with them. There must be other explanations.

Much of the motivation for marriage has to do with our education, the way we have been socialized. This is suggested by the fact that the rate of marriage varies from one culture to another. In those cultures where the marriage rate is lower, people are exposed to alternatives. In the cultures where almost everyone marries, people don't seem to recognize or accept any other lifestyle—marriage is ingrained in people as the norm, the "natural" way to be, the way to be fulfilled. This is what we tell our children, just as it was told to us.

The idea that marriage is the norm has been communicated through succeeding generations since humans lived in very primitive societies, when it was established as a matter of survival. In early cultures, marriage existed as an integral part of the human division of labor. Someone had to do the hunting, the fighting, and the protecting of the territory; someone else had to care for the babies and prepare the food. Since the women were having the babies—almost continuously during their fertile years—it fell to them to remain at home. If either the man or woman failed to fulfill the expected functions, there would be little chance of survival for both. In modern society, sheer physical survival is no longer the significant motive, but emotional survival needs are still valid motives.

In *Marriage and Morals* (1929), Bertrand Russell has described better than most social scientists what he thinks are the reasons people marry. He asserted that marriage is the principal means of escape from the loneliness which afflicts people throughout their lives. "There is a deep-seated fear," he wrote, "of the cold world and the possible cruelty of the herd; there is a longing for affection, which is often concealed by roughness, boorishness or a bullying manner in men, and by nagging and scolding in women. Passionate mutual love, while it lasts, puts an end to this feeling; it breaks down the hard walls of the ego, producing a new being composed of two in one. Nature did not construct human beings to stand alone, since they cannot fulfill her biological purpose except with the help of another; and civilized people cannot fully satisfy their sexual instinct without love. The instinct is not completely satisfied unless a man's whole being, mental quite as much as physical, enters into the relation." Russell was wise as are few people, and his works were more than rhetorical. He tried marriage four times during his long life. He believed to his dying day that "nine out of ten who have a conventional upbringing in their early years have become in some degree incapable of a decent and sane attitude toward marriage and sex generally" (quoted in Jager, 1972).

What Kind of Marriage?

Since people do not tend to be clear about their reasons for marriage, it shouldn't be surprising that they also do not consider what type or form of marriage they might have. Most people, in fact, do not even consider that there are alternatives. There is only one way to be married, they reason, and so there is nothing to think about. They also tend to think there is only one kind of acceptable partner to consider as a possible mate. Sociological research consistently shows that Americans grant themselves few choices regarding acceptable marriage and partner. These are socially restricted. For example, only 3 percent of women feel free to marry, or even to date, shorter men. Only 3 percent of men feel free to date or marry a taller woman. Fewer than 5 percent of both sexes would marry outside their own racial group. The majority of women and men want the husband to dominate in making the decisions. Almost 70 percent of the women surveyed want their husbands to be more intelligent, better educated, older, more knowledgeable, and better paid than themselves. Women want their husbands to come from equal or higher socioeconomic class families, but men want their wives to have equal or lower socioeconomic backgrounds. Almost everyone wants their marriages to last their lifetime (Bernard, 1972).

Long ago, when the idea that marriage was for life first achieved general public acceptance, a lifetime was about 30 years. Therefore, the duration of a marriage which would begin at puberty was usually less than 20 years. Now marriage for life typically means more than 50 years. Despite such self-imposed restrictions, most couples say they are open-minded about marriage; they say they want companionship and equality when they speak in the abstract. The trouble is that most people are not trained to deal with the specifics. It takes skill, knowledge, practice, and positive role models for individuals to acquire the ability to negotiate, share equally, and be companions. Yet most people are still socialized to accept one type of marriage and one type of partner; the traditional marriage is what most people still want, to an over-whelming degree. This is the "father knows best" marriage. He makes the decisions, earns the money, determines the lifestyle, and dominates the wife. She adjusts, accommodates, sacrifices, depends upon, and looks up to her husband. Few people say this is what they really want—again in the abstract sense—but they always seem to raise their eyebrows at those who deviate from this expectation.

But what are the alternatives? Most people are only subliminally aware that there can be other ways of living to achieve the same ends that they seek to get in marriage. Most who are aware of alternatives believe them to be wholly unacceptable, intolerable, immoral, or un-natural. Of course these alternatives have all been the predominant life-styles in various cultures, and the people of those societies seem to function adequately. Indeed, the people from these cultures tend to view marriages which are different from their own as unacceptable or immoral, too.

Alternative Marriage Forms

Possible marriage forms include lifetime monogamy, serial monogamy, multilateral or group marriage, open marriage, and polygamy. Lifetime monogamy is the one most Americans think is the only possibility worth considering; it is by far our most popular marriage form, but by no means our only one. Monogamy literally means "one marriage" but in popular parlance it has come to denote sexual and emotional ex-clusiveness as well. Its fundamental premise is that one's emotional and sexual needs are to be met by the marriage partner. The limitation of monogamy, indeed a reason traditional American marriages may so of-ten be troubled, is because so much is expected of the relationship.

Is it realistic to expect two people to spend a lifetime together, al-ways and completely meeting each other's needs? This assumption was made when the marriage took place (Whitehurst, 1977). Many do, of course, but when they do, it may be because one or both partners are able to accommodate their expectations. They succeed because they communicate their needs and are willing and able to meet those needs. Sometimes they succeed by openly or furtively seeking to meet needs outside the marriage without ending it. Many succeed only by suppressing the wish for anything other than what already exists in the marriage. It is remarkable, given the opportunity Americans have to end their marriages, that so many remain in them in the face of all these demands.

The most common alternative to this traditional marriage or lifelong monogamy in American culture is serial monogamy. This is the expectation of sexual and emotional exclusiveness for the duration of the marriage. Actually, serial monogamy in its true sense is a legal or social sanction in which the marriage is not expected to last a lifetime. Another marriage is expected to supplant it. Most people who divorce and remarry in the United States have not made prior decisions to be serial monogamists; they are unprepared when divorce happens. They find it unpleasant, in large part because few social institutions reinforce or support the divorced and remarried. Our society is so "wedded" to the notion that traditional monogamy is the ideal that our social efforts are confined to the perpetuation of lifelong exclusivity. We justify this view with the dubious claim that traditional monogamous marriage promotes affection between the partners and that it provides a loving context for child-rearing (McMurtry, 1977). Others argue that affection between partners can be achieved with equal or sometimes better success in the other forms of marriage, and that half the span of a typical monogamous marriage involves no child-rearing at all.

Society seeks to preserve the traditional marriage, so it discourages its most common alternative (Knapp, 1975). But many social scientists believe that serial monogamy can be positive, an institution to be encouraged. They propose formal social sanctions for serial marriage to accommodate the life stages through which everyone passes. Each person could choose to have a different partner every time a new life stage is entered, and choose to remain in or leave that marriage at the next stage. The first stage would be "individual marriage," in which the couple would legally live together but would not have children. The second stage, called "parent marriage," would last through the years of child raising. It would be easy to end the first stage individual marriages, but difficult to dissolve parent marriages. Since couples wouldn't enter into a parent marriage without marital experience and since they know they would be able to dissolve the relationship when the children are grown, there might be less inclination to divorce (Duberman, 1974). A third stage of marriage would occur, if the individuals chose, during middle age when companionship is a high priority. There might also be marriage stages for the elderly, providing a different form of relationship. Social scientists recognize that society is unlikely to sanction or encourage such radical changes, but they often predict that there is an evolutionary trend in this direction anyway (Olson, 1972). The fact that society would still control these marriages is important; it is desirable that legal protections continue to define the obligations and rights inherent in these relationships and in the fair distribution of property.

Another alternative to monogamous marriage is called "nonmarried marriage" or sometimes "open marriage." The term "open marriage" here does not have the same meaning as the version used in the O'Neills' influential book, *Open Marriage* (1972). The O'Neills refer to open marriage as freedom from traditional role patterns, often within an otherwise traditional marriage form. But open marriage—or nonmarried marriages—as used here refers to a voluntary non-legal association without state supervision or sanction (Greenwald, 1970). This view holds that legal marriage cannot guarantee to protect the children or property rights anyway. Only the couple's love, mutual respect, and wish to be together can provide such assurance. If society abrogated its legal control of marriage, people would stay together or separate because they want to, which is probably the only viable justification for marriage in the first place. Divorce is nonexistent in this system; no one would tolerate the expensive, sometimes humiliating, always anxiety provoking legal experience of the adversary system. The problem with this form of relationship is that, to retain stability, any civilization must exercise some controls, some sanctions, some protections over its members. With the protections and rules about human relationships, many people might give a second thought to their impulses to enter and leave relationships. This form of relationship is now the third most common pattern after monogamy and serial monogamy in the United States; it is cohabitating without benefit of marriage or "common law marriage" (Stein, 1969). Society, once frowned on such conduct, calling it "living in sin." Gradually society is tolerating it, first among some "lower" socioeconomic classes and more recently among every economic group. There are presently over one million couples living together in the United States without being married; over 10 percent of all adults between ages 21 and 30 now live this way. It is becoming more acceptable to some as a way of testing whether the couple could be happily married before giving it legal sanction (Watson, 1983). Living together does not mean total absence of obligation to the partner, as the "palimony" cases are demonstrating. But for some who choose this relationship form, which is often based on love and the desire to remain together, it has many advantages over its alternatives.

Another marriage form, group or multilateral marriage, has been discussed and studied more than practiced in the United States. It is the relationship in which three or more individuals, in any distribution of sex, share sexual and emotional intimacy as a single unit (Constantine and Constantine, 1973). Its idealized version is that of sharing responsibilities and resources within the group. The children may be communal and may have several surrogate fathers and mothers, regardless of biological relationship. Multilateral marriages are probably the oldest form of marriage in the world; they have been successful enough to survive for centuries. They come in many variants, from large communes in which everyone shares intimacies and responsibilities, to triadic forms in which one man or one woman has two partners of the opposite sex. The argument in favor of group marriage is that it may be an effective vehicle to achieve growth and personal satisfaction in relationships. Rigid role patterns would not be so likely; one would not place every demand on a single other person. The responsibilities are shared. An individual can have different partners, depending on who is best suited to meet a particular need. If a person wants information the most knowledgeable partner would be consulted. If sex or physical intimacy is sought, the sexiest or most sensuous partner's attentions are sought. The argument against this form is that it becomes another bureaucratic relationship, with specialists and eventually informal job descriptions and assigned divisions of labor. Practically speaking, group marriage seems unlikely to become a possibility for most Americans. It is still considered immoral, impractical, legally complicated, and alien to our values.

One version of multilateral marriage which is becoming less alien, however, is occurring among older people. At its extreme it would be polygamy, in which one man is married to two or more women (Kassel, 1970). There is a dramatically skewed sex ratio among older Americans. Since there are so many more older women than men alive, and since there is a continued need for older people to belong and share love and intimacy, this relationship pattern might make sense for some. Shared living arrangements can be more economically, emotionally, and productively rewarding. On limited incomes, many older Americans are already living without benefit of the legal or social sanctions of marriage. The arguments against it are the familiar ones: It seems immoral, it might cause jealousy and competition between the two or more women, and it is "unnatural" since it is not monogamous. It might also be unacceptable because the adult children could fear complications in financial and inheritance issues. Polygamy among younger people seems even less likely to achieve social and legal acceptance. The sex ratio is more evenly distributed, so available potential partners do exist. The idea that society might sanction polygamy and replace its bigamy laws, given the tenacity of its values, seems remote (Osofsky, 1972).

Alternative forms of marriage are highly suspect in the United States. The more they are advocated or practiced, the greater seems to be the reaction against them. Even with increasing acceptance of serial monogamy, society still presumes that there is no true alternative (Whitehurst, 1977). The pressures of the traditional form of American marriage are increasing, however, and may eventually lead to some evolutionary changes. The pressures derive from the unrealistic expectations we place on marriage, expectations which may be unreachable and probably undesirable if they could be reached. Many people who enter marriages with such expectations eventually feel they failed because they didn't get what they expected. Realistic expectations will do much to enhance the status of marriage, no matter what its eventual form.

Chapter Three

The Client in Marital Therapy

Who is the client of the marital therapist? This deceptively simple question might cause most marital therapists to form a mental picture of a couple, a man and woman who are married or committed to one another. "The couple and their marriage is my client" would be the typical response. But the answer is an oversimplification. The marital therapist's client includes, but is not limited to, the couple or the marriage. This is illustrated in the following transcript:

> "Now remember, Dr. Jones, you swore to tell the whole truth before this court. So let me ask you again; did the defendant, Mr. Harris, tell you he was seeing another woman?"
>
> "Objection, Your Honor. The witness should not be compelled to violate the confidentiality of his client. We have already established that this is against his professional ethics."
>
> "Objection sustained."
>
> "But Your Honor, the defendant was not Dr. Jones' client because Dr. Jones was not representing the interests of Mr. Harris. Therefore no confidentiality should exist. Doctor, which of the Harrises were you treating?"
>
> "Both of them. I wasn't treating them as individuals."
>
> "But Doctor, that means the marriage was your client, and not Mr. Harris."

"No. He was also my client."

"But he wanted out of the marriage and you were trying to save it. So you weren't doing what he wanted, were you?"

"Well, marital therapists don't try to save marriages if it harms the individual. I was trying to help both of them be happier as individuals and as a couple."

"Now, Doctor, you are giving us a platitude. If Mr. and Mrs. Harris had different ideas about what would make them happy, you would have to choose sides. If one wants a divorce and the other doesn't you have to help one and not the other, don't you?"

"Not if one changes."

"Okay, but Mr. Harris never changed his mind. He was sure what he wanted from beginning to end. Only Mrs. Harris changed her mind. Did you get her to change?"

"Not really. I spelled out her alternatives. She made her own decisions."

"Is that a 'yes' or a 'no,' Doctor? Didn't you convince her to divorce?"

"No, I wouldn't try that. No reputable marital therapist would talk a client into divorce. I believe marriages should stay together whenever possible. I believe in marriage."

"Once again, Doctor, this makes me wonder who your client is. If you advocate marriage to a man who doesn't want it, how can he be your client? You may have been representing Mrs. Harris and maybe the interests of society itself, but you certainly were not representing Mr. Harris."

"Sir, I reiterate. Both the Harrises were my clients."

"Then tell me, what's your definition of a client?"

"Ummm . . . let's see. A client is someone you provide professional services for when they need help. They, uh, they have . . . problems and, er. . . ."

"Let me help you, Doctor. In my law practice, clients come to me voluntarily. If they don't want me to represent them, I don't. When I help clients I don't get it mixed up with helping society or serving the interests of anyone else but my client. You, on the other hand, are serving everyone but Mr. Harris. You are serving society, the institution of marriage, Mrs. Harris, and your own values. By that definition I suggest that Mr. Harris is not your client. Don't you agree, Doctor?"

"I object, Your Honor. The witness is being led and harassed."

"Objection overruled."

Who Is Being Treated?

The marital therapist is compelled to serve many masters; this is because a marriage is so much more than just two people. So much more than the well-being of those individuals is at stake in working on their marital problems. Since marriage is basically a foundation upon which much of civilization rests, all of society will have a vested interest in its outcome. Out of marriage has emerged much of the essential economic, educational, procreational, political, and psychological structure of society. These institutions would have had little viability without culturally sanctioned marriage. Thus, if the marriage did not extend beyond the interests of the couple, there would be no need or support for legal and religious involvement in the marriage or divorce process. There would be little impetus for marriage or influence as to how those marriages should be conducted. Society would have little legal or moral obligation to protect those who are vulnerable to the harm of family members. There would be few public funds spent on strengthening the family, no money for those agencies where marital therapists are employed, and none for the education of marital therapists. There would be unclear frames of reference by which to provide standards, expectations, or goals about how the couple might achieve greater growth and harmony. There would be no values which the couple and the therapist could consider in establishing their goals and means of achieving them. The marital therapist needs to recognize the competing and contradictory social and individual forces before embarking on an effort to treat couples in marital crisis.

It should be taken for granted, therefore, that society and its institutions will inevitably have much to say about marriage and the work of the marital therapist. Whether therapists recognize this fact or not, society itself is going to be one of the many other "clients" which are relevant, each of which compete and covertly "lobby" for the therapist to help protect their respective interests.

The Client-Set

For every marriage treated, there is a set of at least seven client-systems which must be served. Each has unique and competing goals, values, and priorities. And within each of these client-systems there are contradictions and constantly changing priorities as well. The seven clients are (1) the marital dyad itself; (2) the wife as an individual; (3) the husband as an individual; (4) those dependent on the couple; (5) society, i.e., the various economic, religious, psychological, and social elements whose ultimate well-being depends on what happens to the marriage institution; (6) the authority which sanctions the work of the marital therapist; and (7) the therapist himself.

If the marital dyad, the couple, is seen as the "client," and if its survival is the prime consideration, then therapy could be devoted solely to its preservation and improvement, no matter how this might affect the individuals. The interests of the marriage and the interests of the individuals are not always identical. In the long run, there are generally far more similarities of interest than there are conflicts—but this is never certain with some individuals. For example, one of the partners could be terribly threatened by the other's wish to go to school or get another job. If the change were beneficial to the individual but threatening to the relationship, a choice must be made. If the therapist views the marriage itself as the entity to be saved, he might attempt to dissuade the individual from such inclinations. The goal would be to change one or the other individual so the marriage could have a better chance of survival. That it might not be in the best interests of the individual to make this accommodation would be secondary. This is the risk in thinking of the couple or the marital dyad as the client.

If the husband or wife as an individual is considered the sole "client," there is another complication. Often what is in the best interest of one will be detrimental to the well-being of the other. Hopefully, a comfortable balance between their competing values and priorities can be found. But balances aren't always possible. If, for example, the husband was raised to believe that marriage is supposed to be the "traditional" type, where the male dominates, makes the decisions, keeps the wife "barefoot and pregnant," and determines the lifestyle for the family, his interests might be served at the expense of his wife's well-being. She might concur in this marital style, but in so doing might develop psychological and somatic symptoms which are clearly attributable to the marital relationship. If the husband were considered the client, the therapist could justifiably help him effectively teach his wife to be more content with her circumstance. Her "symptoms" could be treated by helping her accept and enjoy conforming to her husband's wishes. If, on the other hand, the wife as an individual were considered the sole client, therapy might help her become more effective in getting her husband to accept an egalitarian relationship. She could be taught to be more assertive. Her husband could be taught to feel comfortable with the change and with her motivation to change her role. If the therapist views the client as an individual, the well-being of the marriage would be secondary. He might seek to influence either partner to do whatever is deemed best, regardless of its impact on the marriage.

The children and other dependents of a marriage may also be considered clients by the therapist. If the interests of the dependents are paramount, the intervention will be different than if the interests of the husband, wife, or marriage were primary. For example, a couple might have serious dysfunctions in their relationship, but be in complete agreement about how they raise their children. If the couple subjected their children to severe beatings to discipline them, the therapist might find it distracting. The couple might be comfortable with this type of child-rearing behavior, but if the therapist finds it contrary to his own or to society's values, he might attempt to dissuade them from the practice. If he does, his client becomes the children. It could be argued that the abuse is a symptom of dysfunction in the marriage and that its continuance would ultimately be harmful to the couple, but this isn't certain. Many parents are not directly harmed by abusing their children—but the children always are. This is not to suggest that the children's interest is to be ignored. On the contrary, they are appropriately to be considered a part of the client-set in working on the marriage. In many states, in fact, marital therapists are legally obliged to consider the children's interests. In those states, therapists and many other professionals are required to report to law enforcement agencies any suspected child or spouse abuse. The requirement supersedes confidentiality provisions in those jurisdictions.

Society is another of the marital therapist's "clients." Social mores are imbedded in our personalities and felt so strongly that often we don't even question their validity: young children don't question the authority of their parents; people do not destroy the possessions of others; one does not always express whatever emotions are felt directly, whenever they are felt; the poor or handicapped are not allowed to starve while others have plenty; adults don't go to public places unclothed; siblings do not have sexual intercourse. The list is endless.

But the list is also contradictory. Different segments of society have different prescriptions for how people should conduct their lives. For example: "You shouldn't drive cars faster than the speed limit," vs. "Test drive one of our hot new muscle cars today. It goes from zero to 80 in just 12 seconds." " People should limit the number of children they have in order to conserve the earth's limited resources," vs. "God gave us sex for procreation, so whenever we have intercourse we should expect to have babies. Besides, God will always provide." "Women should be afforded equal opportunity and responsibility," vs. "Women are different from men and need special protections and considerations." The list of these contradictory pressures is also endless.

The influence of these expectations on marital therapy cannot be ignored (Fisher and Sprenkle, 1978). They are the basis for determining what is "normal" or "healthy" marital functioning; therapists as well as clients use them as their standard. It is considered "normal" in some Eskimo villages for a host to share the sexual favors of his wife with an honored visitor. But the same behavior might be labeled pathological in other cultures. If the Eskimo did not make such an offering he might be seen as selfish and miserly by his peers (Mead, 1977). On the other hand, an Appalachian bootlegger might be considered abnormal if he didn't fight someone who partook of his woman's sexual favors.

The therapist's attitudes and treatment approaches are as much influenced by societal norms as are the client's. For example, despite assertions to the contrary, therapists are highly vulnerable to sex-role stereotyping. Many therapists recognize that clients and other therapists engage in such thinking, but doubt that they themselves may be so inclined. However, research has demonstrated that both male and female marital therapists, as well as their clients, have preconceived notions of what is healthy or appropriate female vs. male functioning (Gingras-Baker, 1976). Studies addressing this question often present to therapists lists of behaviors or responses to given situations. Some therapists are told that these behaviors and responses were made by a woman; a matched group of therapists is given the same list and told the responses were made by a man. Therapists who believe the behavior to be a woman's are usually more likely to consider it abnormal, symptomatic of problems, or worthy of further inquiry. Other studies show that therapists will more likely seek to have the woman accommodate to the man's needs than vice versa. So if a woman wanted to deviate from prescribed roles in order to grow, learn, or reach her potential, therapists would probably question her motives more rigorously. If society seeks to keep the sex roles intact, and if the therapist supports this, then it is society's interests, not the wife who is the client. Therapists can find "proof" — or at least compelling arguments — that one or another norm for the marriage is the healthiest. And when they seek to influence the husband and wife toward such conduct, they are serving the interests of society.

The sixth type of clientele served by the marital therapist is the therapist's employer or the auspices under which the work is sanctioned. This includes the therapist's agency, professional association, state regulatory or licensing board, and special interest groups who help finance the work of the therapy. For example, if the therapy is conducted in a church-sponsored or privately financed social agency, the values of those sponsors must be considered. To continue to receive funding, the therapist's employer must demonstrate that the providers are getting their money's worth. If the funder holds that the preservation of the marriage is the sole criterion, the agency must show that so many marriages were saved during the fiscal year. Some organizations which help finance marital therapy could not tolerate much deviation. A conservative or fundamentalist religious organization might not be inclined to sponsor a marital therapy operation in which the couples were encouraged to form more egalitarian relationships.

Finally, the therapist's own values and beliefs are also served. He cannot help but refer to his own values as the standard of well-being for the couple. For example, suppose a husband and wife agreed that they would enhance their sexual relationship if they both participated in extramarital affairs. This lifestyle has not been accepted in the United States and, in fact, has been condemned by most of its moral leaders. It is seen as abnormal or indicative of pathology, even though many other cultures of the world have endorsed and supported extramarital sexuality. It cannot, therefore, be considered inherently pathological but only a deviation from the acceptable norms of this particular society. If the couple sought therapy in an agency or church which believed that such behavior was immoral or sinful, the therapist might attempt to show that this behavior is a symptom of mental illness or instability. His measure of therapy progress would be the couple's growing reluctance to participate in extramarital sex. Rather than attribute the goal to such value-laden considerations as "morals," the therapist might ascribe it to unhealthiness, or to the ill effects such deviant behavior might have on the participant. The values of the therapist rather than the needs of the couple being treated would be taking precedence.

Obstacles in Treating Client-Systems

It is not easy to consider serving so many different interests whenever a marriage is treated. Therapists face at least four major obstacles to such thinking. One is that the conscientious therapist is usually devoted and committed to the individuals he serves; he wants to be single-minded in his zeal to help them and wants their interests to be paramount. The husband and wife are real entities, present in his office, with flesh and blood needs. The other "clients" are less visible and not immediately apparent. The demands made by these competing interests are more subtle, and the response to them is often outside the conscious awareness of both the therapist and the couple.

This dilemma is vividly demonstrated in examples in which conduct considered appropriate by the therapist is not identical with that of the client. For example, a husband and wife, both of whom were physicians, were treated in marital therapy. In an early session they revealed that they believed it was healthy for their two young children to sleep with them in the parental bed. All four members of the family had always slept together and planned to continue doing so. Though the clients were born in this country, their parents had emigrated from a nation whose culture accepted this bedroom propinquity. It was a poor nation where most people had no alternative but to share. The therapist was concerned about frustrated oedipal conflicts in the children and suspected that the psychodynamics of the choice of sleeping arrangements was more pathological than culturally derived. He remained impassive about the issue, believing that its "inherent pathology" would force it to the consciousness of one or the other partner, and then into the therapy. But it never seemed to come up. The therapist finally began to ask questions. "Do you find that you have sexual inhibitions when your children are beside you?" "Do the children want to get between you during foreplay?" "Are they very upset during your intercourse?" But the couple didn't seem as concerned as was the therapist. "No, we have a good sex life," they responded. "We're not inhibited because we've never hidden anything from them. They aren't upset at all. They're used to it. Sometimes they want to cuddle with us and sometimes we cuddle back, and sometimes we just push them out of the way."

The therapist tried other questions: "How long will this go on? Will they still be in your bed when they are teenagers?" "Have you ever heard of oedipal problems? There are some serious mental health issues here, don't you know?" But the couple remained unconcerned. "Sure they can stay in our bed until they are out on their own. Why not? We said they are used to it. It is as natural to them as our eating dinner in front of them. Sure we have heard of the oedipal complex. But that's an unproven hypothesis, originating in a sexually repressive Victorian culture. We don't think it is going to cause mental illness in our kids. There is a lot more mental illness in this country, where sleeping as a family unit is a no-no, than there is in the countries where it is accepted."

The therapist could offer many rejoinders and counter-arguments, of course. But he knew further debate would be counterproductive to the therapy. He continued to work with the couple; when they terminated their sessions they were happy with the results. The therapist, however, always believed that treatment was not really concluded successfully because he didn't help them solve their "problem" of sleeping with the children.

A second obstacle to thinking about the conflicting client system is that it appears to confuse the issue. The job of the marital therapist is already immensely complicated without having to consider such arcane matters as social norms and implicit values. Treating couples requires considerable knowledge of the psychic and social influences on the husband, the wife, and the interaction. This can be far more confusing and demanding than is work with an individual. There is an overwhelming mass of relevant information in the marital therapy situation; the therapist must choose which of it is going to be in the forefront of his attention at any given time. Some important information will have to be relegated to a secondary place. The therapist copes by keeping as much of the clutter of irrelevant information from his thinking as possible. Information which is considered to be of less immediate impact, such as the other elements of the client-system, gets placed in this category.

A third obstacle to thinking about the client-system is the result of the marital therapist's training. Most practitioners are trained, not as marital therapists, but as members of other professions or academic disciplines. In most of these disciplines, such as psychology, psychiatry, social work, pastoral counseling, and the education and guidance specialties, the training has generally followed the model of individual treatment. All the marital therapy disciplines, some more than others, train their members to consider social influences as they interface with the individual being treated; but the individual is still the primary consideration. The training is disproportionately devoted to helping the individual "get well"—which is usually seen as adapting to society. It is less oriented to helping society change to accommodate to the individual. Given such training, it is not reasonable to expect marital therapists to think about client systems as much as about individuals.

The fourth obstacle occurs through the influence of the professions with which marital therapists identify. Most marital therapists are members of at least one other profession, and their primary allegiance is to that other body. Even those practitioners who are not members of other professions, who are exclusively marital therapists, still identify with the other professions which primarily serve individual clients. They model their form of intervention after the other "helping professions." But the other professions have more clearly defined clients than does the marital therapist. The doctor or lawyer, for example, does not have to represent the interests of society when working with the individual. The only thing that counts, during that interaction at least, is this client's well-being. The other professions have a more quantifiable or objective way of determining how much they have succeeded in behalf of their clients. How long did the patient stay sick? How many patients died? Did the client win or lose the case? How many cases were lost? These are objective criteria, and the only basic ones which are relevant. When members of these disciplines also engage in marital therapy, as they frequently and happily do, they are inclined to use the same criteria for the different kind of clientele with whom they are working. And they influence others who are also engaged in marital therapy to view clients this way. The professional associations and legal regulatory bodies which sanction the work of these professionals also contribute to this view; their codes of ethics invariably indicate that the individual client's interests are paramount. They would have a difficult time developing a clear, consistent ethical code which might suggest that there are many additional and contradictory values which have to be considered as well.

Benefits in Treating Client-Systems

With so many obstacles to thinking this way, why should the marital therapist want to reorient his view to encompass an entire client-system every time a couple is treated? Some therapists might feel they are better off concentrating on the complex task at hand without obfuscating the issue at hand with such things as social norms, competing value priorities, and client-systems. They might believe that they will be more effective in their work if they are unaware of the conflicting pressures. But as in most things, added knowledge obviously doesn't cause problems. Knowing about this is no more dangerous than a pubescent child knowing about sex. Knowing how it works, what its implications are, and what the various consequences of it might be do not automatically assure that the child will become promiscuous. The child, in fact, will probably be better able to deal with it than if ignorant. So too is it with the marital therapist. Recognizing that there are many masters, many different clients all seeking a voice in the marital therapy intervention, does not mean that the therapist is performing a disservice to the couple. Indeed, this awareness enables the therapist to more effectively resist influences which are antithetical to the goals of therapy.

The marital therapist's awareness of the client-system is analogous to the psychoanalyst's awareness of the transference phenomenon. Knowing what is implicitly going on is equally important for both. Many therapists, particularly those who have a psychoanalytic theory base, stress the importance of the unconscious and of transference and countertransference in the treatment relationship. They recognize that the relationship between the client and the therapist contains many feelings and behaviors which have no apparent rationale if appraised superficially. The dynamic interaction between them is something more than the explicit words they are speaking. If only their words were considered relevant, it would be almost impossible to account for some of the interaction taking place. It could only be explained by knowing of some of the unconscious dynamics which are contributing to the relationship. Some of the feelings about the other person are based on factors in the therapist's or client's memory or unconscious impulses. If the therapist were ignorant of the phenomenon and unaware that part of the interaction was based on it, the treatment would be confused. The analytically oriented therapist would find it very difficult to conduct a therapeutic relationship without such knowledge. So too should the marital therapist find it difficult to treat couples while ignorant about client-systems.

Armed with the awareness, however, the therapist can potentially be far more effective. He can be more objective and can recognize when the treatment is proceeding inappropriately. The different elements of the client-system will not evaporate if the therapist tries to avoid them; the best alternative is to be aware and find some balance between them. Choices have to be made, and the choice is always implicit at any given moment in the therapist's work. He must continually be asking himself, "Who am I serving at this moment?"

Choosing Sides

A cardinal principal of marital therapy is that the therapist should not take sides. He should not favor the husband over the wife or vice versa, even if he is firmly convinced that one is right and other is not. Even if he is sure that one is more healthy than the other, or that one has values more similar to his own, this should not determine the direction of the therapy. All clients and all of the clients' values deserve respect and freedom from the imposition of contrary values. This principle is easy for marital therapists to learn and practice; it is relatively rare to have a therapist blatantly choose sides between the husband and wife. The only exception should occur when a paradoxical ploy is built into the treatment plan. In such instances the therapist might align with the husband or wife in order to upset unhealthy positions which otherwise are locked in place. But paradox is not the same as choosing sides between the partners.

Therapists rarely violate this principle unless it is temporarily part of the treatment plan, because the results are so clearly counterproductive. It is more difficult to avoid other kinds of choices. A therapist can't always avoid choosing among other elements in the client-system; he must take a position. He has to know just whom among the many who seek his support he is representing at any moment. It is an over-simplification or meaningless platitude to say that his concern for the couple is paramount, but the idea of dividing loyalties is troublesome. It seems wrong and unethical to choose a side, to represent one of the clients at the expense of the others. But wrongdoing or unethicality can only occur when the perpetrator has an option and chooses inappropriately. In marital therapy an opportunity to choose doesn't exist; it is not possible to avoid making decisions, conscious or otherwise, about which of the clients one is serving at any given time. This is not to say, however, that the therapist has no ethical problem in serving the clients. On the contrary, the dilemma is very great, perhaps more so than that confronted by any other discipline. The required need to deal with so many compelling but contradictory demands is fraught with opportunities to make unethical decisions—but this is going to occur when there are choices to be made. And the choice which is always implicit at any given moment is who is my client at this moment.

To the extent possible, the therapist should make explicit who the client is. If this is done at all times, then the wife and husband will know what is behind the therapist's activity. If it isn't explicit, then the husband or wife might think that the therapist is representing one of them when in fact the client is someone or something else. Armed with this knowledge, the man or woman may make a realistic choice. Knowing the primary concern of the therapist at a given moment, they can more clearly choose to accept or reject the thrust of the therapist's ideas, or possibly seek treatment with someone whose values are more closely attuned to their own.

This is easier to accomplish in some therapy settings than in others, and it is easier with the theoretical orientations of some marital therapies than of others. For example, if a couple goes to an agency which is sponsored by a church, and if everyone knows the church is adamantly opposed to divorce and adamantly in favor of the preservation of traditional marriage styles, then the couple can assume that this value will also be served in the intervention process. It is reasonable for an agency to specify its values and make clear to potential clients that it provides service with specific objectives in mind. This means there is no hidden agenda. Similarly, the agency known as "Save-A-Marriage" might be expected by its clients to work more toward finding ways of reconciliation and compromise than would an agency known as "Divorce Guidance Center."

Some theoretical orientations in marital therapy are more amenable to this kind of explicitness than others. Therapies with behavioral orientations might find no difficulty in being clear about specific objectives and means of reaching them. But the psychoanalytically oriented therapist may want to keep his values and positions on any social issue more or less to himself. This orientation works largely through getting the husband and wife to project their own conflicts, needs, and ideas onto the therapist; they would be less inclined or able to do so if they were aware of the therapist's values. The question, "Who is the client?" is more complex than it first appears. The answer is that all the seven components of the client-system are, whether we feel they should be or not. The therapist should endeavor to be aware who is being served at any given time in treatment. He should establish what his own priorities are and how his own standards impinge on the treatment. If his own values are recognized and are paramount, he owes it to his clients to inform them what his values are and that they are not the only possible considerations. If his values are inevitably biased in favor of the man or woman, this too should be made clear. If he is not inclined to support the values of the agency or profession under whose auspices he works, this should be made clear. Then the couple has an informed choice to make.

Therapists cannot always be aware of their own prejudices. Biases are bound to occur no matter how alert or insightful the therapist is. Conscientious therapists find various means of minimizing the risk, including the use of supervision, team interventions, videotapes, and one-way mirrors to permit objective scrutiny of their work. All are beneficial, but none are completely satisfactory. Supervision of the marital therapist, no matter how experienced he is, can be a very useful tool in keeping biases from creeping in. Discussion of each interview—or the whole case—with a supervisor or colleague helps the therapist gain a different perspective of a situation. Unfortunately, this practice is limited by its costliness and by the feeling of many practitioners that supervision is only for the novice. It is also limited in that the therapist will not be able to accurately portray the dynamics of the therapy, especially when the action was not in concordance with the supervisor's values. Using a team approach, where more than one therapist works with the couple simultaneously, can also help preclude some biases. Two or more therapists will be able to evaluate one another after the session and will make a more objective treatment possible during the session. The liability of the team or conjoint approach is that there is often an implicit or explicit power and authority structure between them. The therapist in the subordinate role is likely to have less to say about his values and have to defer to the values of the more powerful therapist (Barker and Briggs, 1969).

The use of videotapes can help some therapists see how their own values and prejudices creep into the therapy situation. If the recording is witnessed by the therapist only, many of the same blind spots in the session would exist in the replay. If it is witnessed only by a few people who are less powerful than the therapist, they might be reluctant to point out any problems. The ideal use of a videotape is to show it to several others of varying power. Some of the therapist's peers, supervisor, consultants, students, and even the treated couple could view it. The disadvantage of this option is that it is extremely time consuming and thus not used as frequently as one might want. Furthermore, the harm caused by the prejudice has already been done before the tape is shown. Although it could be useful to the therapist and his other clients to have his blind spots revealed, the couple concerned in the observation have not had the same benefit.

Use of the one-way mirror and a consultation team observing the work of the marital and family therapist can be quite useful for minimizing such problems. It is, however, a very expensive and time-consuming process; thus it is seldom done outside of teaching situations. This method is used by Jay Haley and Chloe Madanes in teaching and practicing their strategic/structural approach to family therapy (Haley, 1977). The therapist or therapy team works with a couple or family while under the direct observation of the consulting team. Team members discuss among themselves the dynamics of the interaction; they comment to one another about the therapy while it is actually transpiring. As the occasion arises, they may signal the therapist and family members that they have an observation they may wish to share. The effect of this observation interaction is to keep the therapist alert and aware of more of the dynamics than would be probable if he were working alone. Commentary by the "outside" therapist to the "inside" therapist has been likened to a Greek chorus, in which outsiders help the participants in the play and the audience keep abreast of everyone's role in the system (Papp, 1980).

Nothing will be as effective in preventing these conflicts from occurring as the awareness of the therapist to their existence. Keeping an open mind and recognizing the limitations of trying to serve so many conflicting parties and discrepant goals is both challenge and reward for the capable therapist.

Chapter Four

Establishing Marital Therapy Goals

Since there will be disparities among those in the client-set who have an interest in the therapy outcome, it is important to define goals at the beginning of treatment. The marital therapist and the couple have to decide what they hope to accomplish; otherwise treatment will meander aimlessly and inefficiently, as it is pulled in a variety of contradictory directions.

Who determines the goals and makes them explicit in marital therapy? Therapists would like to think that the husband and wife, themselves, do this. It would be most convenient if the couple would simply say what their goals are. In the first meeting, when the therapist asks why the couple wants professional help, whatever they answer could be considered their list. However, as most experienced marital therapists know, goal setting can't be left entirely to the couple. There are six major reasons why this is so.

Obstacles in Goal Setting

The first factor which prevents the marital therapist from relying on the marital partners to explicate goals is that they often aren't sure or can't articulate what they want. The husband or wife might say things like: "I just want to be happy." "I want to get along better with my spouse." "I want to feel more fulfilled in the relationship." "I want to feel the romance that used to be there." "I want my partner to quit making me unhappy." These are important as abstract ideals, but can't really be used as objectives in specifying the direction of therapy; they must be redefined in operational terms to be useful. It is the therapist's job to help the couple restate and reformulate objectives in terms which can lead to a workable plan. The therapist must ascertain, for example, what the client means by "being happy" or "getting along better with my partner." He helps the couple determine what factors in the relationship contribute to the way each defines happiness and which do not. Redefining and breaking goals down to workable parts is a major part of the marital therapy process. But in the course of doing so, the therapist realistically cannot avoid determining as well as explicating them.

The second obstacle in goal setting is the likelihood that the objectives of the husband and wife will conflict. The husband, for example, might want his wife to initiate sexual activity more often, while she wants her husband to be the sole initiator. He wants leisure on weekends and she wants them to get the chores done. By the time many couples reach the marital therapist's office, they have gotten into the habit of working toward competing goals. They are frustrated at their failure to make their individual hopes the goals of the relationship. Eventually they become determined to reject any of the partner's goals simply on principle. For many clients, an overriding but implicit goal is to obtain the support of the therapist against the spouse. When both husband and wife have such opposite objectives, they are in no position to solely determine the goals of marital therapy. The marital therapist must intervene and help redefine their objectives. The most convenient way to do this is by identifying those goals which are fairly compatible and by focusing the treatment on them; after they are reached new goals may be added. When the husband and wife achieve some goals together, they are more amenable to adding new ones.

Third, goals are usually interrelated and cannot be easily divided into desirable and undesirable parts. For example, a husband wants his wife to maintain a comfortable home and be there on demand; then he is displeased because she isn't an accomplished and highly paid professional like the women in his office. A wife may want her husband to be more forceful or dominant; then she insists on having an equal voice in all family decision making. In most successful marriages, the partners recognize that the bad must be taken with the good. It is the therapist's job in goal setting to make this apparent, to show how certain of the couple's goals are inextricably related. This knowledge permits the couple to make more rational decisions about whether or not they really want to achieve those goals.

The fourth obstacle is that each marital partner has mixed and changing feelings about what is wanted. What is a goal one minute may not be the next. The husband or wife may want to leave the marriage one day, and improve it the next. The marital therapist cannot rely solely on the what the client describes as the goals of the moment, since they may not typify what the client's goals really are. Moreover, the goals cannot remain synchronized between the partners even when they start out together. Their experiences are unique and influence them with different levels of impact; their rates of change vary. The therapist takes all this into account when the goals are being explicated. There must be enough flexibility about the goals so they can continue to be relevant to the changing circumstances of the couple, yet they must be consistent enough so the therapy is not aimless. To accomplish this, a procedure for changing goals after treatment is under way is established before change actually occurs. If the marital partners agree that they no longer hope to achieve a certain goal, the treatment plan can be modified accordingly.

The fifth obstacle is that the marital partners and the therapist might have very different views of what the goals should be. Couples often want to achieve a goal which the therapist believes is not in their long-term interests; this is not uncommon. Recent studies show some disparity between what therapists and clients consider to be healthy family functioning (Fischer and others, 1982). Because of such disparities, it is challenging but particularly important to explicate marital therapy goals in advance. The couple and therapist may never agree about all the goals, but clients are better served by clearly knowing where each wants to go. For example, one couple's goal was "to stop arguing." They wanted marital therapy only to help avoid this. It was their united belief that arguing indicated a poor relationship and the eventual risk of divorce. The therapist soon learned that the couple always seemed to feel and communicate better after each argument; the therapist saw their arguments as healthy safety valves. Despite some unpleasantness while they took place, the arguments seemed more beneficial than harmful. This couple's kind of argument was a catalyst for subsequent communication and not an indicator of a poor marriage. So the therapist helped them modify the goal. The revised plan was not to stop arguing, but to argue in a more fair and less manipulative way. The therapist obviously was instrumental in determining and explicating this new goal.

The last obstacle to setting marital therapy goals comes from the therapist's conceptual orientation. Marital therapists are by no means in agreement about what the goals should be. Differences largely stem from their underlying theoretical or conceptual orientations. The defined goals are often as much a product of this conceptual orientation as they are of the specific needs of the couple. It is vital in marital therapy goal setting, therefore, for the therapist to have a clear and consistent notion of the theoretical influences which are the foundation of the practice.

Most marital therapists are influenced by one of five orientations. They might belong to one of the three marital and family "schools" or consider themselves "eclectic" or "pragmatic." The three schools are known as the systems, psychodynamic, and social learning orientations. The systems approach takes into account a myriad of social, psychological, and environmental influences. It views the couple and the family as a unit whose every part is influenced by every other part. Goals are defined in terms of changing the power balances and communication lines among the family members so that the reciprocal influences between them are more healthy. The basic goal of the psychodynamic orientation is that of reconciling intrapsychic conflicts which lead to problems in the dyadic relationship. The goal of the psychodynamically oriented therapist might be to help a husband and wife understand how an unconscious personality pattern leads to unhealthy interpersonal relationships. The goal of the social learning or behavioral orientation is to teach the couple to behave in ways which are more consistent with their explicitly stated objectives. The goal would not be to determine why personality patterns lead to conflict but to identify and change observable behaviors which harm the relationship, regardless of why.

Marital therapists are ethically obliged not to impose goals on their client couples. This means the husband and wife must actively participate in the goal-setting process and have the last word about the objectives. Therapists faced with the aforementioned obstacles recognize the complexity of this ethical obligation, as well as its seriousness. They realize that they are going to be very influential in establishing the goals, whether or not they want to be. Since the therapist influences the choice of goals, the clients deserve to know what influences the therapist.

Five Orientations in Goal Setting

Most marital therapists are influenced by and derive their conceptual orientations from a composite of sources (Sprenkle, Kenney, and Sutton, 1983). A therapist rarely adheres strictly and exclusively to the tenets of one theory or school of thought. Instead of being "members" of one of the three predominant schools or of the myriad variations within the schools, some therapists tend toward the eclectic, espousing portions of the different orientations. Others avoid all theoretical foundations. Each of these five possibilities has merits and faults.

The approach by marital therapists which stands in greatest disrepute seems to be the "pragmatic" or atheoretical orientation. This is so even though its history is longest by far and its adherents outnumber all the others. It is mostly practiced by non-mental health professionals, lay people, and various advice givers who rely on "common sense" and the "wisdom of the ages." The premise is that, if couples keep mindful of the appropriate maxim, their troubles will be over. The ideas are usually platitudes or witty bon mots—and are rather inconsistent. There is no conceptual orientation behind the advice but rather a series of disjoined ideas about what seems to work to achieve a specific goal. Some of the more durable of these aphorisms include the following: Love conquers all problems; A person who desires to get married should either know everything or nothing; Marry in haste and repent at leisure; Whether you marry or not, you will regret it; Anyone not worth the wooing is not worth the winning; If you're losing an argument with your wife, tell her how wonderful she is; Common sense would prevent many divorces—and also many marriages; A woman gives sex to get love and a man gives love to get sex; For every woman who makes a fool out of a man, there's a woman who makes a man out of a fool; The ideal man is as numerous as there are women to describe him; The happiest couple is a deaf man and a blind wife; The woman who thinks no man is good enough for her may be right, but more often she is left; Before marriage a man yearns for a woman, but after the wedding the "Y" is silent; Many a man loves his wife still; Women are to be loved, not understood.

Truth exists in many of these and countless other epigrams, but they are usually accorded more attention than they merit. Their purveyor is sometimes considered profoundly wise and perceptive by troubled couples who seek a functional relationship. So if the goal is to convince a naive couple about the wisdom of the advisor, they are indispensible. But if the goal is to facilitate more understanding, better communication, and a more adaptable relationship, they are not very helpful—and in some cases harmful. The pragmatic approach is destined to remain a static field whose function is to preserve the status quo. An atheoretical therapist is hopelessly consigned to a career of repeating ideas which have been around for centuries, never growing, never learning about more effective means of helping troubled couples. Obviously there is nothing wrong with a little of this, and probably every marital therapist, serious or otherwise, states some of the platitudes on occasion. But if the advisor's entire professional repertoire of helping activity is at this level, it is rather meaningless in any professional sense.

The orientation called "eclectic" comes from the Greek "eg lego," to choose. An eclectically oriented therapist is also pragmatic but uses theories and theory-based techniques from a variety of sources to provide his unique form of treatment. For example, one eclectically oriented therapist assessed a husband and wife who had a long history of violent arguments. He discovered that both of them were raised by violently abusive parents. He also learned that one or the other of them tends to pick the fights whenever reminded of certain childhood episodes. A psychodynamic therapist might have helped the husband and wife to work through and resolve their traumatic emotional conflicts with catharsis. The eclectic therapist appreciates the importance of the developmental psychic conflict, but also recognizes that such treatment would take longer than the couple can or will endure. So he uses behavioral modification techniques instead; in order to encourage different behaviors, he assigns several tasks for the couple to use whenever a fight is about to start.

The value of the eclectic approach is debatable. Its detractors say it is conceptually inconsistent in that it often uses theories which are contradictory. They also point out that its results are limited to practical and short-term expedients. Always borrowing the ideas of others affords little room for the development of an integrated conceptual scheme of one's own (Colapinto, 1979). Furthermore, the therapist cannot determine whether the method was effective. If several contradictory premises are used, one can't be sure which of them accounted for the results. Therapists can, and usually do, surmise that improvements are the cumulative product of their entire composite of skills and knowledge. But this cannot be certain unless the therapist analyzes each discrete element to see which accounts for the desired outcome. Moreover, say the detractors, an eclectic therapist cannot easily teach any

orientation or methodology. This means every new generation of eclectic therapists virtually has to begin all over again.

Proponents of this approach say that those who are helped don't
mind that they were treated with a variety of concepts, if they get the
results they want. What counts to consumer and practitioner is that the
goals are reached. It is argued that different techniques seem to work
for different people, even if we don't yet know why. They also say that
there are so many problems with all the available conceptual orientations that it is best not to adhere to one until further refinements or
proofs are obtained.

The Conceptual Orientations

It is true that each of the three major theoretical orientations in marital
therapy, the approaches known as psychodynamic, social learning, and
systems, is founded on some questionable assumptions. There have
been thoughtful criticisms of the inhibiting effects of theory on clinical
practice (Whitaker, 1976). Nevertheless, a theoretical orientation offers greater potential for systematic inquiry, growth in methodology,
and testing for efficiency, than does the eclectic or atheoretical orientations. The serious marital therapist will probably be more effective and
be able to make greater contributions to the field if he becomes familiar
with all of them and chooses one as his foundation for practice. But
how does one choose?

No attempt will be made here to advocate one or another of the
theoretical orientations. Making a rational decision about which approach is best is challenging and may ultimately be rather arbitrary.
Most marital therapists seem to arrive at their choice of theory base as a
result of greater exposure to the ideas of one or another school, rather
than through an objective comparison of them all. No choice can yet
be based on a preponderance of evidence which clearly shows the su-
periority of one or the other.

Still, if one wanted to make a systematic comparison he might attend some of the many workshops, graduate schools, seminars, and
special lectures devoted to each. If he lacked the resources for this, he
might read the more important works describing each approach. For
example, thoughtful reviews of the psychodynamic theories and methods used in treating couples in marital crisis can be found in works by
Meissner (1978), Nadelson (1978), and the Blancks (1968). Dicks' per-

ceptive book, *Marital Tensions* (1967), is still the basic source for the object-relations aspect of psychodynamic theory. The social learning or behavioral perspective is thoroughly documented in Stuart's excellent book, *Helping Couples Change* (1980). And some of the most influential works which fit under the general rubric of systems approaches include books by Bowen (1978), Haley (1977), Madanes (1981), and Minuchin (1974), to name only a few. It must be remembered, when using the term "systems theory," that a single orientation is not being considered. There is considerable diversity and controversy between those who are considered "systems thinkers."

The student who wishes to learn about these approaches should read these original sources. For the most part, their work is at least as readable as that of their "interpreters" and "disciples." They tend to be quite persuasive in behalf of their respective orientations, even though many who do not share their enthusiasms sometimes consider some of them to be too dogmatic. It is also helpful to read the more thoughtful comparative analyses. Those who have objectively described the theoretical orientations, critiqued and provided a comparative analysis of their respective goals, deficiencies, and prospects include Sundland (1977), Ritterman (1977), Gurman (1978), Foster and Hoier (1982), and Green and Kolevson (1982).

The goals of the psychodynamically oriented therapist might seem as ambitious as curing the underlying emotional illness of each partner. But, in practice, their goals are less devoted to the individual restructuring of the couple's psyches than toward the restructuring of the internally based perceptions, expectations, and reactions each spouse has of the other (Nadelson, 1978). Personality reconstruction doesn't occur in brief interventions, and most marital therapy is of short duration. Psychodynamic therapy might assume and encourage regression so that the client can rework development conflicts, but the typically more constricted time frame of marital therapy usually precludes this. Fostering transference would be a problem in couple therapy because of time constraints, the presence of the third person, and the need for the therapist to be more directive and focused. Most psychodynamic therapists point out that their theory is mostly used as a framework for providing understanding and appraising the internal workings of marital problems. Psychodynamic marital therapists heed Karen Horney's statement, "Analysis is not the only way to resolve inner conflicts. Life itself still remains a very effective therapist" (Horney, 1945).

The premise of the social learning theory of marital therapy is that successful marriages occur when each partner provides sufficient rewards to the other for satisfying behavior. There are positive reinforcements and reciprocal rewards to encourage desirable behavior in one another. Marriages which are not successful are those in which the reciprocal rewards are out of balance, often because of coercion by the spouse. The view is that marital dysfunction is situation-specific and based on the immediate behavior of the other spouse. This may be rewarding or reinforcing for one but not for the other. Goals center around changing this pattern through a gradual solving of one problem at a time. There will be "spillover" into other areas when the couple learns to interact in reciprocally rewarding ways in similar problem situations. It focuses specifically on observable problem areas in the couple's relationship. The therapist is often very directive with the clients. Objectives are stated at the outset in a very precise manner. Outcomes can be tested more satisfactorily than in the other approaches.

The various "systems" approaches tend to seek to work out overt shared agreements about covert rules of the relationship. Bowen might call this process working toward the better "differentiation of self" and away from "ego fusion" in which the family members are not autonomous enough to function independently in a healthy way (Bowen, 1978). Strategic/structural therapists (Minuchin, 1981; Haley, 1977; Madanes, 1981) look at negative feedback loops which alert the system when one is exceeding tolerable limits of family rules. The focus in the systems orientation is not so much with the origin of the conflict or misperception, but with the current organization of the interaction. The understanding is that couples communicate at multiple levels simultaneously and paradoxically. They exchange mixed messages, and the spouse risks responding at the wrong level or to the wrong component of the message. The therapist helps by delineating the different levels and contradictory messages, reframing the messages, and paradoxically exaggerating the communication to make it more easily observed. The premise of this orientation is that changed relationships between the husband and wife cause a change in subjective experience.

A Couple Compares Orientations

The way the orientations compare is illustrated with the following case: A newly married couple wants marital therapy primarily because of serious sexual problems. The husband is inorgasmic whenever intercourse occurs in the front-to-front "missionary" position. The wife invariably becomes nauseous whenever alternative positions are attempted or even suggested. If a therapy goal is partly to help the couple achieve harmonious sexual functioning, the particular theoretical orientation of the therapist would strongly influence the direction the therapy would take.

The psychodynamically oriented therapist might explore with the couple the developmental experiences which led to each of their current feelings about the act of intercourse. The therapist learns that the man was exposed to a series of traumatic events during his oedipal developmental phase. From the age of three to six, he witnessed a profusion of men having intercourse with his mother, always in the "missionary position." The child watched with fascination and horror, and whenever his presence was noticed by his mother or her lover, the boy would be soundly thrashed and ejected from the house. The psychodynamic therapist hypothesizes that the emotional conflict set up by this recurring experience still remains within the man and is activated whenever intercourse is contemplated. He defends against the conflict primarily with the denial and reaction-formation mechanisms. He attempts to pacify his libidinous urges through intercourse, but avoids duplicating the way he witnessed it as a young boy. The therapist's goal is to work through the conflict by allowing the man to emotionally relive the experience and abreact the tension. This method might preclude the presence of the wife during this working through phase of the husband's treatment; she might be provided individual therapy at the same time to achieve similar goals.

If the couple had gone to a behavioral therapist, the goal might be to extinguish the aversion to this coital position. The therapist might suggest that the couple refrain from intercourse for the next month. Meanwhile, during the first week after their training begins, the couple would be asked to hold each other face-to-face in bed. They would gradually increase frequency and amount of time they do this each day. The therapist instructs the couple to be mutually supportive during this experience, and under no circumstances attempt intercourse, no matter how strong is the desire. The assumption is that the man will gradually lose his fear of intercourse if he comes to associate something pleasurable and rewarding with the position rather than suffering the threatening or fearful feeling. In ensuing days, the therapist might suggest gradually escalating activity, such as lying atop one another without intercourse, fondling in the front-to-front position without engaging in intercourse, and finally having intercourse face-to-face.

If the husband and wife had seen a systems therapist, they would work toward more clear communication and explicit role definitions.

They might tell one another what they think intercourse means to the partner and themselves. Each partner would describe the fear of intercourse and relate it to the relative expectations and feelings of power and powerlessness it instills. The couple might be asked to sit together for a few minutes each day and describe in detail what they feel about sexual intercourse, and about the various positions which they have tried to use. They might be asked to describe their fears about the front-to-front position and detail what they think would help ease some of this conflict. The therapist gets the couple to define their rules about intercourse and to look at the rules from different perspectives. The husband makes explicit his fear that his wife will reject him as did his mother. His wife's perceived power will have to be restructured. He would be helped to see himself as the equal of his wife and not as a little child who can be hurt by her.

Outcome Goals

No matter what the therapist's theoretical orientation, the work begins with a specification of goals. Goals may be explicit, in writing, or implicit and simply kept in the therapist's mind. The problem about writing the goals in advance is that they can be so extensive, complex, and interconnected that a written list might fill a volume. Moreover, goals are often so flexible and transitory that a written version of them would technically require constant rewriting and a very large eraser. Nevertheless, the advantages of written goals are great. The list may be long and changing, but when written, it is so much more clear and consistent than when kept in the mind alone.

Marital therapists, like other psychotherapists, work with two types of goals called outcome and process (or mediating) goals. Outcome goals are the ultimate objectives of the couple. They include idealizations and need not relate to any means of achieving them. They are more static and can be specified with some assurance that they will not continually change; they become the standard against which to measure progress. One kind of outcome goal is the resolution of the specific problem the couple wishes to work on (Weakland, et al., 1974). This goal may be delineated when the couple defines what to them is happy marital functioning and what is the obstacle to their enjoying it. However, since most couples don't assess their situation well enough to do this, the therapist helps them define the outcome goals, too. Some of the following statements represent outcome goals of different couples:

> "We want to know what to expect from each other."
> "We want to feel laughter, pleasure, and joy in each other's presence."
> "We want to know what the other person means when they communicate with us."
> "We want to give and receive sexual gratification through pleasurable intercourse at least every few days."
> "We want a traditional relationship where he makes the decisions, provides the financial support, and makes the rules and she is the supportive helpmate."
> "We want our arguments to lead to tension release, and further understanding, but we want them to be fought fairly and end quickly and conclusively."
> "We want to divorce, causing a minimum of emotional and situational harm to one another and our children."
> "We seek to know if the other person will be the best possible future spouse and to know what are the areas which might become trouble spots in our future marriage."

Each couple, of course, can provide a long list of such goals. They can be used as the framework within which to provide marital therapy services. At this point they need not be operationally defined unless it is not clear what they want or unless goals are contradictory.

The different theoretical orientations emphasize or deemphasize some of the major outcome goals commonly used in marital therapy. The psychodynamic orientation attaches great importance to such goals as increased intimacy, role flexibility and adaptability, toleration of differentness, improved sexual relationships, resolution of presenting problems, balance of power, increased self-esteem, clear communication, and resolution of neurotic conflict. This orientation gives only moderate emphasis to improved relationships with children and one's own parents. The behavioral approach emphasizes role flexibility/adaptability, toleration of differentness, resolution of presenting problems, balance of power, and clear communication. The communications/systems orientation gives low emphasis to increased intimacy, toleration of differentness, improved sexual relationships, gender identity, and resolution of neurotic conflict, but high emphasis to adaptability, balance of power, clear communication, and resolution of present-ing problems (Gurman, 1978).

Process Goals

The process goals of marital therapy are the more specific and opera-tional definitions of the outcome goals. They break down the outcome goals into "do-able" parts. They make it possible for the couple to de-fine what they specifically seek; they define what each of the partners wants the other do be able to do to reach the objectives. Process goals usually are the means to reach the couple's ultimate goals. More often than not, however, process goals are seen as desirable ends in them-selves. To achieve them is often sufficient for the couple.

A list of all the process goals sought in marital therapy would obvi-ously be endless. However, some coherence has been made possible through the findings of researchers David Olson, Barbara Fisher, Douglas Sprenkle, and their colleagues. By systematically investigating responses from marital therapists and their clients, they have delineated the major types of goals under three categories. They find that the basic therapy effort is designed to help husbands and wives adapt, become closer, and send and receive information more effectively. For our pur-poses in briefly summarizing their findings it is convenient to think of these three categories as the "A-B-Cs" of marital therapy goals, for (A) adaptability, (B) bonding or cohesiveness, and (C) communication.

A. Adaptability Goals

Adaptability goals are based on the recognition that people keep chang-ing. They are never the same from one moment to the next, and cer-tainly not over the lifespan of the usual marriage. No one is able to re-main with the person he/she married for long; that person has become someone else. It is essential in working marriages to accept this and adapt to the differences. Adaptability goals essentially are to help the couple modify the interaction patterns, roles, and rules defining the re-lationship.

The goals that therapists use to help couples adapt to one another (Olson, Sprenkle, and Russell, 1979) are:

    1. Become more flexible. The couple is able to find new ways of

interacting when either the situation or their way of understanding it changes.

2. Become more democratic. The couple moves away from authoritarian or laissez-faire leadership patterns. Neither individual rules.
3. Become mutually assertive. The couple moves toward balanced aggressive and passive interactions.
4. Become able to negotiate. The couple can reach decisions which are mutually acceptable. They arrive at consensus.
5. Become able to modify rules. The couple can redefine their rules and expectations to meet their changing needs, values, and wants.
6. Become able to modify roles. The husband/wife can change the way they have been required to act to meet the changing needs of the family.
7. Become able to use feedback. The partners can receive positive and negative feedback and respond appropriately.

B.   Bonding, or Goals Toward Cohesiveness

The objectives of cohesion are to strengthen the emotional bonds, the cathexis, which the husband and wife feel toward each other (Fisher, Giblin, and Hoopes, 1982). They are to help each spouse to care, to be involved, to be interested in recognizing and meeting the needs of the other. The cohesion goals are to help a couple:

1. Feel emotionally attracted to each other.
2. Respect the autonomy and self-responsibility of the partner.
3. Permit the partner to take care of oneself when appropriate.
4. Provide for each other's emotional needs verbally and nonverbally.
5. Assume responsibility for protecting the spouse and family against intrusive forces.
6. Provide psychological safety, security, and trust in each other's presence.
7. Honor agreements and commitments to each other.
8. Enhance both partners' sense of identity with and belonging to each other.
9. Take care of the physical needs of each other.
10. Pleasurably interact with each other.

C. Communications Goals

Communications goals are the most well known and understood of the marital therapy objectives. They are to enable the husband and wife to clearly inform each other about their respective expectations, needs, and potential responses (Sprenkle and Fisher, 1980). They include listening as well as transmitting skills, and include the ability to convey to the partner that messages were received and understood. Of the 17 communications goals which marital therapists help couples reach, six have to do with listening, seven concern sending out clear messages, and four are general communication skills. The therapist helps a couple to:

1. *Listen effectively.* The goals of receiving the partner's messages are to (a) listen and observe attentively while the partner speaks; (b) demonstrate that the message was heard and comprehended; (c) indicate understanding by being able to paraphrase the partner's message; (d) clarify the partner's meaning to assure proper reception; (e) attend to the affect of the message as well as its content; and (f) consider the sender, message, and one's own self to be important and worthwhile even when a disagreement occurs.

2. *Send out clear messages.* The communications goals of transmission are to (a) speak for oneself and avoid the pattern of speaking for the other; (b) specify or provide specific data while avoiding generalizations and misunderstandable labels; (c) express thoughts openly and clearly; (d) express feelings openly and clearly; (e) express intentions and wants openly and clearly; (f) report expectations as completely and appropriately as possible; and (g) send messages which have verbal and nonverbal congruence.

3. *Communicate well.* The four general communications goals are to help enable a couple to (a) be spontaneous in conversation; (b) provide each other with relevant feedback or information about the other's behavior; (c) discuss and process the way the couple communicates (metacommunication); and (d) receive feedback or encourage the spouse to disclose information about how the information was received.

Each of the outcome and process goals of marital therapy are equally important. But not all of them are equally important for every individual or every couple. Once the therapist and couple delineates the potential range of working goals, they are able to select those which seem most relevant and needed. After these goals have been specified, they are periodically reviewed and used as a continuing guide for the therapy process. The goals are modified as needed when the agreed procedure for their modification is followed. How the therapy proceeds to achieve the established goals is then influenced by the particular treatment format used and the way the therapy process is structured.

Chapter Five

Marital Therapy Models and Formats

Marital therapy takes many different forms. Some practitioners structure their sessions very loosely and have very ambitious, almost unlimited goals. Their time frame is open-ended, and they continue working with the couple as long as the couple wants. Other therapists are very constricted in their procedures. They define, in advance, all the goals they hope to achieve, all the specific tasks which will be used to reach the goals, and the number of sessions they will require of their clients. Some therapists use written contracts to specify the mutual expectations between therapist and marital partners, while others prefer to keep everything more open and spontaneous. Some practitioners model their work after that of individual psychotherapy while others use approaches which are alien to traditional psychotherapy or counseling. Others base their orientation on group therapy and sociometric formats, or on "enrichment" and "human potential" encounters. Different approaches largely depend on the theoretical orientation of the therapist as well as his personal preferences and style, and not on any overwhelming evidence that tells him his orientation is without peer. No one has yet convinced all marital therapists or consumers that one or another approach is best.

How, then, is one to know which approach or marital therapy format is best? There are, of course, articulate proponents and ample documentation for virtually every model now in general use. But the studies which attempt to show that one is more successful or effective than the others consistently achieve rather ambiguous results (Frank, 1979; Luborsky, 1975). One reason is the problem discussed in Chapter One: Success is in the eye of the beholder. With many different views of what marital therapy success is, there can be no single answer as to which format can lead to such results. To say this or that type of marital therapy is most effective requires consensus about goals and more consistent outcome criteria than is now available. Meanwhile, arguments about which is preferable will continue to be based on inference, impression, and inconclusive empirical studies.

Still, marital therapists carry on spirited debates about different formats and procedures. They speculate with one another about techniques and treatment models, knowing that they aren't soon likely to find unequivocal answers. The questions most frequently discussed include the following: Should the goals be ambitious and modifiable, or specific and limited? Is it better to explicate the goals in advance, or let them emerge as the treatment progresses? Should the sessions be short term with specific agendas for each session, or open-ended and spontaneous as is often the case in most individual psychotherapy formats? Should husbands and wives always be seen in therapy together, always apart, or some of each? Is it better to see the couple as a single unit, or to see them with a group of other couples? Should they be seen with their children or not? Should the therapy be conducted by one professional or by a team? Some discussion about these formats is in order.

The Time Frame for Marital Therapy

Time is an important ingredient in successful marital therapy. One of the recurring themes in marital conflicts is about time. Husbands and wives complain that their spouses waste it or spend it inappropriately, or never give enough of it to the partner. The marital therapist has an opportunity to assist in these problems if he uses time in the therapy situation as a model for the couple. The time frame in marital therapy consists of the amount of time given to each session and the duration of the therapy.

Individual psychotherapy has traditionally taken place in the therapist's office with specific time constraints on each session, but not on the overall duration of treatment. Appointments are established in advance and sessions tend to last 45 or 50 minutes. Because many marital therapists also provide individual psychotherapy, they have been inclined to use this familiar model with couples in marital therapy. Thus marital therapy typically occurs in weekly or twice-weekly sessions lasting the same amount of time as the therapist uses in individual sessions. Their fees are usually the same for couples seen together as for individuals who are seen in the same amount of time.

Some marital therapists question the rationale of using this individual model for treating couples. They say the sessions should be longer than the 45 or 50 minutes because two people interacting require more time than does one. They say marital therapy is more analogous to group therapy where the sessions are more typically 90 to 120 minutes long. Accordingly, some therapists see couples for longer sessions. Each of these sessions typically lasts either 60, 75, or 90 minutes, and their fees are proportional to the greater amount of time spent. Other therapists acknowledge the merit of longer sessions but, because of schedules and other practical problems, retain the time frame they use in individual sessions. Few therapists condone having variable times for each session, however. Those who do suggest that the complexity of working with couples is so varied and unpredictable that there must be room for flexibility. But the great majority of therapists say that a consistent, structured time frame is more important than the benefits which might accrue from this flexibility.

Many less experienced marital therapists find it difficult to truncate a session which seems to them to be going well. This is particularly true when they have no other commitments at the normal conclusion of the sesssion. But prolonging a session vitiates the therapist's opportunity to use time as a treatment tool. This is illustrated in the Baxter case:

> Mr. Baxter was reluctant to participate in marital therapy and was there only to appease his wife. Not an articulate person, he spoke haltingly, slowly and concretely. Mrs. Baxter was more expressive verbally and could communicate about abstracts. The therapist was soon coaching Mr. Baxter, helping him get his thoughts across and get equal time and attention. The second session had only five scheduled minutes remaining when Mr. Baxter finally started to express his feelings. He tearfully related how he felt defeated, beaten, intimidated by his wife. Mrs. Baxter attempted to correct him or change his story. The therapist, believing this was an opportunity to make progress with their communication and to understand the reticent husband, decided to extend the session. They continued for 20 more minutes and, indeed, Mr. Baxter was able to express more in the extra time than expected. Then, in the following session there was little talk from either of the Baxters for the first 45 minutes. The therapist began coaching both the husband and wife and received only short, con-

crete responses from each. As the session was about to end, Mrs. Baxter began crying, describing some apparently deeply imbedded thoughts and fears. Suddenly the therapist became aware of the dilemma. If the session is ended, it might be interpreted as showing partiality to Mr. Baxter. If the session is extended, what would happen the following week? No matter what the therapist does, it will convey that there are questionable time limits on the therapy, and with the Baxters as well as many other couples, this is a duplication of the problems which exist at home.

Experienced therapists have learned, often the hard way, that the length of treatment sessions must remain constant, no matter what the clients *seem* to need. Almost every therapist has broken this rule on occasion; there are always going to be unique circumstances that require some deviation. But usually it is understood that the client will use time to manipulate, control the session and the therapist, or move in directions which are counterproductive. Many clients find they can't seem to get started until they near the end of the session. Often they are attempting to hold onto the therapist to obtain a demonstration that they are more important than others or that their problem is so serious that they need special consideration. Every session must end sometime and, if the time is not standardized, the couple might misinterpret the reason for stopping. A client might conclude he was less interesting this week than last, or he had displeased the therapist. Husbands and wives, if seen separately, might compare who had the longest session and read meanings into it which weren't intended. Moreover, as in work with individuals, clients could soon learn how to manipulate the therapist into extending or retracting the session. Many therapists would also find that variable-timed sessions would play havoc with their schedules, administration, and payment system.

There is less consensus in the field about the overall duration of marital treatment or the optimal number of sessions to be required. The major individual psychotherapies historically were of unspecified treatment durations. The rationale was that, since no one could be certain in the beginning what might be learned about the client's psyche, it was not possible to predict how long treatment would take. Most marital therapists have followed this model and do not specify or even predict the time required to treat any given couple. But in more recent years there is a clear trend toward a more specified and limited time frame. Many marital therapists now suggest seeing couples no longer than 16 weeks in once or twice weekly meetings. It is possible, they point out, to specify a limited number of sessions only when the objectives of marital therapy are also limited and clearly spelled out in advance. When the goals are clear and specific, and the tasks to reach them are explicated, the length of the therapy can be anticipated. It is when the goals are unspecified and the criteria for termination are vague that the duration can't be predicted; in such cases the decision to terminate occurs when the couple simply feels they are no longer accomplishing anything. Many studies show most couples terminate their marital therapy after only a few sessions anyway, whether the therapist recommends it or not. In any event, much of the decision about time frames depends on how much the therapist is inclined to be nondirective in his treatment of couples.

Directive or Nondirective Therapy?

In nondirective marital therapy, as in nondirective work with individuals, the therapist is inclined to let the marital partners talk about anything they deem appropriate. The couple determines the rules, the time frame, and the goals and means of achieving them. In the directive approaches, the goals are determined precisely, in advance, and the methods of achieving them are assigned by the therapist. The therapist is more confrontative and often follows a prescribed agenda for each session. Psychotherapists who use psychoanalytic or psychosocial orientations in their work have tended to be nondirective with these couples, while those who use systems and social-learning theory approaches tend to be more directive. Therapists of either persuasion offer strong arguments. Nondirective therapists say that clients cannot be truly understood when the expectations are spelled out in advance. When a therapist is directive, they say, it is the social context of the therapy which largely causes the couple to behave and think as they do. In such circumstances it is impossible for the therapist to know where the client leaves off and the outside influences begin. The nondirective therapists believe their way is the only way to keep from imposing therapist's values, goals, and methods on the client. To direct is to interject someone else's objectives into the situation.

Therapists who use a more directive approach are also persuasive. They suggest that the client who doesn't know what to expect is going to behave and think in ways that are atypical; they are going to be cautious until they determine what factors will lead to the therapist's approval and what will not. They will search the therapist's behavior for clues which tell them they are behaving appropriately. The therapist may attempt to remain inscrutable, but this will only prolong the time spent in search of the clues. The therapist who thinks he can conceal his expectations, says the directive therapist, is deceiving himself. Clients will learn that some behaviors are unacceptable even in that supposedly accepting situation. For example, the client who decides to walk around the room instead of staying on the chair or couch is more likely to be asked, "Why are you walking around right now?," much sooner than would the seated or reclining person be asked, "Why are you seated or reclining?" Since even the most nondirective therapist is going to communicate some of his expectations, the directive marital therapist suggests doing so openly. They cite mounting empirical evidence indicating that couples in marital therapy want direction and expect it (Gurman and Kniskern, 1978).

Conjoint or Separate Sessions?

Most marital treatment models have the therapist seeing the couple together during some sessions and separately at other times. The recent trend, however, seems toward more conjoint and fewer individual sessions. In fact, many therapists now strongly recommend that husbands and wives should never be seen separately in marital therapy (Stuart, 1980). Not many years ago the reverse of this was true. Mittleman (1948) was among the first to provide a conceptually integrated view of the dynamics of treating married people, and his approach was to see them separately. His rationale was consistent with his psychoanalytic orientation: each spouse is an individual, subject to unique, neurotic conflicts; these conflicts are subsequently brought into the marriage; each individual develops insight which will eventually help each understand how to relate to the other; working the conflicts through will lead them to more mature rather than infantile responses to the spouse; transference is disrupted by present reality conflicts if the spouse were present in the interview; seeing the spouses individually permits the therapist to better determine which conflicts between them are caused by reality factors and which are caused by neurotic ones (Meissner, 1978).

The trend toward treating the spouses together exclusively has been gradual. In the late 1940s some Family Service Agencies and other organizations whose theory base was more sociological than psychoanalytic experimented with it. Several variations of the form emerged in the late 1950s and early 1960s: In conjoint marital therapy (Satir, 1965) couples were seen together with one therapist. In "collaborative therapy" each spouse was treated by a different therapist, who then discussed respective observations and plans with the other (Greene and Solomon, 1963). There was "collaborative combined therapy," with one therapist for the husband and one for the wife; all four would regularly meet for joint discussions, and sometimes the therapists would see the other spouse alone. This approach is commonly practiced by sex therapy treatment teams (Masters and Johnson, 1970).

Group therapists have also been treating couples. Some group therapists see the husband in one group and the wife in another (concurrent marital group therapy). Other group therapists treat couples in the same group (conjoint marital group therapy). Therapists have had couples in groups with other members who were single (Gottleib, 1960). But the most common form of conjoint group therapy is with several couples in one group.

Obviously not all forms are worthwhile or equally effective, but empirical evidence is scant. Two of the more important studies were conducted by Beck (1975) and Cookerly (1973). Dorothy Fahs Beck compared different types of marital therapy in Family Service Agencies and concluded, without much equivocation, that conjoint marital therapy based on predetermined criteria led to better outcomes than did forms which treated spouses individually. Cookerly compared six treatment models and also gave a high rating to conjoint therapy. It was, he said, the most successful for couples who remained married well after treatment ended. However, for those who eventually obtained divorces, conjoint therapy led to the poorest outcome in terms of the husband's and wife's emotional well-being. Conjoint groups were rated second best for couples remaining married and best for those who eventually divorced. Individual therapy with a different therapist for each spouse was considered worst for those who remained married and second best, behind conjoint groups, for those who divorced. The worst model for those who remained married was treatment in which the same therapist sees each spouse individually; this model was also deemed next-to-the worst for those who divorced.

Despite such conclusions, it still seems premature to unequivocally state that conjoint marital therapy is the treatment of choice by all therapists for all types of clients. Obviously this judgment cannot be made until there is consensus about what is the "desired" outcome of marital therapy; the research is still subject to many qualifications. Above all else, it seems likely that the therapist's own experience and preferences are overriding. The therapist who has used the model of treating the husband and wife separately might be more effective doing so than if he started working with the couple conjointly. There is still much room for variegated orientations in marital therapy.

Conjoint Therapy Pros and Cons

Whether the choice is to treat the couple together or separately, there are advantages and disadvantages. For example, in separate therapy the individual client can work through conflicts in part through transference, or by projecting words, feelings, and values onto the therapist. It is then possible to understand the thought processes of the client by examining these perceptions. But this can be dangerous in conjoint treatment. If the husband and wife see the therapist separately, they would likely report, as fact, their distorted perceptions of the treatment to their partner. One could misinterpret or intentionally deceive the other. Then the spouse would either believe incorrect information about the therapist, or disbelieve the spouse and have more trouble with trust in their relationship. If the therapist expects that an observation will be transmitted to the spouse who was not present, it is impossible to know if the message was accurately conveyed or not; and if the communication between the therapist and one spouse is not transmitted to the other, the spouse may feel left out or rejected. If the therapist assigns a task to one spouse, he cannot know if the outcome was really effective. He would have to rely on the subjective impressions of the reporting spouse rather than see objectively the way the two subsequently interact. If the assignment were not effective, the therapist would not be sure why. It might be because the individual who was given the assignment relayed the information inaccurately to the spouse; or it might be because the method itself was ineffective; or it could have actually been effective, but was not perceived as such by the reporting spouse. Since an important part of marital therapy has to do with improving communication skills, this model can sometimes offer a negative role model. If, on the other hand, the assignment were given to both simultaneously, chances of misinterpretation would be reduced. It would permit clarification if there are questions and permit corrective action should the task seem ineffective.

There are three major arguments and possible disadvantages in seeing couples exclusively together. One is that spouses may be reluctant to disclose relevant information or "secrets" in the partner's presence. Another is that some spouses simply refuse treatment, so the other is disadvantaged unless the conjoint model is circumvented. Also, treating couples together might not lead to the kind of "deep" and enduring personality changes that are an objective of individualized approaches. But each of these is dubious.

Many therapists insist on seeing couples separately, at least sometimes, because they believe it is the best way to learn all the needed facts. Many spouses may think or behave in ways which might be deemed harmful to the marriage if the information were known by the partner. This is, however, a debatable premise and, if valid, the cure may be worse than the disease. Even when the partners are seen separately, the therapist will certainly not get all the relevant information. No therapy exists in which everything is revealed; there isn't enough time. Therapists recognize that they can help their clients without knowing everything about them. Moreover, the information clients do reveal is very subjective and biased. What they say apart from the presence of their partner may be as much a distortion of reality as what they reveal in the spouse's presence. If they have secrets they want to keep from their spouses, doing so will alter the relationship and their work in therapy. But it is also true that the relationship is altered if they revealed it confidentially to the therapist. The therapist who shares a secret is put in a precarious position. "Can he be trusted?", wonders the one who shared the confidence; can the other trust the therapist if the revelation ever comes out? The therapist is working in collusion with one partner and essentially deceiving the other. He is advocating honesty and openness between the spouses, but doesn't practice what he preaches. His actions can be justifiably interpreted by both partners as condoning the secret behavior, encouraging dishonesty, discouraging openness, and in some ways working at odds with the marital well-being.

The argument suggesting that individual work is more likely to mean deeper insights and longer-lasting personality changes is also debatable. There is not yet scientifically validated evidence to show that individual psychotherapy leads to greater or longer-lasting personality changes than may any other form of therapy (Thomas, (1981). Nor is there evidence showing that therapy with groups or couples leads to superficial or shorter-lived outcomes. But even if such evidence is eventually found to show that treatment through individual sessions is a more effective way to change personalities, it still doesn't mean that this is applicable to the marital disturbance; the objective of marital therapy is interpersonal rather than intrapersonal. To attempt to achieve "deep" personality changes in one spouse without regard to the needs, values, and well-being of the other might not be effective for either—or for the marriage—in the long run. The spouse who is already an outsider in the therapy relationship would have to contend with a partner who is becoming a rather different person, without having any input into whether those changes are in the best interest of either spouse.

The last argument about conjoint therapy derives primarily from a practical problem. Often one partner wants treatment for the troubled marriage but the other refuses. If the conjoint model is the only one permitted, then the motivated partner is disadvantaged. But every marital therapist has to confront this problem, and usually becomes adept at minimizing the difficulty.

Spouses Who Refuse Therapy

Many spouses refuse the entreaties of their partner to partake of marital therapy. They justify their reluctance with the belief that everything is their spouse's fault, so they don't need it. Or they are concealing a fear of therapy or an aversion to receiving help no matter how much it is needed. More often than not, in the American culture, it is the wife who seeks help while the husband is unwilling. This is undoubtedly because there is greater social acceptability for women to ask for and receive help.

Therapists who are faced with the refusal of one spouse to enter marital therapy which the other needs do not refuse treatment. In this case, they usually treat the individual rather than the marriage. After individual therapy has progressed, it is not uncommon for the other spouse to confer with the therapist. If this happens soon after the partner has started treatment, there may be no problem changing the format from individual to conjoint therapy. But if the individual work has gotten well under way, it may be ill-advised to make the change. Many clients would find it awkward if the therapist abruptly ended individual sessions to begin conjoint marital ones; the focus and orientation would drastically change. It would also be difficult for the latecomer spouse, who might find it difficult to ever "catch up," or to feel an equal of the partner in the eyes of the therapist.

Rather than switch roles, the therapist might consider some alternatives. He could see the new partner in individual therapy just as he is seeing the other partner in separate sessions; he could refer the new partner to another therapist for individual or group treatment; or he could delay the entry of the new partner into therapy until the treatment of the other spouse has been concluded. If they have both finished their individual treatments, the therapist could then see them to-gether. At this point it might be advantageous to use another therapist; the new therapist would work with the partners as a couple from the beginning, and there would be decidedly less role confusion.

To minimize the need for such complications, the reluctance of spouses to enter marital therapy should be addressed before individual therapy is undertaken. The therapist can do much to encourage the re-luctant spouse to participate. The therapist's effort is illustrated in the following case example:

> Mrs. Appleby has just had a violent fight with her husband. She impul-sively telephones a marital therapy center. The therapist to whom she is referred says he would like to see both Mr. and Mrs. Appleby in the first session. Mrs. A. says her husband won't do it. He doesn't want treatment or believe in the value of therapists. The therapist then asks Mrs. A. if her husband recently told her this or if this was her overall impression of his views. Mrs. A. isn't sure. The therapist suggests that Mrs. A. ask her hus-band again. If he agrees, an appointment is made. If he doesn't, the thera-pist coaches Mrs. A. in some arguments to present to him: that marital therapy works best when both participate; that one person is not singled out for blame or "ganged up" on by the therapist and spouse; that no one is going to imply that one or the other spouse is crazy; that both partners' input is important; and that changes will be a mutual process and change in one will inevitably affect the other. The therapist asks Mrs. A. to say this to her husband in her own words to get his consent to a one-time in-terview. If Mr. A. still refuses, the therapist asks Mrs. A. if he, the thera-pist, may be permitted to talk with Mr. A. If he comes to the phone, the therapist relays the above information directly and stresses that his input will be very important in treating the wife. He need not return for further sessions after the first one, unless he so wishes. The therapist might also stress that the purpose of the visit is primarily information gathering, and that the information will not be used in any way against either partner and will, of course, remain confidential. Mr. A. is much less threatened by the therapist with the direct telephone contact.

If the Applebys come in for the initial session, a decision among several alternatives can be made at its conclusion. They may return for marital therapy together, or Mrs. A. may see the therapist for help in resolving individual problems. The door is kept ajar for Mr. A. to enter therapy at a later date, either with the same therapist or someone else. In any case, the therapist would only offer marital therapy to them if they both agreed to start together.

Couple Group Therapy

Group therapy for couples is often an efficient and effective way of helping couples. As with all group approaches, marital therapy groups have many different formats, themes, sizes, goals, and theoretical orientations. Some are open-ended; new couples are added to the existing membership. Some are closed, with all couples starting at the same time and with a specific ending time established in advance. Some groups consist of paired couples exclusively, while others are made up of individuals who have marital problems as their central theme. Some are very large, with as many as 15 couples participating, while most are in the range of three to six couples. Couple groups might be structured to last for 90, 115, or even 200 minutes per session. There are marathon couples groups lasting more than 24 straight hours. In other words, virtually all the myriad forms of individual group therapy have been emulated in couple formats.

The way group treatment conceptualizes about human social interaction is generally quite compatible with marital therapy conceptualizations. The orientation to interpersonal dynamics, socialization, role modeling, and providing reciprocal help is similar in both formats. If the therapist is as skilled in group therapy as in dyadic marital therapy, there is no reason to think the outcome for any given couple will be less effective when derived from couples groups than from dyadic treatment. Groups have been shown to be as effective as individual work regardless of people's ages, the nature of their problems, educational and socioeconomic backgrounds, and level of intellectual functioning (Rutan and Alonso, 1982).

What criteria, then, does the marital therapist use in deciding whether or not to include a couple in group? Primary considerations are whether the therapist and couple want group or individual work, the expense involved, the special interests and skills the therapist might have with groups, and the effect of the new couple on other members of a prospective group.

Some couples may have strong reservations against going into a couples group and sharing their problems with others. If the therapist is committed to group intervention and believes the couple can benefit best by marital group therapy, he might be persuasive with the clients. He can show them how group therapy can achieve rapid results, be less costly, and can give the couple the benefit of the combined wisdom of many. He can point out that group members have a stake in preserving confidentiality, noncensoriousness, acceptance, and mutual support. The members will learn from one another about many successful techniques for solving relationship problems. He can invite the couple to enter a group on a trial basis; if they don't find it a positive experience, they can drop out in favor of other forms of treatment. The therapist may be successful in persuading couples who had not considered groups before.

However, when a couple enters group therapy, it is necessary to make sure they are both willing to participate; they should not be manipulated into joining. If one spouse is not enthusiastic about joining but the other is, it is best not to force a group on either of them. The risk is that the less motivated one might want to drop out, which imposes a hardship on the one who wishes to remain. The more motivated partner might well have developed a good working relationship with the group but then feel compelled to drop out when the spouse does so. The pressure to leave the group would be great if the remaining group members were all paired. In such cases, the therapist usually allows the partner to leave the group and enter individual therapy or a non-couple group. The alternative is to postpone further therapy until the partner wishes to resume group work.

Couple Therapy or Family Therapy?

How does the marital therapist decide to see the couple only or to include the children in the sessions? As outlined in Chapter One, the usual considerations include the ages of the children, the nature of the problem, and the particular preference of the therapist. Most family therapists suggest that only children over the age of six, or sometimes nine, be invited to participate. If the offspring are adult and not affected by the parent's marriage as when they were children, they might not be included. When children are of appropriate age to participate, the nature of the problem is the crucial factor. If the problem is such that the children would have little input or derive little gain from discussing it with the parents, they might not be included.

If is far more common for therapists to begin work with the couple dyadically and eventually add the children to the treatment than it is to start with the whole family and later exclude the children. To overtly exclude the children after they have been involved in the work could have ill effects on the children and the whole family.

Nevertheless, individual situations, needs, and priorities usually make stronger arguments than do any generalizations about including or excluding the children. Much of it depends on the skills and interests of the therapist. If he is equally skilled and experienced in both formats, the decision will be based on the family needs. If he is less skilled in one format and believes that model is best for the family, he would refer the family to the therapist with that expertise.

Close collaboration between those who practice marital and family therapy is becoming more common; there is really no competition between those who say they are family therapists and those who say they specialize in marital therapy. Most of their history is in common. Most of the techniques used by one are used by the other. The goals, values, and education of the practitioners of each subspecialty are virtually synonymous. When therapists who are skilled in one or the other work closely together it is almost moot as to whether the choice is family or marital. In these circumstances it can and should be both.

Solo Therapists or Teams?

While it's not unusual for a couple to be treated by two therapists working together, most marital therapy is still conducted by therapists working alone. This likely is due more to economic factors than anything else; it costs twice as much for two therapists to treat a couple. Agencies or churches may not want to pay for two therapists to do what was once apparently done by one. Private practitioners often don't want to share their profits with another therapist. And many marital therapists don't know other therapists with whom they can form teams. Even so, there is some evidence to suggest that therapy teams, for some couples at least, might be more effective and economical in the long run. Many studies demonstrate that teams can extend the range of services far beyond what any individual therapist could offer (Barker and Briggs, 1969). Masters and Johnson (1970) convincingly demonstrated the efficacy of the male-female treatment team in working with sexually dysfunctional couples. The rationale they used applies equally to working with couples who have problems other than sexual (Brent and Marine, 1982).

There are several obvious advantages to the male-female team approach. For one thing, there would be less controversy about whether one or the other of the marital partners is disadvantaged in the therapy situation. As we shall discuss in the next chapter, many therapists and consumers believe gender makes an important difference in therapy outcome. Says this view, when the marital therapy is conducted by one person, it will be by someone of the same gender as one of the marital partners; the client of the same sex may have a different therapy experience from that of the client of the opposite sex. The same sex client may have a greater sense of identification, rapport, and in some ways a better understanding or perception of understanding. There may also be greater rivalry and jealousy-provoking situations. The opposite sex client may be more flirtatious, as perhaps will be the therapist. There will be more likelihood of sex-role stereotyping. But if a marital therapy team is involved, with both male and female therapists, none of these dangers are as likely to occur.

Apart from the economic disadvantages, the only other reason for solo therapy with couples is the therapist's preference. Some therapists don't feel comfortable working in teams. Some can't because they get involved in power struggles of their own with the other therapist. When this is likely, it is unquestionably better for the couple to work with a single therapist than with a team. Otherwise, marital therapy teams have much to commend them.

Chapter Six

The Treatment Process

Marital therapy is a process. It is always a transition, always moving from one phase to another, never remaining just as it was even a moment before. Every part or event is influenced by many others which precede, follow, and envelop it. Marital therapy is more like a movie than a still photo. The metaphorical camera may be stopped to scrutinize each picture on the reel in detail, which permits an observation of elements that would otherwise pass by too rapidly for observation. But looking at a still photo without seeing its relationship to the other pictures doesn't reveal its true nature; it is the movement and the relationship of these elements to one another which is most vital. So the following description of the process of marital therapy is stated with an important caveat: None of the elements are discrete, static entities— they are flowing, changing, interrelated systems.

The marital therapy process consists of at least seven overlapping developmental phases which couples go through to achieve their goals. These are called (1) preliminary facilitation, (2) the initial encounter, (3) goal setting, (4) overcoming resistance, (5) implementing functional change, (6) termination, and (7) follow-up. During the earlier phases, treatment is oriented toward establishing the ground rules and facilitating an understanding about how the process is to work. Then the work tends toward involving the couple in the treatment effort and dealing with each person's reluctance to participate. Once these objectives are achieved, the process concentrates on the specific means used to achieve goals. Toward the end of treatment there is the weaning process, and a post therapy review to assure that results are sustained.

This seven-stage process occurs, not only over the span of the treatment, but within each interview session as well. In the allotted time rules are established, goals and methods for the day are reviewed, resistances are overcome, and alternative changes are implemented. Follow-up occurs at the beginning of the next session. Each session is an entire course of therapy in microcosm. More will be discussed about marital therapy interviewing in Chapter Eight; for now the attention is on these overlapping phases of therapy.

Phase One: Preliminary Facilitation

Couples tend to seek marital therapy at a time of acute stress. They might have considered therapy for months, but when they actually call for the appointment it is because they have reached the last straw. They want help *now*. The problem is acute, and the couple wants emergency attention. It is during these times of acute stress when change is most likely to be rapidly achieved (Caplan, 1960). The individual or couple is in a state of flux; their old ideas or perceptions haven't been working and must be replaced by something else. In many ways they are more amenable to change than they were before the crisis started. Soon, however, they find new adaptive mechanisms and new ways to cope. They become relatively comfortable once again and are much more reluctant to change, even though they might intellectually recognize the value in so doing. This means there are certain times when the initial therapy encounter is optimal. If the therapist and couple begin at this time, the prognosis for change and improvement is more optimistic.

Marital therapists, like all other busy professionals, cannot usually make initial appointments to coincide with this optimal moment. Schedules have already been set and time is offered when it is available, not necessarily when it seems most therapeutically desirable. Both client and therapist must accommodate to the practical realities. Treatment usually will begin some time after the acute stress has abated, when the couple has again become guarded and more rigid. They will be comfortable enough to avoid anything which might upset the balance they have recently and temporarily achieved. They are more on guard with the therapist; they don't have a precise knowledge of what to expect, are no longer enthused about being there, and are reticent about making sudden changes at the suggestion of a stranger (Bent, et al., 1975). Perhaps it is no wonder that premature termination among marital therapy clients is very high in the first few sessions (Fiester and Rudestam, 1975).

A compromise between the practical and the ideal time to begin treatment is achieved when the therapist provides some "preliminary facilitation." Basically, this first phase of marital therapy consists of an exchange of as much relevant information between therapist and couple as possible before their first face-to-face contact. It has a three part goal: to engage the couple in the therapy process as soon as possible after the initial contact is made, hopefully during the time the acute episode is still "hot"; to obtain enough preliminary factual information so that some differential treatment can begin immediately; and to prepare the couple with information to minimize the time-consuming guardedness.

To engage the couple in the therapy process almost immediately after the call for help is made, some means for exchanging important information must be established. If the husband and/or wife has a chance to state some of the problem, perhaps to ventilate a little, and get some reassurance that help will be forthcoming, the first meeting will be more productive. When the couple knows what might be in store for them in marital therapy, what the therapist is like, and what the facilities are about, they will be more amenable to getting into the hard work of therapy. When the therapist has acquired in advance some factual data, there will be more focus on the real problems at the outset.

There are many acceptable variations of this preliminary facilitation. In larger marital therapy-providing agencies, clients who call are asked to come in immediately. They can discuss the matter with an intake interviewer, fill out questionnaires, and read about the organization and its staff. This fulfills a useful function; it enables the couple to start soon and affords less apprehension about what might be in store for them. They have already "opened up"; by the time they see the therapist, they are still likely to be more open. In smaller agencies, churches, and private marital therapy practices, it is somewhat more difficult to readily engage couples. Some therapists attempt rapid telephone call returns and then spend some time asking and providing information to the clients by phone. Others have receptionists who are instructed to obtain predetermined "face sheet" information by phone, and to provide answers to specific questions asked by the caller.

Some therapists in these circumstances request that the couple come to the office on the day of the call or soon thereafter. They may not be given an appointment that soon, but are told they can see the facilities, pick up some information about the program, and complete a questionnaire which will help the therapist in the initial assessment. It would be preferable during this "drop-in" for both husband and wife to come, but if one simply cannot or will not do so, the single spouse may come in for the information and then relay it—one hopes, accurately—to the partner.

When the client comes to the office before the initial meeting with the therapist, it is useful to have an information packet and a questionnaire available. The receptionist may give this to the client, or a sign may indicate where in the waiting room the information/questionnaire packets may be obtained. The packet is only a large envelope containing three or four pages of information about the facility and the questionnaire. On the first page of the packet may be a warm, informal note from the therapist which explains the situation and the reason for the procedure. It may be similar to the one which follows, borrowed from a therapist's office:

Hello.

Welcome to my office. I'm sorry I can't see you now, but I hope we'll meet soon. This packet will answer some of the questions you might have about our program. It will describe how the sessions work, how long they will last, what you will be asked to do, and what you can get out of it. There is also some information about my background and philosophy of marital therapy. There is a statement about our fees, insurance considerations, and payment plans. There is also a pamphlet about this agency. After you have read this material, you can decide if you want to set up an appointment with me. If you decide you want one, you may let the receptionist know or call me later to arrange it. If you want an appointment, please fill out the enclosed questionnaire. This will let me know something about you so we can get started more quickly. I hope that both you and your spouse can come for our first visit. Please try to find an appointment time which is convenient for both of you. I look forward to seeing you both very soon.

Sincerely,
Dr. Roger Jones

The next page includes a description of the program to be offered. It states how long the first session will last and that no commitments for ongoing therapy will be made until then. It concisely states that the session will consist of the therapist asking pertinent questions about the relationship, that it will be confidential, and will not attempt to find someone to blame. This statement might also describe the therapy contract, its purpose and implementation. The part of the contract which applies to all marital therapy clients may be contained in the packet for the couple's preliminary perusal.

The third page might contain information about the therapist. A description of the therapist's credentials, background and experience, philosophy of treatment, and typical approach is described. If the couple will be seeing two therapists conjointly, of course, there would be descriptions of both. Potential clients have the right to this information before making any commitment to work with the particular therapist or agency. This page might also describe a typical marital therapy case which has been treated by the therapist(s) or agency. It might discuss the problems which are typically treated, the usual methods in treatment, and an overview of potential outcomes. Some packets include the therapist's code of ethics, history of the agency, and bibliographies or reading which might be helpful to the distressed couple. Most marital therapists prefer to limit the size of the packet to avoid overwhelming the couple; they are given additional information as therapy progresses.

The preliminary facilitation phase is a propitious time to obtain as well as provide information. The couple wants to give information to someone to begin the helping process, and factual data must eventually be acquired. If information gathering comes later, it can be needlessly costly and distracting. The questionnaire acquires information about both the husband and wife, their relationship, and their relevant others. Usually it requests facts about the clients: names, addresses, birthdates, status of the family members and important others. It elicits historical information, such as social, educational and vocational experiences, previous marriages, and the background of the present relationship. Information about physical health is also sought, not only regarding the couple, but also about their progenitors and offspring. Marital therapists often coordinate their work with the couple's family physician to rule out health problems as a contributing factor to the relationship problem. The therapist may include in the questionnaire a standardized form about the individual's health history; these forms may be obtained from the mail-order houses which specialize in printing for physicians and professional offices. The questionnaire which pertains to the problems of the relationship is usually designed by the therapist to suit his own diagnostic and therapy orientation.

Naturally, this approach is impersonal. It might turn off some potential clients who want to and expect to see the therapist right away. And, if the therapist's time permits, a personal encounter is a better way of connecting with the couple at the optimal time. Otherwise, this is a practical alternative. If the clients complete the questionnaire at this point, they have started to work on their relationship problems. They are likely to remain more open to the therapy process until the first face-to-face meeting takes place. This preliminary facilitation is integral to the therapeutic process; its usefulness is especially appreciated by therapists who are alert to the apprehension faced by all potential therapy clients.

Phase Two: The Initial Encounter

If preliminary facilitation has succeeded, the therapist and couple will know something about each other when they first meet. This allows them to proceed more rapidly with assessment and goal setting. If there has been no prior facilitation, some preliminary steps toward acquainting the couple with the expectations of therapy will have to take place during this phase when there is much else to be done. The therapist spends the first few minutes describing the program, the methods to be used, and some administrative matters. The therapist and many clients might want to start the session with a description of the problem—this is sometimes ill-advised. It doesn't alleviate, and may contribute to, the couple's uncertainty about what to expect in therapy. Without prior successful preliminary facilitation, the therapist should devote the first few minutes of the encounter to a description of the facility, his approach, and expectations. This gives the couple a chance to relax, consider the therapist and the office, and gather their thoughts. It also signals to the couple that the therapist is going to be active, directive, structured and goal-oriented.

The major objective of the initial encounter is to get the couple involved. At this early stage, the partners are usually preoccupied with their own relationship problems, are cautious, guarded, or fearful of embarrassment or unpleasant therapy outcomes. It would take little to discourage them from returning or being open about their difficulties.

The therapist's primary objective is to help the couple become engaged in the treatment process, or, as Cashdan (1973) calls it, "hooking in." Others refer to it as the cathexis or bonding which enables the clients to stay in the therapy relationship despite some unpleasantness or adversity. To a great extent, "hooking" comes when the couple perceives that the therapist is not a detached, mystical figure but one who is warm, caring, and involved.

Fishermen learn there is no single best way of hooking what they are after. They find different techniques, movements, bait, and circumstances are most effective on specific occasions or with varied species. Experienced therapists likewise know there is no single best way of "hooking in" the couple, getting them involved in the treatment process. Beyond certain fundamentals, it is quite individualized. The fundamentals include the demonstration of competence, seriousness, concern, and devotion to working with the couple to help them achieve their goals. Some therapists readily engage couples with a light-hearted, humorous approach, while others are more effective with a no-nonsense businesslike manner. It is probably better for therapists to use the manner which is most comfortable for them. The one exception is that many therapists might be more comfortable with a more passive, nonstructured approach. Since considerable empirical evidence shows that couples end marital therapy prematurely and achieve less successful results when marital therapy is less structured, therapists who want a better chance of successful outcome will provide a more structured therapy atmosphere (Gurman and Kniskern, 1978).

To actively involve the couple, the therapist needs to make the initial encounter a rewarding, positive and pleasant experience for them. Diagnosis, treatment planning, and treatment implementation are of secondary importance at this phase. These objectives would be pointless if the couple didn't care enough about the therapy to return. Obviously diagnosis and treatment have already started, even in the preliminary fact-gathering phase, but the therapist does not emphasize this until after the couple has become somewhat committed. To make the contract rewarding, positive, and pleasant, the therapist asks the couple to describe the strengths and positive aspects of their relationship, the assets and the appreciated attributes of the other person. Many marital therapists devote much more time to this in the first session than to a recitation of problem areas; doing so encourages the couple to consider what is healthy rather than sick about the relationship. It is more pleasant for each to hear what the spouse appreciates; it stimulates them to pay more attention to what is good about their partner in the future.

After some time is given to this positive exchange, attention turns to a discussion about how goals are set and reached. This is another departure from those traditional therapy approaches in which first sessions are explicitly organized around data gathering and assessment. Most marital therapy clients expect short term intervention and hope for immediate results (Noonan, 1973). If they are disappointed, they may discontinue. The therapist tells the couple that improvements will occur in steps rather than leaps toward complete marital bliss; then the therapist describes some of the steps. These include having the couple clearly define their goals for the marriage, their reasonable expectations of the partner, and the growing awareness of the positive attributes of the partner. Some of these steps will occur in the office starting with the first session; others will be part of a homework assignment. Assignments to complete at home before the second session will be made by the therapist and couple together.

The first encounter then turns to questions about the nature of the problem as seen by both the wife and husband. It is delayed until after the preliminary work has taken place and tasks have been delineated. This has probably taken half of the session already, and the therapist needs to reserve some time at the end for wrapping up and possibly for discussing the contract. A rather limited time for problem discussion will thus be available, but it is important that some time, perhaps ten minutes for each spouse, be given to it. Otherwise the encounter may be as confusing for the clients as if the session were devoted solely to data collection; the partners would wonder what was going on if they didn't have some chance to discuss specific problems. The therapist can limit the amount of time and detail given to problem explication by asking each partner to list, without examples, five major problems they feel exist in the marriage, in the partner, and in themselves. Or, if the preliminary facilitation questionnaire acquired this information for the therapist, he could go over each item for some elaboration and illustration. This compels the couple to describe an overview of the problem in a highly focused, less threatening way. The therapist asks the other partner for additional information, but generally inhibits either from challenging or refuting the spouse's list of problems.

The initial session concludes with a discussion of overall outcome goals, homework assignments, and the contract. The therapist asks each partner what goals they wish to achieve. He makes it understood that the goals are not yet finalized and can be modified as circumstances warrant. The couple's first homework assignment is to spend some time thinking about goals during the week before the second session. Each is asked to list goals and break them into "do-able" parts. For example, if a wife's goals include having more fun with her husband, she would list what activities meet this criteria. The therapist suggests that each partner lists ways they believe the goals can be achieved, too. The partners need not show their spouse what they have written, though it is understood that disclosures will be forthcoming in the next session.

Finally, a contract may be presented to the couple. It is not formally signed during the first session; there will be too many subsequent modifications and the couple needs time to decide if they want to make this commitment. Some therapists give the couple a sample contract to take home and examine during the week. During the second session it can be developed and completed in writing. The goals, methods, and mutual obligations are written on the contract before it is signed. During the contract signing, it is agreed how many sessions there will be as well as what the ongoing format will be. The initial session can end on a hopeful note when the therapist has summarized what has already been accomplished by the couple, what they have done to make their objectives clear, and what is anticipated about their work in the forthcoming week. Therapists often schedule a second session within a week of the first so that the momentum which has already been developing can be maintained.

The initial encounter phase, in sum, is designed to eliminate uncertainty, develop some commitment or "hooking in" of the couple, achieve an overview of problem areas, prescribe some "do-able" tasks to give the couple a positive sense that they can be successful, and discuss goals and contracts (Margulies and Havens, 1981). While each interview is unique, the order and time spent on each of these components may be as follows in a 50-minute session:

Minutes into the Session	Therapist Activity	Couple Activity
0–5	Describes program	Asks questions about program
5–10	Goes over question-naire data	Confirms accuracy of written data
10–15	Asks wife (or husband) to describe other's positive attributes	Wife describes and husband listens
	(makes sure both stay with positives)	No interruptions when spouse is talking

15–20	Asks husband (or wife) to describe other's positive attributes	Husband describes and wife listens
20–25	Asks one partner to list five marital problems	Spouse lists five problems without elaboration
25–30	Repeats with partner	Other spouse lists problems
30–35	Asks each to define goals	Both describe goals
35–40	Describes how some couples achieve these goals	Listens, asks questions
40-45	Suggests specific tasks, gives examples of tasks	Agrees to return, asks questions about tasks
45–50	Describes contract for couple to consider	Asks questions about contract
50th minute	Words of encouragement and salutation	Concludes session

Obviously, a great deal needs to be done in the initial encounter. To accomplish it all, one needs to be rather firm and organized. There will be more time to recapitulate, dwell on specific problem areas, and do other work in subsequent sessions. Of course, if the session is designed to take longer, say 60, 80, or 90 minutes, then commensurately more time for each of these activities can be planned.

Phase Three: Goal Setting

Goal setting is listing outcome goals, listing process goals or methods of achieving the outcome goals, and defining the treatment plan. It is primarily during the second meeting that the objectives of treatment are spelled out, divided into outcome and process goals, and formalized in the contract. To do this earlier or later would be less effective. If done sooner, it would take place while the couple is still unsure of what therapy has to offer and before they are committed to it. They have, of course, started defining goals in the first two phases, but it is formalized at this phase. To delay it beyond the second session suggests that treatment is not goal directed, and subject to subsequent changes in direction.

In this session, couples have a good idea of what to expect. They have been told in the previous meeting that goal delineation is important and that it will be formalized next time. Their homework was to list goals and criteria for achievement; the contract was to be developed based on the goals. The agenda is quite full. The goal lists are the primary focus of this second meeting.

Sometimes one or both partners will not have prepared a list for this second meeting; the therapist must consider what this means. It might reveal that there are formidable problems of apathy or cohesiveness with the couple, and that it just isn't important enough for them to do. It might mean that the assignment is alien to them. Many people are so uncomfortable with writing, or with being specific about such abstract subjects as goals, that they find the assignment too difficult to complete. Failure to carry out the assignment might result from the therapist's failure to clearly communicate its importance.

If it is determined that the couple is uncomfortable putting words onto paper, the therapist goes through it with them during this meeting. The therapist asks them about their goals, paraphrases or restates them in a concise way, and perhaps writes them on paper for each client. If he does it for one, he will do it for the other; this is so even if the other has no trouble with writing, in order to maintain balance between them. If the therapist is facile about it, the partners will not realize that this is not the normal procedure for all clients; this way one partner is not made to feel deficient or inferior.

If it is determined that the assignment was not completed because the couple is too apathetic to bother, the therapist has to find alternative assignments which are easier and more accomplishable, even for apathetic people. If this cannot be accomplished, it is likely that marital therapy has nothing to offer them as a couple. If they still want therapy, they could partake of individual treatment or different therapy groups.

If the assignment was not carried out because the couple didn't understand or appreciate its importance, the therapist can clarify. If the therapist finds that a high proportion of his clients somehow fail to get around to doing it, the therapist himself is probably not convinced of its worth and conveys this to his clients. Most goal-directed marital therapists have little trouble getting the majority of their couples to fulfill this assignment, at least verbally.

When the outcome goals have been written and everyone concerned agrees that they are the ones to be worked toward, the couple and therapist turn to discussing ways of reaching the goals. The therapist describes the techniques, homework assignments, and procedures to be completed in the office toward the achievement of the goals. The couple then knows what to expect, so they can decide whether or not to participate. The couple has still not been invited to focus on problems other than in the ways they relate to goals. This subordinates the focus on problems and negative aspects of the relationship and maintains a more hopeful and positive direction.

The talk about problems, symptoms, or the deficiencies of the spouse which occurs in this session is done in the context of the explicated goals. For example, a wife lists one goal as "being able to spend more time with Jerry." The therapist asks if this is a problem for them now. The wife then describes this problem and its proposed solution without going into any of the other problems. Focusing on goals permits the partners to tell what is wrong with the relationship, but in a structured and specific way.

The therapist then asks the couple to consider the contract. Together they examine its components. The conclusion is that the husband, wife, and therapist state what their goals and expectations are, what they will be willing to do in therapy to reach them, and what the mutual obligations between the therapist and the couple are to be.

The therapist may then suggest a series of assignments, to be conducted first in the office and then in the couple's home, which can help with the particular problem. Descriptions of these specific assignments are found in Chapter Ten. The second session concludes, then, with the signing of the contract or handshake about the verbal agreement and the assignment of homework to facilitate efforts toward some of the goals which were outlined. The ongoing therapy work and refinement of diagnoses and process goals will be the next phase in the intervention process. However, it is also at this time when the therapist must deal with the couple's resistance to bring about the desired improvements.

Phase Four: Overcoming Resistance

People are generally uncomfortable about radical changes even when their present circumstances also cause them discomfort. This fact is most notable among long-term inmates whose institutions attempt to release them; many find the prospect frightening and regress to avoid their freedom. Perhaps the fear of the unknown accounts for people's reluctance to change. Perhaps change is avoided because we hate to admit that we have allowed ourselves to get into the unpleasant position. Perhaps a major reason for resistance among married people is to avoid an admission of wrong-doing; if an individual is urged to change, it implies that he is presently deficient, or not entirely okay. So the person who refuses change may be saying, "It's not my fault. I should not have to change because my spouse caused the problem."

Resistance in all forms of psychotherapy, including marital therapy, is any behavior or phenomenon which rises from the client's actions which thwarts the change process (Luther and Loev, 1981). In marital therapy, it is of two major types. One is the same as that which exists in individual psychotherapy—the intrapsychic reluctance to give up one's way of thinking or relating to others, the unwillingness to disrupt one's more comfortable, predictable way of being. This form of resistance manifests itself in such varieties of behavior as being unwilling to keep the appointments; finding excuses for being late; being unable to afford the therapy; never being able to complete homework tasks; not really exploring oneself; answering questions with terse "yes, no, or I don't know" answers. The client is "frozen" and wants to remain that way. He sees the therapist as jeopardizing that status.

The second type of resistance, which is more common to marital than to other forms of therapy, is that in which one partner attempts to influence the other to avoid change within the self or within the relationship. This is here called an "interpsychic resistance." A resistant spouse points out to the partner some of the therapist's deficiencies; describes some marital therapy philosophies which are alien to the couple; repeatedly reminds the partner about the costliness or ineffectiveness of therapy. The resistant spouse interrupts the partner, suppresses or challenges everything the partner says. The resistant husband's or wife's goal is to effect the same noncooperativeness in the partner. If the resistant person is successful, he or she can not only prevent change, but can cause everyone to attribute the lack of change to the partner or the therapist.

"Interpsychic resistance" is most likely to emerge before the first appointment and during the early phases of treatment. Therapists have little to do with client resistance before the first contact. The client is unwilling to come into sessions. Therapists often don't see such people at this point but hear about them when the spouse calls for help and indicates that the partner is not interested in participation. Many marital therapists have to work with individuals who have troubled marriages because of the partner's reticence; they would prefer to treat both, but can't overcome the spouse's initial resistance. The therapist who values conjoint marital therapy will attempt to persuade the reluctant, resistant partner to join his or her spouse in the treatment. If the effort is fruitful, once the resistant spouse has reluctantly started treatment, the therapist concentrates on overcoming the resistance. This process begins with the initial contact, but the need for it and specific techniques to cope with it become crucial during this phase.

Prior to the third session there hasn't been much emphasis on what's wrong with the partners or their relationship. Therapy has been positive and goal directed. Tasks have been assigned which are "doable" and the partners have been encouraged to think positively about the potential in their relationship and working for it. But the honeymoon is over by the third session. It is natural that the resistance would be heightened at that time.

Overcoming resistance in marital therapy uses the same methods as in working with individuals, but with some modification. In both cases, the therapist avoids responding to the resistant client in ways as do two laymen engaged in a communication dispute. The therapist does not debate with or try to trap the client. Some therapists might feel that, if only they can convince the client that he or she is wrong to resist, the individual will no longer do so. Neither does the therapist coax or cajole, hoping that this will cause the nontalkative client to open up. The therapist does not provide meaningless encouragements or false platitudes (i.e., "Come on, John, we know you can talk."). Nor does the therapist overcome resistance by extolling the virtues of therapy or by shaming the client into more cooperation (i.e., "Mary, if you would just stick to the subject it would be better. Therapy can really help if you do it right."). It is sometimes very tempting to attempt such behaviors because it seems so natural, but to do so is to miss the point of the resistance. The client fears change, fears the unknown realm into which he is being asked to go, fears being ridiculed or blamed for being the one at fault. Psychodynamically oriented therapists say he resists because his psyche doesn't want to lose its control. Whatever the reason, therapy which uses a frontal assault on resistance not only will be unsuccessful, but will heighten the resistance itself.

There are more effective ways to overcome resistance. One is to find a more healthy way of meeting the needs which were fulfilled by the resistance. If, for example, it is ascertained that the client resists out of fear of blame or humiliation, the therapist doesn't say to the client that he is just scared. Instead he emphasizes that the purpose of the session is not to find fault or to convict one partner of wrongdoing while supporting the other. The therapist says that everyone makes mistakes, that doing so is only a sign of being human and a sign of willingness to take risks. If the client is resistant because of fear of the unknown, or of change per se, the therapist assuages anxiety by concentrating on expectations, goals, and predicted outcomes. The future becomes more predictable, so it is less fearsome. If the client resists out of fear of ridicule, he can be made more comfortable when the therapist engages in mildly self-deprecating humor. He shows the client it is okay to laugh at oneself and not take oneself too seriously.

When a client is defensive, the therapist does not attack the defense but helps the client save face by attributing positive intentions to his action. For example, a wife complains that her husband "always laughs at me in front of our friends." An ineffective response would have the wife and therapist turning to the husband and confronting him with a stern, "Why do you do such dastardly deeds?" The husband would naturally be defensive. He would deny, justify, or withdraw. One hopes this is a gross exaggeration, but many therapists sometimes engage in milder versions of it. The therapist might instead attribute positive intentions to the husband's actions no matter what the actual intent might have been (i.e., "You know, Mary, I'll bet John doesn't do that to hurt you. He probably just wants to get everyone at the gathering to enjoy themselves. He knows you can get them laughing when he does that, and he knows you can take the kidding. Maybe his doing that is a real compliment to you. But now that he realizes that it hurts you, he can find another way of getting everyone in the group to enjoy themselves. What do you think, John?").

Combatting resistance in marital therapy diverges from the same effort in individual therapy when one spouse attempts to influence the other to resist. The therapist must exercise great caution in the way he responds to clients who do this. He does not want to allow the resistant spouse to compel the other to emulate that behavior, nor does he want to confront or attack the resistant partner's behavior. For example, in the following excerpt a resistant husband attempts to get his wife to follow suit:

JERRY: "I don't think Sarah or I should answer that question, Doctor. Is is really relevant?"

SARAH: "Oh, Jerry, shut up. I don't mind. No, Doctor, we haven't had intercourse for two weeks. We never do when we are in a fight, and this one has been going on for quite some time."

JERRY: "That's not the problem we are here for and I don't see what

> business it is of Dr. Jones' anyway. So, Sarah, you just keep quiet
> about my business. I'll decide what I want to tell about when it con-
> cerns me."
>
> DR. JONES: "Maybe you're right, Jerry. Let's not get into that now. I
> think Sarah made a good point when she said the fight goes on for a
> long time. Let's just concentrate on that. Okay, Sarah?"
>
> SARAH: "Well, okay. When we fight we don't have anything to do with
> each other. We don't talk, we don't have fun, we don't even
> sleep . . . ."
>
> DR. JONES: "That must be pretty difficult for both of you. Jerry, what do
> you think brings you both out of these episodes?"
>
> JERRY: "I guess when I really get horny . . . ha, ha, ha."
>
> DR. JONES (laughing): "Then what happens?"
>
> JERRY: "Well, then I start to make up so that everything is back to nor-
> mal. We have sex again."

The therapist does not permit one spouse to determine what the
other says. In the example, the therapist reinforced the wife's right to
say whatever she wants, but he provided a face-saving way out for the
husband which included supporting his rights as well as hers. The husband, in this case, was permitted to get back to the very subject he had
been trying to avoid. It is not always possible for the therapist to successfully walk this tightrope between the rights of the partners, but it is
an effort which must always be made.

Some therapists attribute too many therapy obstacles to client resistance. Sometimes they label behavior as resistance when, in fact, the
client simply doesn't agree with the therapist's goals for the therapy. Or
sometimes clients are labeled as resistant when they are only correctly
perceiving that the therapist doesn't have their basic interests at heart
or is not sincerely attempting to work toward the goals which have
been explicated. Clients are not necessarily the cause of resistance;
sometimes the conscientious marital therapist will recognize that he is
causing it. Unfortunately, he will sometimes not even realize his part in
the phenomenon. This is another reason why marital therapists should
work closely together, in teams, or by using one-way mirrors, or at
least by taping sessions and having close supervision.

The fourth phase of marital therapy, overcoming resistance, is perhaps most visible and crucial in the third session, but by no means does
it begin or end there. It continues throughout the treatment process.
Often, after it seems under control, it returns intermittently and with
annoying persistence. It is most likely to return whenever new methods
are considered, or when new stages of the treatment process are about
to take place. It also occurs when things haven't gone well or when

there have been setbacks. But the patient therapist will recognize that this is an inevitable part of the process and will be quick to employ those methods which are most effective with the particular couple in overcoming it.

Phase Five: Implementing Functional Change

At first glance, the fifth phase of the treatment process, that of bringing about needed changes, might appear to be the heart of the intervention. It has this appearance because it is the longest lasting of the phases. If the treatment has been defined as consisting of, say, sixteen sessions, it might occupy twelve of them. If the sessions are open-ended, it might be all but a few. But it is no more or less important than any of the other phases. In fact, if the other phases have been given proper attention and adequate implementation, this activity can be more easily achieved.

This part of the marital therapy process consists of four therapy activities which occur simultaneously and in mutual reinforcement. First, it includes the interview strategies which help couples understand themselves, their partners, and their relationship. The interview facilitates change by permitting the couple an opportunity to objectively assess their situation, talk about it, debate its meaning, and discuss alternatives. Second, it includes the working relationship which helps couples experience, understand, and work with the effective aspects of their marriage and the therapy; the feelings experienced in therapy reflect and influence those between the partners. Third, it includes the tasks and techniques which therapists assign to the couple. These tasks are selected to give each partner some practice at finding alternative and healthier ways of relating to one another. Finally, it includes the therapist assuming different roles to bring out relevant understandings and behavioral changes. For example, the therapist sometimes acts as a mediator in disputes between the partners, a side-taker to restore power imbalances, and a focuser to keep clients from digressing. Each of these four components of the process are of such complexity that they are discussed in the next four chapters.

The following example demonstrates how all four of these components exist in the marital therapy process. It is part of an interview in which their relationship is crucial to its outcome. A technique is used and the therapist assumes such roles as "structure provider," focuser, and catalyst.

THERAPIST: "All right, an assignment for this week is for you both to pay three compliments to the other person each day. Do you both understand?"

JERRY AND SARAH: "Yes, sure. Okay."

THERAPIST: "Well, let's practice anyway. Can you pay each other a compliment right now?"

JERRY: "Uhhh, let's see. Well, Sarah is wearing a pretty necklace."

SARAH: "Huhhh. Some compliment. He bought it for my last birthday. He's really complimenting himself."

JERRY: "Well, TO HELL WITH IT, THEN! Why should I compliment someone who just turns it around?"

THERAPIST: "I think we should put some ground rules on this assignment. Let's say that this week's compliments should not be about personal appearance and they should always be sincere. And let's say that the other person will respond to the compliment only with a simple, "Thank you." Let's say every compliment should be brand new, different from any other compliment used during the week. And finally, when one pays the compliment, the other will not immediately respond with a compliment. Okay? Do you understand?"

JERRY: "Not exactly. I don't know what to say if I don't tell her how she looks."

THERAPIST: "Okay, Jerry. Let me give you an example. Pretend I am Sarah paying you a compliment about something which has nothing to do with your appearance. I might say, 'Jerry, that was a terrific idea when you suggested lighting candles with dinner.' Or, 'Jerry, I really like the way you always wrestle around with the kids when you get home.' See what I mean?"

JERRY: "Yeah, I see."

THERAPIST: "Okay, let's try it. Pay Sarah a compliment."

JERRY: "Uhhh—Sarah really did a nice job on her hairdo this . . ."

THERAPIST: "Not about appearance."

JERRY: "Let's see—oh, yeah. I like the way she always laughs at my . . ."

THERAPIST: "You're on the right track, Jerry, but tell her, not me."

JERRY: "Sarah, I like you way you always laugh at my jokes, no matter how cornball they are."

SARAH: "Thank you, Jerry. And I like the way you . . ."

THERAPIST: "Remember the ground rule about waiting for a while before paying back the compliment, Sarah."

Phase Six: Termination

The conclusion of therapy is as important as its inception; the way termination occurs can negate or solidify any gains made in the therapy.

The last scheduled interview occurs when any one of the following conditions is met: (a) when goals have been achieved; (b) when the contracted time period has been reached; (c) when one or the other partner or the therapist fails to adhere to the explicit agreement or obligations; or (d) when it is agreed by the clients and therapist that there is nothing further to be gained by continuing. The therapist wants termination to occur only when the first of these goals have been reached within the time frame established. This is more likely to occur if the goals have been explicit, reachable, modest, and if the time frame is long enough to realistically achieve them.

The major objective of effective termination is to assure that the results have been stabilized. One hopes that this phase will solidify the healthy changes, and not constitute a new crisis for the couple which will lead to their reverting to unhealthy patterns. Therefore, termination should never take the couple or therapist by surprise. It should be an integral, predictable process.

Stabilizing the outcome suggests that goals should be reached fairly well in advance of the final session. A target date to begin work on new changes should probably occur at least a month before the last scheduled meeting. This gives the couple an opportunity to solidify, integrate, and consolidate the changes and practice them while still active in therapy. Stabilizing results also suggests that the couple and the therapist are discussing the treatment methods and results throughout their work together; they are continually evaluating their progress. The therapist is providing considerable feedback and suggestions for further refinement and improvement, and he encourages the spouses to do this with each other. Thus, by the time the termination phase occurs, the couple is well aware of where they are. They have planned for it, expect it, and look forward to it. The disengagement process then becomes less problematic.

Perhaps disengagement is not as difficult in couple therapy as in effective individual therapy. The one-to-one relationship between therapist and individual client accentuates an intense interpersonal connectedness, mutual empathy, transference and countertransference, and strong reluctance to give it up. But if the marital therapy is effective, the therapist plays a subordinate role to the couple's relationship. He encourages and fosters more awareness, empathy, and connectedness between the marital partners than between himself and either of them. His intentionally lower profile and the husband's and wife's growing preoccupation with each other makes the disengagement process easier. Of course this is not always going to be true. Some partners will form attachments, transference, and cathected bonds with the therapist no matter how much he encourages focus on the mate. Nevertheless, the marital therapist sticks to the game plan. The goal is not to "work through the transference" in marital therapy; termination must go on as scheduled.

Whether difficult or not, disengagement may be facilitated when the therapist expects and is prepared for the usual manifestations of the client's wish to prevent termination. These client manifestations include denial that termination is about to happen, regression or "flight into pathology" so that new sessions can presumably take place, premature flight, and subtle or blatant pleas for further therapy.

The therapist deals with these client efforts by casual reminders about the termination date approaching, frequent references to the gains that have been made, and encouraging words about the prognosis for the future. The therapist does not even hint that there is a possibility of extending the sessions. At most he can schedule a new series of treatments based on the need to achieve new goals, but this does preclude termination of this treatment.

During the final session, the couple and therapist recapitulate the work they have done together. They review the problems, the methods they used to overcome them, the setbacks, the leaps forward, and the achievement of their objectives. They talk about the future, how to make it brighter, and how to prevent the problems which led to the therapy. The results will be more stable when the therapist acts as a celebrant in commending the couple for their accomplishment. Many therapists put in writing the fact that the goals have been reached, or write on the couple's contracts that each of the objectives have been accomplished. These documents constitute something of a diploma which can provide the couple with some solace in the future when they feel somewhat discouraged—and some happy nostalgia as well.

Basically, termination is a happy experience. It is like a graduation or a wedding, a sign of moving on to a new, probably more fulfilling stage of life where the couple is in greater control of their destiny. For the therapist the termination is sad, like a parent feels when children get married or graduate, but it is mixed with considerable joy and a feeling of accomplishment, too.

Phase Seven: The Follow-Up

During the termination phase, the therapist has given some specific suggestions and homework assignments of things the couple might do when they encounter certain problems. He urges that they adhere to these exercises for at least several months after the final therapy session, and is confident that if they do so they will further stabilize the successful results of their therapy. This begins the final phase of the intervention process, that of follow-up.

There is considerable variation in the way therapists approach this important phase of treatment. Some don't bother doing anything; they reason that further involvement fosters client dependency, or it suggests that the therapist is not sure the couple can make it on their own. Some see it as an indication that the therapist wants to hold onto the couple. Other therapists who want some follow-up simply suggest that the couple call with a periodic message about their well-being. In this case they might simply leave a message with the receptionist or on a phone answering machine indicating that all is well. Other therapists tell the couple they will call at regular future intervals with no indication of personal visits. And still other therapists build into their intervention process one or more follow-up personal interview sessions. However, this is not really follow-up, but part of the disengagement or termination phase, with greater time separating the last sessions.

There is no single best or worst way in any of these models, and no conclusive evidence to demonstrate that any one is preferable. Probably the best solution is for the therapist to individualize the follow-up to suit the unique needs and circumstances of each couple who successfully terminate treatment. Some couples will be called periodically, some will call in, some will be left on their own, and others will return for follow-up sessions.

What does seem clear, however, is that an abrupt ending of the work with no further connection seems to contradict the whole point of the effort. If the therapist and couple really care, really are involved in bringing about changes together, really are devoted to achieving and maintaining results, it is hard to imagine that one would be satisfied with no further contact. Furthermore, the therapist who truncates the sessions forevermore can never be sure of the outcome, never know if what he did was effective or not. How would he know what tools and techniques to use if he never followed through? Follow-up is the phase which gives a sense of completeness to the extensive effort which went into the entire therapy process.

Chapter Seven

Interviewing and Communication Strategies

The interview is the procedure which holds the marital therapy process together. It is the primary vehicle in which information is given and received, diagnostic understanding is acquired, and treatments are prescribed. It is the principal means used by the therapist to directly observe how the husband and wife interact. It is used to demonstrate how both partners might communicate more effectively with one another. And it is important for improving needed listening and comprehension skills. The following excerpt from a marital therapy interview illustrates these elements:

> THERAPIST: "Now I want both of you to describe what you like about the other person. Why don't you go first this time, Ted?"
>
> TED: "Who, uh, me? Well . . . okay . . . but I don't know what to say. Uhh, Janet is pretty and she's a good cook, when she wants to be. And she's good at her job. In fact, she's so good she never wants to come home. That's where she sees that guy. I want her to quit, but she won't give him up and uhh . . . ."
>
> THERAPIST: "Ted, remember, we are just talking about the good things right now. What other qualities do you like about her?"
>
> TED: "Uh, yeah, sorry, I forgot. It's hard to think of good stuff after what she's done to me. . . . Well, it's true, Janet! Why don't you talk and tell him my good qualities?"

THERAPIST: "Ted, can you tell us some other good things about Janet?"

JANET: "Of course, he can't. He's so negative, all he knows about is bel-lyaching and put-downs and . . . ."

TED: "You rotten cheat! Where do you get off talking like that about me? Why should I bother trying to straighten this marriage out?"

THERAPIST: "Okay, folks. Let's remember the goals we talked about last week. We agreed that one goal was to reduce the tension so you could start talking in a more friendly manner. Do you remember? We agreed one way to do that was to look at the positives. That's why I'm asking each of you to describe good qualities in your partner. Janet, perhaps you can say what qualities you appreciate about Ted. Then we'll come back to Ted."

JANET: "Hmm. Let's see. I don't believe I can think of anything. Ted is . . . uh, well, he's handsome. And he's a real man, not a wimp. You know, the macho type. He's a little too bossy at times, but I think the man should be the boss, mostly. And he's a good lover. He is a little rough, sometimes, but basically he's good in bed. What are you smil-ing about, Ted? And he's a good provider. He doesn't drink too much and he's a very good father. I don't want to make him sound perfect, though. He's got lots of faults. Like the time he. . . ."

THERAPIST: "Let's stick to the good things for now, Janet. Can you think of some other qualities?"

JANET: "Well, I don't know. I want to hear what he says about me be-fore I say any more good things about him."

THERAPIST: "You mean that what you think is good about him depends on what he thinks is good about you?"

JANET: "Gee, that sounds kind of dumb, doesn't it? If it's good, it's good, no matter what he thinks of me."

THERAPIST: "Good, Janet. That's exactly right. If you see him as good only when he does what you want, then your version of what's good is shaky. Now, can you think of some other good qualities?"

JANET: "Yeah, sure. Now that you put it that way, I can think of good qualities he has, no matter how terrible he thinks I am. He's decisive. He's kind to my mother, even though I know he can't stand her. He always does his share of the housework. And I thought he was pretty accepting of my going to work, too."

TED: "Well, dammit. If I'm so terrific, why in hell are you screwing around with that lawyer in your office? What's he got that I don't have?"

THERAPIST: "That was a good job describing Ted's good qualities, Janet. Ted sounds like a good guy. Now, Ted, can you think of some other good qualities in Janet?"

TED: "Hey, why are you ignoring what I just said? Let's get to the point. That's what we're here for, isn't it? How come she's messing around with some other guy? How come she just sits there all sweetly and tells you what you want to hear and then goes home and treats me like shit again? Why don't we get to that instead of just talking about all this lah-te-da good stuff?"

THERAPIST: "Ted, we are going to talk about those things. But we all agreed to concentrate on this for now. Do you want to change our game plan? We can talk about that in a little while, if you both want to change it. But let's stick with this for a while first, okay?"

TED: "Yeah, I guess. But it's hard. I am really bugged about the whole thing and I really wanna let her know that I don't like it."

THERAPIST: "Just the good things, Ted. . . ."

TED: "Okay, okay. Let's see. Well, first of all, she's real pretty, like I said before. And she's a good cook, and she's good at a lot of other things. Like tennis, she's good at that. I have a good time with her when we play. She's a good athlete and not a sissy at all. She's a lot of fun when we go to parties. Everyone likes her and it always makes me proud that she is my wife."

JANET: "I didn't know you liked those things about me."

TED: "Well, sure I do. I always have."

JANET: "But you never say so. How am I supposed to know?"

TED: "Awww. You know me. I never show my feelings except when I'm mad."

JANET: "Ted, if only you would show me some of those other feelings, it would make such a big difference."

Psychotherapy vs. Marital Therapy Interviews

The excerpt shows some of the differences and similarities between individual psychotherapy and marital therapy interviews. The two treatment modalities are usually more alike than different. However, the differences are important. The therapist who uses individual psychotherapy interview skills interchangeably with marital interviewing might have difficulties (Berman, 1982). Most marital therapists also work with troubled individuals. They have learned to use their skills in psychotherapy interviewing as a foundation for interviewing couples in crisis. The competent psychotherapist has learned how to effectively pose questions, reframe answers, provide structure and coherence, and get the client to respond honestly. The psychotherapy interviewer learns to know when to speak, when not to, what speech patterns and physical gestures to note, and how to listen effectively. These also are essential attributes of the marital therapy interview.

There are other similarities as well. In both instances the therapist seeks to create a therapeutic environment and relationship. The interviews are almost always conducted in the therapist's office where proper working conditions can be assured. The office is comfortable and free from outside distraction. The interview is scheduled in advance, has a specified length of time before it concludes, and is oriented to the needs and interests of the client rather than those of the therapist. The interview is conducted under some regulatory auspices to which the therapist must adhere. If it takes place in an agency, the therapist is obligated to conform to the requirements of that auspice. If the therapy is by private practitioner, the work is regulated by licensing laws and/or professional codes of ethics and sanctions.

Clients seek the therapy of their own volition. Since motivation must occur to reach goals, there is nothing to be gained by somehow forcing therapy on a couple or individual. Fees are paid to the therapist or his agency employer for the service provided. The funds come from the client and, increasingly, from third party financing institutions which thereby have growing influence in the way the therapy is to be conducted.

Many of the same psychodynamics and behavioral patterns are seen and dealt with in both individual and conjoint marital therapy sessions. It is assumed here that the reader is generally familiar with the techniques of individual interviewing. This knowledge is useful and basically applicable to work with dysfunctional couples and thus will not be recapitulated here. However, those who wish to review the literature of individual psychotherapy interviews are particularly encouraged to read Benjamin (1981), Reik (1977), Garrett (1972), Combs, Avila, and Purkey (1978), Kadushin (1983), MacKinnon and Michels (1971), and Knapp (1978).

While knowledge of individual psychotherapy interview techniques provides the foundation of conjoint marital therapy interviews, it is not all one needs to know. There are important differences which the marital therapy interview must utilize and accommodate if the interview is to be effective.

Major Differences

A difference between individual therapy and conjoint marital sessions is that the interviews themselves have a different relative impact. It is almost everything in individual work and only an important part of the marital therapy process. The interview has been described as the "base of therapeutic interaction" (Edinburg et al., 1975, p. 1), but in conjoint marital therapy, much more of the treatment interaction goes on outside the therapist's office. What happens between the therapist and client is usually the therapy centerpiece and the most important factor in individual treatment. In marital therapy, what happens between husband and wife, often outside the therapist's office between sessions, is equally important. The marital therapist often instructs the couple in "interviewing" each other, or communicating together. They go home to implement the recommendations. Their interaction with each other is far more important than that which exists between the therapist and one or both of them.

It is conceivable, though not likely, that a successful marital therapist could be a terrible interviewer. If he is a good diagnostician and can determine methods which will be effective in helping the couple achieve their goals, much of his work would succeed. Conversely, if the marital therapist is a fine interviewer, but lacks the ability to design programs to help the couple work through their difficulties in their time between sessions, the outcome might be less positive. A good interview is important in both formats, but is not the be-all and end-all in marital therapy.

A second difference is the physical setting. If the therapist is primarily oriented to individual therapy, he may have his office set up with one comfortable chair for his client and one for his own use. When couples are brought into such an arrangement, a second, less comfortable chair is used. This causes an imbalance. The husband or wife who has the more comfortable chair, the more "official" one, or the one located closer to the therapist or in a more permanent location, has some inherent advantage or the perception of such.

Many studies demonstrate that the physical arrangement of the therapist's office has a profound influence on the course of therapy (Hall, 1966). So, for example, if the husband sits in the "best" chair, the wife is subordinate, no matter what goes on outside the office. The therapist who often sees couples conjointly would serve them more effectively by having two permanent, identical interviewee chairs placed equidistant from the therapist; this is an important but not crucial factor. Many agencies where marital therapy takes place cannot provide such accommodations. But the interviewer who has to make do with such an arrangement could at least make sure that the husband and wife alternate where they sit in subsequent weeks, in order to equalize the physical arrangement. If the format is conjoint with a male and female therapist, then ideally there will be four approximately equal chairs set equidistant from one another.

The marital therapy interview room should be larger than that used for individual sessions because marital therapy more often uses role playing, stand-up physical demonstrations, and encounters. Marital therapists also benefit from the use of one-way mirrors. One therapist can be in direct contact with the couple while another can be unobtrusively observing and providing more objective information. Therapists frequently use video-tapes as an adjunct to their therapy; they should have the room arranged for easy and unobtrusive monitoring.

A third difference between individual and conjoint marital therapy interviews involves the relative activity of the therapist. In marital therapy interviews, the therapist has to be more verbal, and more inclined to determine what direction the discussion will take. The interview requires greater therapist activity, because the husband and wife will often influence each other in deleterious ways if the therapist does not counter with therapeutically effective ways. In most individual psychotherapy the therapist encourages the client to say whatever is on his mind, ventilate his worries, and apply his newly acquired insights to the outside world. But in marital therapy the interviewer is concerned with the influence the two people have on each other. If one is allowed to freely associate or determine the direction of the sessions, the other will be excluded. The marital therapist has to seek a balance between the husband and wife and is more concerned about the interpersonal relationship than intrapsychic phenomena. This requires more activity and directiveness.

Fourth, the marital therapy interview is primarily devoted to the "here and now" rather than the "there and then." If the therapist devotes much time to history taking or to listening to the husband and wife recite events in their past, the process is more likely to be obstructed, rigidified, resisted, and ineffective. Couples quite often want to spend the interview describing what the spouse did in the past. Their premise is that the therapist will better understand why they now react to the spouse as they do.

But the marital therapist soon learns that focus on the "there and then" is a needless diversion. Clients will relate past events with some inaccuracies. This isn't a problem with individuals because their inconsistencies eventually are revealed. In marital therapy, the other partner won't passively wait for this to happen. The partner usually listens selectively for those inaccuracies and then points them out to the therapist, along with the implication that the other doesn't tell the truth or is prone to faulty memory. Then each partner's pride is at stake; neither wants to be humiliated in front of the therapist, so they will seek to substantiate their respective views about the situation described. Their resulting exchange could be a transactional game called "yes, I did; no, you didn't."

Rather than encounter the problem, marital therapy interviews can be more successful with attention to what is going on between the couple at the present moment. What happens is visible, accessible, and more reliable than biased reconstructions could ever be. The husband could make a convincing case that his wife is always nagging him, is domineering and shrewish, when only past events are considered. But the therapist may see that, in their relationship in the office, it is the husband who has such inclinations. Basing assessments and treatment plans on what he sees rather than on what is reported is more reliable.

A fifth difference is that marital therapy interviews have a more positive orientation. Much of the focus of individual therapy is on problems, failures, inadequacies, and grievances. If this becomes the focus of marital therapy when two people are in treatment, each partner can discourage the other. A focus on possibilities, strengths, and satisfactions is the way to circumvent this. Most couples who finally reach a marital therapist are pretty discouraged, rather bitter about the spouse, and not very optimistic about a future with the other person. They need little confirmation of this by devoting the therapy time to dredging up the hurt and suffering they have endured. Therefore, the therapist keeps the interview positive, up-beat, hopeful, and mutually supportive. He does this by encouraging the couple to spend at least as much time talking about the positive aspects of the relationship as about the negative. If they tend to move toward negatives a great deal, as couples are often wont to do, the therapist interrupts and stresses a return to the positive. Sometimes the partners will be angry with the therapist for preventing more discussion about problems, as was illustrated in the script which opened this chapter; but in the long run, the results make it worthwhile.

One way to encourage positive exchange occurs early in therapy when the therapist asks each partner to tell the other what qualities, attributes or activities are most appreciated. To do this, couples usually have to think hard for positive considerations, since their minds are cluttered with grievances and hurts. So they have to look more carefully at the partner, more objectively and more optimistically. Their selective inattention to the partner's good qualities is defused.

The therapist might suggest that the husband and wife pay each other a compliment. Compliments are to be honest statements about qualities which are recognized and appreciated. They are to be said sincerely, without sarcasm or barbs. They should not be duplicates of what the other partner has said. It is tempting for many couples asked to do this to compliment some aspect of the partner's appearance, such as saying, "That's a pretty dress." For couples who are prone to think of compliments exclusively as expressions about appearance, the therapist might specifically exclude such compliments from the assignment. He might recommend, instead, that the couple should pay compliments about personality characteristics, or ideas, or clever ways of saying something. Success in carrying out such an assignment not only helps the recipient feel better about himself or herself, but it encourages reciprocation.

The interview can encourage many different types of positive exchanges in addition to compliments and describing appreciated characteristics. It is positive to be recognized. When the interview situation is structured so that the speaker is given undivided, uninterrupted attention, at least for a specified amount of time, the speaker is inclined to upgrade the quality of the speech. The partner speaks with more thoughtfulness, more care, better delivery, and more respect for the effect it will have on the other. It is positive to hear the partner's ideas and act upon them. If the husband or wife makes a suggestion about what would improve the relationship, the therapist might encourage them to try it for a week. This is recognition for the partner with the idea and positive approbation when it is successfully implemented.

One final difference between the individual therapy interview and that of marital therapy has to do with balance. It is not necessary for the client in individual therapy to talk during the sessions; silence is as meaningful as verbalization. It is not necessary for individuals to be assertive, submissive, controlling, or controlled; the therapist can accept the client as he is. This is not usually possible in the interviewing of couples. The therapist must see to it that both partners have relatively equal input, and that neither is dominated by the other. One of the crucial aspects of the marital therapy interview is the therapist's effort to achieve this balance.

Implementing the Therapeutic Balance

The marital therapist has several impartial strategies for assuring that each partner has an equal say in the therapy process. They basically center around the way the therapist asks questions, where the questions are directed, how they are rephrased, and some nonverbal communications.

One of the most important techniques to maintain this balance is posing "duplicate questions." A duplicate question is not the same as a "double question" asked of an individual (i.e., "Where did you stay and was the room nice?"). A duplicate question is the repetition of a single question to both partners (i.e., "Was the room nice, Ted?" "Janet, do you also think it was nice?"). It is established in the beginning of many marital interviews that one partner tends to be the spokesperson and the other the endorser. It becomes tempting for everyone, the therapist and both spouses, to let this happen; but it can lead to problems. The therapist might get a distorted picture of the actual situation, seeing mostly through the eyes of one spouse. Or he might fail to see that gaps exist between the way each perceives the situation. Or the client who was not asked the question may feel left out and relatively less important to the therapist.

To counter this, the therapist asks questions of either the husband or wife, and he usually asks almost the same question of the other fairly soon. The therapist confirms the answer given by one by asking the other if the same answer is appropriate. For example:

> THERAPIST: "Ted, what do you usually say to your wife when you first come home from work every night?"
> TED: "Well, usually I like to see the kids first. They come out to the car and we start talking. Then I go into the house with them and say hello to Janet."
> THERAPIST: "Janet, is that how it seems to you when Ted comes home?"

After a very short while, the therapist who keeps asking for confirmation will have "trained" the couple to be ready with confirming or denying remarks. After each spouse answers, the therapist can simply look toward the other person; the other spouse may nod and the interview can proceed. If concurrence does not occur, the therapist directs the questions back to the first partner until clarification about the discrepancy is achieved or at least that the gap in interpretation is explicitly known to exist.

Another strategy is to prevent monologues, or dialogues between therapist and one partner, and encourage dialogues between the spouses. If one partner enters a lengthy monologue or dominates the talk, the therapist often interrupts and directs some of the attention to the other partner. If one partner frequently interrupts the other, preventing a flow of ideas or obfuscating needed data, the therapist gestures or speaks so as to limit this pattern. He might interrupt the interrupter. Sometimes he might wait until the interrupter is through and then resume with the other partner at the point where the interruption occurred. The therapist sometimes facilitates better listening and less interrupting by being a good role model. The therapist listens attentively to the speaker and does not readily countenance efforts by the partner to garner attention out of turn.

Balance is also achieved through nonverbal communications. One of the partners may want to talk with the therapist to the exclusion of the spouse. The therapist responds by eye contact with the quieter partner. The two silent ones continue looking at one another until the talker notices. When all are again included in the discussion, the therapist may look at both partners equally.

If one partner attempts to dominate by moving closer or situating himself/herself so that the partner is excluded, the therapist changes his position to restore equidistance. Since everyone is generally seated, this primarily occurs in the way each person leans or angles themselves in the seated position. The therapist may imitate the physical mannerisms and gestures of one or the other partner in order to achieve more closeness or distance from either person, depending on the balancing needs.

The third way of effecting greater balance between the partners in the marital therapy interview occurs when the therapist actively takes sides or mediates. He might want to encourage the less dominant partner by speaking in his/her behalf or pointing out to the other how he is in greater agreement with the other. If one is more articulate, intelligent, or sophisticated than the other, the therapist may need to take this person's spouse's side to a greater extent, regardless of the actual merits of their respective positions. More will be said about the therapist's roles in these activities in Chapter Nine.

Enhancing Communication Skills

One of the major virtues of the interview is the teaching of the couple to communicate; few people have had enough systematic training to do it well. Effective communication is a highly complex skill. Most couples with marital dysfunction have problems with it and seem to accept the need for its improvement. The interview lets the couple see how they could talk with one another more effectively; it helps them learn to listen, understand what is being said, respond to certain cues, and ignore others. A substantial part of the marital therapy interview consists of the therapist encouraging the couple to dialogue while he notes their communication patterns. He subsequently instructs them in how to change their patterns so that their information exchange is more accurate.

Skill in communicating includes the ability to both convey and receive information (Nierenberg and Calero, 1973). Every message transmitted and received is multidimensional; it consists of many layers of overt verbal content and many more layers of implicit messages conveyed verbally and nonverbally. Couples are prone to responding to many more of these layers than they recognize. Consequently, they often convey information to their partner which is distorted, unrepresentative of their feelings, and internally inconsistent. When couples have difficulty with reciprocal understanding, it is largely because they are interacting at different levels, responding to the wrong cues, and transmitting inconsistent messages.

The marital therapy interview devotes considerable attention to unraveling "mixed messages." Marital partners often incorporate into a single message many contradictory or inconsistent elements. One partner says to the other: "I think your mother has been terrific in dealing with her menopause." The one who responds must choose which of the elements to acknowledge. "Thanks for saying she's terrific," is one possibility. "What's wrong with my mother?" is another. The speaker is in control. He/she can deny any negative intent and thus be the "innocent" party in any subsequent argument. This control is unhealthy because it is based on manipulation and confused information.

Marital therapists are aware of the many variations of mixed messages. One is the "barbed compliment." A barbed compliment is a positive statement about the partner with a hook in it. For example: "Sure, he tells me he loves me . . . when I ask." "Mary is a good sexual partner, when she doesn't have a headache." "Harold earns a good salary, for someone with so little education." Some couples are not consciously aware of doing this. The therapist can point out the pattern, and demonstrate a similar compliment without the barb. "Yes, he tells me he loves me and he always cares enough to say it when I clearly need it." "I really enjoy sex with Mary because I love her and want to be as close as possible." "Harold has overcome a great many obstacles to get where he is today, and I'm proud that he includes me in his life." It feels better to receive non-barbed compliments. After some of the anger has subsided, it feels better to deliver them, too. It is not hard to keep them going once the momentum has started.

The marital therapy interview encounters many problems of this type and is the most accessible means of treating them—by asking for clarification about the meaning of the message, rephrasing, listening well, and transmitting clearly.

Transmitting Skills

The interview is important in teaching couples how to send out clear messages so the partner can respond more accurately. Transmitting information is, however, much more than using words well. Communication is the product of nonverbal as well as verbal expressions. The content of words has relatively little to do with what is actually being communicated. Mehrabian (1972) estimated that of the total feeling conveyed in one spoken message, 55 percent comes from facial expression, 38 percent comes from the feeling tone in the spoken words, and only 7 percent from the words themselves. There are many other nonverbal cues—such as posture, timing, activity going on during the speech, and the history of the relationship—which transmit information.

Couples and other people who are close develop more awareness of nonverbal cues as the relationship intensifies. They attend even less to the words and more to the nonverbal aspects. This is why more therapists ask couples to write letters to one another to get away from those cues which obfuscate the messages.

It is important for marital therapists to understand the meaning of nonverbal transmission of information between couples in order to "speak the same language" as the spouses. Nonverbal communication has many components. It includes "paralinguistics" (the vocalizations which accompany words, i.e., "tone of voice," loudness, pitch, pauses, and tempo of speech); kinesics (the movements of the body and facial expressions to reveal added information about the speaker's thoughts); and proxemics (the use of space, distance, and position to emphasize one's feelings).

Nonverbal communication is determined to a great extent by the culture or subculture in which it was learned. There seem to be few, if any, nonverbal communications which mean the same thing in all possible cultures. Therefore, while the therapist is alert to nonverbal cues, it is more difficult to generalize about them (Birdwhistell, 1970; Hall, 1966; Watzlawick, 1976). Nevertheless, when they are included in the marital therapy interview, more complete and accurate information is possible. This is illustrated in the following excerpt:

> THERAPIST: "Janet, you frequently seem to move away as Ted moves toward you on the couch. What do you think this means?"
>
> JANET: "I don't do that. What are you getting at? That I don't like to be close to him or something?"
>
> THERAPIST: "I was just noticing that you do it. Was I getting at anything? Do you think you do it?"
>
> JANET: "Well, I get a creepy feeling sometimes when he comes at me. He scares me with his roughness. Yeah, now that I think about it, I guess I do it. What does that mean?"
>
> THERAPIST: "What does it mean to you, Ted?"
>
> TED: "That she doesn't like to be close to me, I guess. I never noticed it before. But now that you mention it, I guess she does it all the time. Now that I think about it, it sort of pisses me off!"
>
> THERAPIST: "But can you see why she might do that, Ted? Rather than get mad, look at the reasons for her doing it."
>
> TED: "Well, I don't want my own wife to be scared of me, for God's sake. Why didn't you tell me I scare you, Janet?"
>
> JANET: "I guess I never thought about it before. I never really felt that you did, but I guess you do."
>
> TED: "Well, hell, let's talk about how to get me fixed up so I don't do that to you anymore."

Couples often do not intend to transmit the information which the other is receiving, and may not be aware of doing so. For example, a husband might dutifully tell his wife he loves her, but conveys the message with indifference or sarcasm. He might say it when he is reading a newspaper or watching television. When he mumbles that he loves her, he is in fact communicating something which is the antithesis of a loving comment. Yet when she tells him in the therapist's office, "You never tell me you love me," his response might be: "Whaddya mean? I just told you I loved you this morning while reading the paper. How often do you want me to say it? I luv ya, dammit, now get off my back."

Therapists contend, with ample empirical evidence, that whenever there is inconsistency between what is spoken and nonspoken, the nonspoken message will be interpreted as the accurate one (Birdwhistell, 1970). When couples learn this, the information they transmit and receive can be clarified. They often communicate by pouting, sulking, or obstructing without words. The intent is to manipulate the partner into initiating an apology. The sulker can say, "But I never said I was upset." Therapists in the marital interview often teach the couple to express their positive feelings both verbally and nonverbally; but when they have a negative message, they should rely on words only. As part of this advice, the other partner should not respond to any negative message from the spouse unless it is explicit and verbal. This compels the sender of the implied negative message to take responsibility for the message, which has to be made explicit in order to be acknowledged (Stuart, 1980).

Listening Skills

It is just as important in the marital therapy interview to teach couples to listen as to help them speak. Every person listens selectively (Patton and Giffen, 1974). We hear only part of what the speaker is saying and add to the speaker's message our own data, which wasn't necessarily intended. When we listen to someone we think we know well, we can't help but interpret their messages in the context of history and our past understandings about them. We speak at the rate of 125 to 175 words per minute (Tubbs and Moss, 1974) but can comprehend words spoken at a much faster rate. Naturally, then, listening to others permits our minds to wander, to take in other data between words, to think our own thoughts, to project our emotions onto the speaker, and so on.

Effective listening is not, as some couples seem to think, just remaining silent or thinking about what words to say the next time the partner has stopped talking. Spouses are poor listeners when they (a) believe they know in advance what their mate is going to say, (b) concentrate on single words or phrases instead of the overall gist of the message, (c) attend to the speaker's appearance or mannerisms to the exclusion of the message content, and (d) reject the partner's words, thinking they are uninteresting, or too simple or complicated (Nierenberg and Calero, 1973).

The marital therapy interview can help couples overcome these attributes of poor listening. It happens primarily through providing a model for emulation. When one spouse speaks, the therapist looks at the speaker and seems fully absorbed in receiving the message. If the spouse interrupts, the therapist ignores the interruption and maintains the interest in the speaker. Eventually the partner notes this behavior and is more likely to imitate it. The therapist gives the spouse the first chance to respond to the speaker. If the spouse wasn't effectively listening, he/she will probably have missed some of the speaker's content. The therapist then responds to the speaker based on a more complete or accurate reception of the message. The therapist doesn't suggest to the listener that he is inferior to the therapist, less intelligent, or less perceptive for missing the content but rather that he just didn't hear all that the partner was saying. The therapist can then discuss the reasons why people sometimes fail to hear what is being said and show how to be more effective at listening.

As the interviews progress, both partners acquire listening skills. They start "hearing" what the partner is communicating and are much less frustrated in their attempts at a clear response. The therapist notes that the partners have more congruence about what is being transmitted and what is received. Unless the speaker has such negative or threatening thoughts that the receiver doesn't want to hear them, the prognosis is much improved when listening skills are improved.

Chapter Eight

Building the Therapeutic Relationship

A relationship is an emotional bond between two or more people who share any interest or concern. It occurs when people experience a similar feeling about something they have in common; the shared experience leads them to connect emotionally. One feels and the other senses the feeling and responds. What they share may be as superficial and time limited as space on a crowded bus on which two strangers are riding. Or it might be as intense and durable as that found in a marriage of 50 years. The relationship may be primarily positive and cooperative or negative and adversarial. Except for very superficial and limited ones, relationships are combinations of different emotional experiences, with all the components, positive and negative, destructive and beneficial, simultaneously or concurrently operating.

Those who work with and understand the concept are not inclined to use the common lay term, "meaningful relationship." All relationships are meaningful. There may be relationships and no relationship, but there are not meaningful and meaningless ones. Those who use the phrase seem to refer to that type of relationship which is positive, clearly beneficial, and satisfying. The opposite kind is destructive, unsatisfying, and negative, but it is still meaningful.

Relationships are always in transition. They often change spontaneously and haphazardly with no intent or design. But as we learn how they are created, how they develop, modify, grow positively or negatively, we find they can be purposefully modified and consciously controlled. Marriages fall into difficulty when the relationship grows, usually without plan, into negative experiences; perhaps this is the only reason marriages become troubled. Relationship is the sina qua non of marriage and the proper focus of marital therapy. The work of the therapist is largely to help the couple understand their relationship and to make it more positive and effective in meeting their mutual and individual needs and expectations (Smith and Hammond, 1980). The therapist and couple jointly facilitate its movement from a mostly negative and unsatisfying one to one which is mostly positive and need fulfilling. Therefore, a fundamental component of marital therapy is to maintain an environment which fosters the effective working relationship.

Not all marital therapists agree that "relationship" is necessary in helping troubled couples (Morris and Zuckerman, 1974). Rather than depend on something as subjective and elusive as relationship, some advocate more objective and observable transactions for effective marital therapy. For example, they say that using tasks for the couple to perform, followed by sufficient encouragements to assure that the tasks will be repeated and extended into other contexts, will reach such goals with greater efficiency. Others say that relationship is the essential ingredient of success in marital therapy. The difficulty with both views is that the field still has not achieved consensus about what successful outcomes are to be. To say relationship does or doesn't lead to success requires a definition of success.

In any case, the therapy relationship is not depicted by many marital therapists as the sufficient condition for improvement of the marriage problem, but only a means toward that end. In other words, when the relationship achieves its potential, it still doesn't guarantee that improvement occurs. It is a vehicle used by the therapist to get to the desired objectives. By itself, it is not a panacea for anything—but is a most important contributor to the helping process (Truax and Mitchell, 1971).

Attributes of the Marital Therapy Relationship

The relationship between marital therapist and marital partners is similar but not identical to other therapeutic relationships. According to

Carl Rogers (1957), in all therapies where relationship is considered important, the therapist demonstrates at least five attributes. These include acceptance, genuineness, warmth, empathy, and caring concern. Several additional components are particularly relevant to the marital therapy relationship, including fairness, noncensoriousness, a working environment which brings people together and encourages interaction, a therapist in whom the couple can feel confident, and a framework in which the marital partners can know what to expect. Each merits some discussion.

Acceptance

The marital therapist has ample opportunity to be accepting during his work with every couple. It means taking each person, the husband and wife, as they are and where they are. The partners may have ideas, values, behaviors, ascribed or achieved statuses, or backgrounds which the therapist finds alien to his own experience or contrary to his standards. Yet, as previously discussed, he does not allow his beliefs to be imposed on the couple. If the behaviors or values of either the husband or wife are offensive to the therapist but not relevant to the problem for which help is sought, the therapist accepts it. He confines the effort to changing that which contributes to the problem. Acceptance creates an atmosphere in which the couple can reveal anything about themselves with the assurance that it will not lead to their rejection or admonishment. This enables them to be more open and provide more relevant data which can be useful in making a sound assessment. If the client does not openly reveal information because he fears he will not be accepted, or because he assumes it is irrelevant, he risks improper diagnosis. He decides privately and subjectively what is relevant and in effect conceals important data.

Acceptance does not mean, as it might imply, that the therapist is a person without bias, values, opinions, or standards of conduct. Nor does it mean that the therapist passively permits clients to say, think, or do anything they want in the session. Clients can't, for example, verbally abuse or suppress their spouses' attempts to speak and still receive the therapist's acceptance of the behavior. Therapists are not always going to feel the same way the client does; the objective is not to avoid having the feeling, but to keep it from interfering with what is going on in the treatment. Sometimes even that is not possible. When the therapist can't accept something about the client, it is usually better to expose the discrepancies in the interview. The working relationship may sometimes be inhibited by the disclosure, but it may also be a useful learning tool in therapy. In any event, the disclosure will be less likely to impede the therapy than would be its concealment.

Sometimes the behavior or values of the client might be so disagreeable to the therapist that acceptance cannot occur without an open discussion about it. For example, family therapist Harry Aponte (1982) describes a therapist's difficulty accepting one family. The stepfather had been repeatedly sexually involved with his two teenaged stepdaughters, while their mother watched. At first the therapist was repelled by the parents but tried to hide his feelings. All the family members were as closed-mouthed about the incest and its condonation as he was. No one in the family openly acknowledged their obvious awareness of the situation. They avoided it, it was later revealed, because they feared the therapist's disapproval. Progress was impeded because the lack of acceptance prevented discussion. Finally, the therapist confronted the family, asking them to explore their feelings about forgiving the stepfather for his incest and the mother for her collusion. They all began to tell one another how they really felt. The disclosures made it possible for the family members to begin to renegotiate their mutual relationships. The therapist could now more sincerely accept the family members and move on to other aspects of the therapy. Had he not brought his own and the family's feelings out in the open, the lack of acceptance might have been terminal to the therapy.

Genuineness

To be genuine is to respond according to one's feelings, rather than to what the perceived situation apparently calls for in order to achieve some objective. It is not something one can achieve, simply through determination or motivation; it is not something one can turn on and off. Genuineness has to do with sincerity, with freedom from pretension. This is not to say that the "genuine" therapist merely says whatever he thinks, or overtly displays whatever emotion he experiences at the moment. In therapy, this kind of impulsive openness can sometimes be disastrous. The therapist who is "genuine" can still withhold words which are thought or conceal emotions which are felt if their disclosure has no therapeutic merit; but when they are revealed, they should accurately reflect the therapist's feeling or thought. They are not expressed merely for the effect they apparently will have on the husband and wife.

Therapists are not "genuine" when they mislead the client. They rarely mislead through overt lies, but more commonly do so by concealing their ignorance, by conveying they are something they are not, or by providing false reassurances. For example, a therapist who affects "street-wise" jargon when talking with couples who communicate this way would probably cause more alienation than closeness in the working relationship. It sometimes happens when the therapist, asked for information which he doesn't possess, might conceal the fact by turning the question back to the client with a glib, "What do you think?"; or it may happen when the therapist responds to questions about which he is ignorant with such obtuse and pedantic verbiage that even the question was forgotten. But the most common form of therapeutic insincerity is to provide false reassurance. Therapists sometimes do this when they have become jaded, burned out, or feel they have heard it all before. They imitate their former theraputic behaviors, the way they seemed when they really were concerned. Their statements such as "everything will work out," or the comforting smiles and reassuring nods, when they are not felt, are simply play-acting. These insincerities usually do more to impede than foster the therapeutic relationship.

Warmth

Those said to be "warm" seem to have an outgoing and ongoing interest in other people, a feeling of pleasure or compassion when in the other's presence. They have an openness, an ability to reveal their own vulnerability, a predisposition to move outside restrictive behavioral conventions with the other person. Warmth is related to self-confidence and to receiving an ample supply of love, respect, encouragement, and empathy during one's life. Warm people may have good prospects for success in marriage, but therapists cannot instruct the husband or wife in being warm; the trait is not easily taught or developed in an adult even though some people can acquire some of its manifest characteristics. One can feign "warmth," interest, love, humor, or almost any emotion by imitating the observed behavior of others who possess these traits. Some therapists and marital partners are not naturally warm people, and if they feel warmth is important to marital success or therapy, they can sometimes convey that it is natural to them. This is usually ill-advised. The perceptive client will easily spot the incongruity in various affects which the therapist would inevitably reveal. Even the client who is not perceptive will have difficulty coping with the therapist's mixed messages and contradictory responses. Feigning of warmth is also ill-advised because it is not necessary. Like other aspects of the relationship, warmth may be useful but may be substituted, replaced, or circumvented. Many therapists seem effective without being or showing a milligram of warmth, but few therapists could be effective with their clients if they pretended something which is not part of their character. So too, many marriages can be effective when one or both partners lack warmth if there are other attributes to replace it. The therapist only displays what warmth he has, as a model to permit the partners to display their own warmth when they have it. There are many other attributes which can supplant or replace warmth in the development of the effective working relationship (Perlman, 1979).

Empathy

The therapist who empathizes is feeling with the husband or wife. He identifies with the feeling one of them has. He not only sympathetically attempts to understand how they might feel, but he experiences that feeling. He imagines himself to be in the other person's self and situation. Not only does this help the therapist understand the client, but it helps a spouse feel supported in an intensely gratifying way. It adds immeasurably to the person's feeling of self-esteem, and it provides a model for the other partner. The partner observes how the therapist is feeling with the other and notes how this leads to a better understanding and appreciation of himself. When both the husband and wife have greater empathy with one another, they are well on the way to a better working relationship with the therapist and each other.

Caring/Concern

It is possible to feel caring/concern for someone without feeling empathy, and vice versa. It is possible to facilitate a positive working relationship without either empathy or caring/concern, but it seems improbable without one of them. In caring/concern, the therapist need not feel with the other person; he need not share the same feeling or identify with the person's situation. Instead, he can observe the client from outside. Sympathy is more closely related to caring/concern than it is to empathy. The caring, concerned therapist can be more objective than the empathic therapist, and the empathic therapist can be more attuned to the feelings of the client than the caring/concerned therapist. The therapist in caring/concern seeks to communicate with the individual or couple about those issues which spell potential trouble, but which haven't yet caused problems and thus haven't yet called for an emotional reaction.

Fairness

It is vital that the therapist be fair to clients in all forms of psychotherapy, but this is especially so when treating couples and families. In individual psychotherapy, the therapist gives undivided attention. During the interview, the client is more important than almost anything else in the therapist's awareness. The therapist identifies with the individual and shows that he is on the client's side, will accept and support, no matter who else believes the client to have failed. But the marital therapist does not have this luxury. He cannot support one person unreservedly when treating a couple because the interests and needs of one might often be in conflict with the other. For example, when the husband or wife unfairly intimidates, manipulates, or suppresses the other in the treatment session, the therapist is not being fair if he accepts it. Fairness requires the therapist to understand the relative power each of the partners has with the other. Power imbalances often prevent treatment progress; the therapist might need to restore the balance so that more goal-directed movement can take place. For example, when one member of the dyad is less articulate than the other, it might be necessary for the therapist to help articulate that person's position more than that of the other person. If one partner dominates through physical or emotional force, this fact could be spelled out in the therapist's office. If one partner seems more attractive or interesting than the other, the therapist might need to make a special effort to give equal attention and concern to both. If the values and interests of one of the partners more closely approximates those of the therapist, the therapist need not change his own interests or attempt to get the partner to change, but must exercise care not to let this fact spill over into relevant issues. To do otherwise is to meet the therapist's needs rather than those of the marital partners. If the therapist rigorously adheres to the dictum that he will be fair to the couple, then the chances improve that they will observe and become more fair with each other.

Fairness, however, is not simply the avoidance of side-taking. At times, in fact, it is necessary for the therapist to take sides in order to achieve fairness. This may sometimes be necessary when one of the partners is more dominant, articulate, intimidating, or persuasive than the other, but no more "right." It also is useful for the therapist to take one spouse's side when both partners are so adamantly stuck in their respective positions and unyielding about their tolerance for the other's views that movement cannot occur (Zuk, 1966). In this instance, the therapist might arbitrarily or genuinely take up for one or the other to intentionally cause an imbalance. This usually causes a renegotiation of their respective positions and a greater regard for each other's well-being (Miller and Geller, 1972).

Noncensoriousness

The trait called "nonjudgmentality" has long been recognized as a major component of the therapeutic relationship (Garrett, 1972). The working relationship can be more effective if the therapist doesn't pass judgment on the client, doesn't blame the clients for the problems in which they find themselves, doesn't reject the client for not doing something better (Meisse, 1965). Perlman (1979) points out that the term "nonjudgmentality" is a misnomer and calls the trait "noncensoriousness." No therapist suspends judgment. What would be the value of going to a marital therapist without some reliance on his judgment? What is really meant is not censoring the person who has made a possible mistake. Censoriousness comes in many forms; the alert therapist can note how it creeps into any working relationship. It occasionally happens with facial expressions or body movements: the rolling of the eyes, the impatient tapping of the feet, the drumming of the fingers, the impatient sighs, and shifting in the interview chair. Often the therapist's actions are unconscious manifestations of his disapproval and may suggest countertransference issues. Whether this is or is not true, it would be better for the therapist to analyze why he feels disapproval for the client than to attempt to conceal any gestures which reveal disapprobation.

The Working Environment

The setting, facilities, and ambiance in which marital therapy takes place are also important in the development of the working relationship. If this environment is comfortable for the couple, secure from interruptions, witnesses, or eavesdroppers, and is arranged to encourage candid expressions of feelings and thoughts, the therapy will have fewer obstacles to overcome. This is not to suggest, however, that the setting is a sufficient or even necessary condition for marital therapy. Obviously competent and successful work has been achieved in less than ideal environments. Alfred Benjamin (1981) discussed such work under battlefield conditions. His supervisors wired him that interviewing could even be done in a tent. He immediately wired back, "Send tent!" Nevertheless, all other variables being equal, the working relationship is enhanced by the environment in which it occurs (Hall, 1966).

By far the most common setting for marital therapy is the practitioner's office. Some therapists hold that any deviation from this is unethical, seductive, or contrary to their theoretical orientation. This is still true even though many therapists report success in working with couples in their homes (Rabin et al., 1982), or in neutral sites such as street corners, cars and vans, restaurants, classrooms, or whatever. There may be circumstances, types of clients, and types of problems which are best served by the marital therapist treating couples in their homes or other locations. Nevertheless, this probably will never be very common among marital therapists because of practical, if not theoretical considerations. It would be difficult for therapists to spend much time traveling to and from various clients' homes. But more importantly, therapy in the couple's home or neutral settings makes it impossible for the therapist to impose the "controls" he might want. He isn't able to limit distractions. He can't easily rearrange the room for optimal communication. He can't be sure that the setting is neutral enough for the therapy work.

However, any advantage to using the office can be nullified if it lacks the desirable attributes for fostering the working relationship. These attributes include, at the very least, the following: a room large enough for comfortable movement and small enough for intimate conversation; a room with enough privacy so that the couple can speak loudly without being heard or without hearing outsiders; suitable heat and ventilation so that the atmosphere is not distracting; furniture which is tasteful enough to be appropriate but not so ostentatiously lavish as to restrict informal and spontaneous expression of feeling; at least two equally comfortable chairs so that neither marital partner is seated disadvantageously; and freedom from the interruptions of telephones, secretaries, or other people. Of course, what is considered "optimal" also depends on the type of work the therapist wants to do and what is most comfortable for him. But sociometric studies have determined some fairly consistent patterns in fostering or impeding the effective working relationship.

The marital therapist's office is ideally arranged so that the furniture and other amenities of the working environment are positioned strategically to bring people together and encourage interaction. Arrangements include tastefully informal furniture of the type more often found in middle-class American living rooms rather than in business offices. The room is usually not dominated by the therapist's desk, and the chairs used by the therapist and the marital partners are located diagonally to one another and between two and five feet apart (Sommer, 1965).

Unfortunately, what is probably the optimal environment for marital therapy may not be best suited for other types of helping intervention. This can be a problem because most practitioners are not exclusively marital therapists. In fact, most of them spend the majority of their work time providing other forms of treatment. Their offices are logically arranged for the type of specialty which constitutes the bulk of their practice. Thus, specialists in group or family therapy may want their offices to be very large with chairs arranged in a circle. Marital therapists who are also clergymen, lawyers, and physicians may need large desks in their offices arranged between themselves and the clients because they must write so many details and perform so many administrative tasks. Marital therapists who work in social service agencies often have little say in the type of furniture which is contained in their offices. This being the case, it is not always possible for the therapist to arrange his office to enhance the working relationship in marital therapy.

Nevertheless, the therapist who is aware of the impact of the environment on the client and on the relationship, whether his practice is or is not primarily marital therapy, would do well to keep the needs of the couple in mind when organizing his office. The conscientious marital therapist will make his office as much a therapeutic environment as possible.

The Sex of the Therapist

A question frequently asked by clients and therapists alike is, "To what extent does the sex of the therapist influence the marital therapy relationship?" The question would be moot, of course, where the treatment model is a male-female team of therapists. But since most marital therapy is done solo, the concern is relevant. The therapist is going to be of the same sex as one of the spouses, and it may make a difference to one or both of them. Many couples choose or are referred to a therapist primarily because he is a man or she is a woman; the premise is that certain clients do better in the care of one or the other. We make such assumptions because we see that gender has great influences on the way people relate; from this we infer that it influences the therapy relationship, too.

The issue is debatable and no one is certain. Many professional writers have claimed it is quite important. For example, in Wolberg's classic text, *The Technique of Psychotherapy* (1954), there is the assertion that certain types of illness, such as alcoholism, psychopathic personality, and borderline cases might be more easily treated by female therapists because of the potential for symbolic gratification of oral dependency needs. Other professional literature suggests that a particular couple or individual might do better with a woman therapist since a woman may be more patient, sensitive, gentle, nurturant, intuitive, and empathic (Rice and Rice, 1973; Turkel, 1976). Others state that some clients need a more masculine source of identification or role modeling, or a more assertive confrontation and so they should see male therapists (Persons et al., 1974). The popular literature also proposes that gender is important. In Phyllis Chesler's (1971) study of over one thousand therapy patients, she concluded that most believed gender made no difference in determining their choice of therapist. However, of those in the survey who said it was important, most would choose to consult a male therapist. Later, she advised women to seek out female therapists because, she claimed, male therapists have limited knowledge about women and are thus ill-equipped to properly treat them (Chesler, 1972).

Most of the research on this issue consists only of the opinions of therapists and consumers. In the opinion polls of therapists, most believe gender makes no difference as to outcome. But more female than male therapists disagree and believe it is important. Of the therapists who believe it is important, they say it matters most with clients who have identity problems, marital problems, homosexuality conflicts, and adolescent adjustment reactions (Mogul, 1982). But these notions are speculative; so far there is little empirical evidence to support such views. Few studies have compared relative outcomes as achieved by the two sexes, and almost none has shown any actual difference in results. Until future research proves otherwise, there is no rational basis for assuming a male or female is best or for referring clients on the basis of gender. The therapist's sex is probably far less important than his or her skills, experience, personality, and self-awareness (Cavenor and Werman, 1983).

What Does the Couple Expect?

The final factor of the marital therapy relationship to be considered here often gets too little attention by marital therapists, even though it is as important as any other in facilitating the therapeutic relationship. Marital therapists must be aware that couples who seek their services aren't quite sure what to expect. Marital therapy is generally far from people's normal range of experience. Much of their impression about marital therapists is derived from stereotype or popular media depictions. In such uncertainty they will most likely be guarded, cautious, and more anxious than usual. Their behavior will probably not be representative, and the therapist may misread the client's personality based on this atypical behavior. Marital therapy is an encounter with the unknown for most people, at least in its early stages, and the therapist must keep this in mind if he wants to facilitate the effective therapeutic relationship.

Imagine the feelings and thoughts which might go on in a person's mind while awaiting a first session with a marital therapist:

Trepidation. It's the only word for the way I feel in unpredictable situations. I feel many emotions now, but they are changing too fast to distinguish as separate entities. Anxiety is part of it, and there's some fear too, though I hate to admit it. I'm angry, too. I'm angry at having to be in this position, of having to humiliate myself in front of a stranger just to help solve a problem which everyone else seems to solve by themselves.

For the past ten days, since we made the appointment, I've been a nervous wreck. I can't wait to get this over with so I can relax again. I always feel a little like this when I wait in a doctor's office. But this is a lot worse. At least there I pretty much knew what the routine would be. But a marriage counselor! Who knows what'll happen? I should've asked my doctor more about it when he referred us. What's a marital therapist like, anyway? Will he blame everything on me? Tell us to get a divorce? Try to get us to stay married? I wonder if he's one of those crazy head shrinkers with an Austrian accent and goatee, like in the movies. Maybe he's one of those religious people who will want us to pray all the time.

I glance up from my magazine and see my wife fidgeting nervously, looking back at me. I quickly return to the pages and study them intently so I won't have to give her any encouragement. The magazine is tattered.

I wonder how many others have fumbled with it, and have also not comprehended its contents. I wonder how many others have used it as a prop to show that they aren't worried about what's going to happen. I wish we hadn't come so early. Then we wouldn't have to wait so long.

I look around the room. It's not what I expected. It's small, not fancy but comfortable. It's more like a lawyer's waiting room than a doctor's. No one else is in the room with us. There's a receptionist desk, with a small sign on it saying, "Please be seated. Dr. Jones will be with you at the scheduled time." Hmm. Can't he afford a secretary? Where is everybody?

I can tell other people are nearby, though. There are voices in the adjoining room, but I can't make out what they're saying. That must be his office. Wish I could hear better. There's music in the waiting room, so it's hard to hear anything. What's that? Sounds like shouting. Or is it loud sobbing? Now long pauses. Now more shouting. Good grief, is that what I have to put up with? Who needs that? I get enough shouting and sobbing at home. I sure don't want to have to pay a stranger to do it here. I look over at my wife again and she returns my glance. We smile and roll our eyes. We feel closer now as though we are about to face a common enemy. Maybe that's how it works. The therapist is so awful that you have to stick together just to stand it.

I think it's about time to go in. What'll I say? If I don't tell my side well, everyone'll blame it on me. Oh well, just so I don't make a jerk of myself and . . . uh, oh, the door is opening. Hmm. That's a nice-looking young couple. They don't seem too unhappy. What could be wrong with people like that? " 'Bye, Doc. See you next week," they both say. Now it's quiet again. Where is he? What's he doing in there? Taking notes? Calling his answering service? Going to the bathroom? Having a drink? Trepidation, that's the word for it. The worst thing is, I just don't know what it will be like. Oooops, there's the door again. It's time at last. "Hello, I'm Dr. Jones. Would you both like to come in now?"

What Should Couples Expect?

Marital therapists sometimes forget that their new clients face such uncertainty. They might assume their clients have more precise expectations about it than they actually do. But those who have never had first hand experience with marital therapy must get their information from sources which therapists might consider dubious. If they get it from friends, or from the popular media, the information may not be accurate. Therapists are often appalled at the way novels, movies, and television depict their work. But we sometimes forget that others have no way of knowing that these depictions are often distorted.

There are three major reasons why consumers often do not have clear expectations about marital therapy. In the first place, marital therapy has a vague and confusing public image. Since it has widely divergent goals, and since there is no single profession to tell the consumer what it does or tries to do, this problem is inevitable. Secondly, consumers are uncertain because there is so much variation in the way marital therapists work. As discussed in Chapter Four, there are many possible formats, so consumers can hardly be expected to have a clear and uniform picture of what therapists do. If a husband and wife asked their doctor or friends what is to be expected in a marital therapy session, the responses would probably vary considerably. They might have less cause for apprehension if they talk only to one other person, but if they talked to two or more people who have been exposed to different therapists, they might have difficulty. It is similar to the old saw: "If I have one watch I know what time it is. But if I have two, I'm not quite sure."

The third reason consumers don't know what to expect from marital therapy is because it is inherently unpredictable. When an individual goes for help he has considerable control over the situation; he can share information or withhold it as he chooses. Thus he can influence and predict the direction of the exchange. But when he goes to a marital therapist with his partner, his control is greatly reduced. He can't withhold information or present it as he might if alone. Neither the husband or wife will be sure what the other is likely to say or do; neither can control the direction or goals that the treatment will take, and neither can comfortably anticipate what is going to happen (Kotlar, 1967).

Until the couple becomes aware of the norms of the treatment situation, until they know what to expect, they will not easily resume what for them is their normal, typical behavior and way of thinking. In their first contact with the marital therapist, therefore, their preoccupation and objective will be to find this out. Furthermore, the therapist might easily misinterpret the clients if he bases his assessment on their behavior under such conditions. Even though treatment begins at the moment the marital therapy relationship starts, the specific diagnosis and treatment plan must be delayed until the framework within which the treatment is to occur is firmly established. All things considered then, the therapeutic relationship is greatly facilitated if the mutual expectations are specified as soon as possible in the first session. The client and the therapist come to a beginning understanding about the nature of the marital therapy process. It establishes how long the sessions are to be, how many of them there are likely to be, whether the sessions will be conjoint or sometimes individual, and what obligations the therapist and client owe to each other. This includes specifying what the fees are to be, and how they may be paid, confidentiality considerations, and the therapist's professional credentials. Marital therapists may also find it helpful to reveal something about their personal style, theoretical orientation, and general values. More marital therapists now spend the initial sessions discussing the couple's unique goals and outlining the tasks recommended to achieve them. They use contracts to delineate the treatment plans and methods to achieve them. When the treatment plan is specified in the initial interview, the expectations for the encounter and the therapeutic relationship are potentially more productive.

Chapter Nine

The Therapist's Varied Roles

No two couples and no two individuals are identical, so the treatment which works best for one individual or couple will not necessarily be best with another. The marital therapist is the medicine, the vehicle whereby change, growth, and improvement takes place. Most medicines contain a combination of ingredients for fast, safe, effective relief.

Some couples enter therapy needing a considerable amount of direction and information. Others cannot abide direction, but need a calm, accepting, neutral environment which permits them to iron out differences. Some couples need their therapist to be challenging, confrontative, and maybe even combative, while others need more support, encouragement, and acceptance. Some couples are stalemated in their relationship and need help getting unstuck. They can no longer communicate because they have stubbornly locked themselves into unyielding defensive fortresses, fearful that any compromise will lead to a weakened position or outright surrender; sometimes they need someone to distort the balance of power so that movement can take place. Others need a referee to help the relationship become more fair, or a mediator to help achieve a better balance of power.

If movement is to occur in the treatment process, then the therapist must recognize that these and many other needs are to be emphasized at various times. The therapist, in sum, must play different parts in order to achieve optimal effectiveness (Andolfi and Angelo, 1981).

Ten Roles for Marital Therapists

Marital therapists perform ten major roles in their effort to help couples in crisis. They are here designated as the roles of (1) host, (2) maintenance person, (3) engineer, (4) focuser, (5) catalyst, (6) educator, (7) reference model, (8) mediator, (9) side-taker, and (10) celebrant. Not all of them are performed with every couple. Some are called upon occasionally during the course of therapy. The therapist's skill is to know when and how to perform each of these roles—and when not to. Some examples are in order.

> Brad and Marge, both 36, have been married for four years. Both are strong, opinionated, and independent people. Neither had been married before, and they have no children or plans to have them. Both want to continue their respective professions at which both are quite successful. Their jobs require them to travel frequently, and they often see each other only on weekends. Even during weekends, they are devoted to rather unique interests. He is an avid golfer and she is a tournament bridge player. Both have had extramarital affairs during the course of their travels, but believed these did not contribute to problems in their relationship.
> They sought marital therapy because of sexual difficulties. Marge has dyspareunia, a painful sensitivity in the vaginal area which is exacerbated by sexual intercourse. She told the marital therapist that she has no symptoms when she abstains from intercourse or when she has intercourse with other men. A thorough physical examination of both determined there was no biological basis for the problem.

The therapy goals will be primarily in the realm of improving their cohesiveness as well as work on the specific sexual problem. Furthermore, this couple is already energetic and hard driving in the way they communicate, so the therapist won't need to be very directive. His role will include providing an environment which is calm, structured, and focused. He will design activities which will cause the couple to become more aware of each other, more willing to meet each other's needs. The therapist could be less verbal and non-confronting with the couple than he would be with a different kind of troubled relationship. Since the husband and wife are strong and independent, and relatively equal in power, the therapist won't need to emphasize such roles as side-taker, catalyst, and reference model, but will provide more effort in the roles of mediator, educator, maintenance person, and engineer.

Mary Beth, 28, and Charlie, 34, experience problems of power imbalance. Charlie is an alcoholic, very domineering, very possessive, and quite disinclined to provide much emotional support for his wife. He denies having any drinking problem and believes the major marital dysfunction comes from his wife's "unreasonable negativism." Mary Beth is depressed and feels quite helpless about getting her needs met in the relationship. Her husband spends little time with her. She can't get him to talk or provide warmth or emotional support. She fears his violent outbursts when drinking.

The process goal is primarily that of enhancing adaptability. Neither spouse is able to deviate much from habitual roles or seems able to accommodate to the needs of the other. The therapist would be more inclined to emphasize his roles as side taker, reference model, and catalyst. The therapist would be more directive, providing homework assignments which would encourage more effective communication and flexibility. He would take sides, sometimes with the wife to even up the power balance, but also occasionally with the husband. The therapist might carefully and selectively take the husband's side in order to paradoxically demonstrate to both how much distortion there is in their relative power balance. For example, the husband is very defensive and becomes offensive in order to avoid being blamed. He berates his wife for saying anything bad about him; the therapist chimes in with words to support his position. The effect is to show how inappropriate is his outburst. This might work to encourage both husband and wife to support each other better, even against the therapist.

Another couple suffered from disturbed communications in their marriage: Dennis, 49, and Polly, 47, rarely felt they understood one another, after 24 years of trying. Polly finally decided to go through with her long-standing threats to leave, since the children were grown. She wanted more fun in life, more opportunity to reap the benefits of their years of hard work. Dennis was a workaholic, serious, responsible, devoted to his children and career as well as to his wife. He didn't want her to leave, but didn't want to give in to her either.

They entered marital therapy with fear, stubbornness, and anger with each other. The couple had spent countless hours discussing their respective points of view; for the therapist to devote much time listening to them describe their mutual grievances would be merely to duplicate their experience at home. The therapist needs to provide something different for them, some mechanism which will enable them to more clearly understand each other's needs, wishes, and goals. The therapist does this by emphasizing the roles of host or structure provider, and gives them assignments to facilitate communication and better understanding of each other.

The effective marital therapist knows which roles to use and how to use them for which purposes. This entails switching behaviors and techniques. Thus versatility is one of the greatest skills involved. The most effective therapists are those who comfortably move among the different roles. Those who find these transitions difficult will be frustrated.

The required versatility can be both the joy and the bane of the marital therapist's professional life. Positively, it means there is more opportunity for variety than is found in most of the other helping professions. Negatively, it can be painful and risky, in that the skills required to do one thing well are not necessarily transferable. For example, the role might call for a therapist to be warm, calm, quiet, and accepting for a while. This is fine if the therapist's personality is inclined in these directions. But when the therapy progresses, a change of roles might be needed. The therapist needs to be stern, aggressive, and confrontative to facilitate the treatment plan. Not all therapists can easily make such changes.

Fortunately, most marital therapists have ample experience in switching roles. They have to become versatile, whether they want to be or not. Therapists who can't or choose not to change roles with sudden regularity tend to move away from work with troubled marriages and into other psychotherapy fields. Often they see individual clients during some of their scheduled time and then see couples with different kinds of problems at other hours. They constantly have to change their roles in these changing circumstances. Each of the ten roles will now be discussed individually.

The Host

A good host provides the environment in which the meeting is to take place. He makes the guests feel welcome, comfortable, and important. He defines the expectations of the guest's behavior, making it clear that some behaviors are welcome while others will be viewed with disapprobation. He conveys when the event is to end and what the plan is for future gatherings. Essentially, this role calls for providing the structure or norms of conduct within which the process is to take place.

In marital therapy, the host role occurs through clearly defining the expectations, showing the couple what their obligations are to be, and delineating the norms in which therapy is to take place, either verbally or with written contracts. It is the only one of the ten major roles which is incessantly being played from the beginning to the end of treatment; in this sense, it may be the most important of the roles. It is probably the easiest one to play, too, since it alone requires no differential diagnosis, nor any particular practice skill, nor experience for knowing when to use it. The therapist's job is to make the therapy rules clear and explicit. He enforces the rules, usually with gentle subtlety, but makes sure the couple operates within these norms.

As we have seen, no couple or individual can function effectively unless they have some idea of what is expected of them. Not only will they be less efficient in working on their problems, but they probably will be so uncomfortable that they may terminate therapy. Or they will try to provide their own structure within it. For them to provide their own structure means they would determine how therapy will proceed. At its extreme, the couple would decide the length and extent of the sessions, and what the therapist will say and do.

Clients rarely try to provide structure to this extreme, but often try to do some of it. They might attempt to get the therapist to play the role of judge and jury, and tell the therapist how something is to be interpreted, and to take their sides in a dispute with their partner. "What she is trying to tell you, doctor, is . . . ." "No, that's not what he really means; he just said it wrong." "Doctor, why don't you ask her what she did night before last while I was babysitting?" The effective therapist prevents this unless it is part of the explicit treatment plan.

This is not to imply that the therapy structure for all clients is identical. The ground rules, the expectations, the ways of enforcement, the consequences for violation, the time frame, the contract, all are tailored for the specific couple and their unique needs. It is possible to set the time frame for one couple at one hour each week for sixteen weeks, 90 minutes weekly for six months with another couple, or open ended with still another. Though there is room for variation in the structure, there should be no deviation from the fact of its existence.

The structure can be slightly modified, refined, or changed during the course of treatment as circumstances warrant. Changes are made, however, according to previously established procedures. The initial understanding is that no changes in therapy are made without the consent of both spouses and the therapist.

One example illustrates how the role of host is performed by the therapist:

Al and Marian were six weeks into marital therapy when a dispute erupted over how treatment should be conducted. A contract had been signed by the therapist and couple in their second session. It was agreed that there would be 16 once-weekly, 50-minute sessions in the therapist's office. The goals were primarily oriented toward communication enhancement and adaptability. The methods agreed upon included homework assignments about spending some time each day discussing positive, non-problem subjects. The spouses were to talk on positive subjects ten minutes daily.

The couple had apparently understood the therapist's rationale for suggesting the assignment. It was based on the fact that both spouses tended to wander in their conversations. In so doing, they would get into subjects which were painful and threatening. Thus they started to dread any prolonged conversation; they knew where it would probably lead and thought it better to avoid the risk. But this meant they were decreasing the quality and quantity of their positive verbal communications. The therapist reasoned that, if the couple began to associate positive outcomes with conversations, their fears would diminish. To achieve this, boundaries had to be placed on the early conversations. The couple had always maintained conversations which lasted a few minutes before fighting, so the therapist asked that they purposely stop their talks after the ten-minute time period.

At first the conversations ended at the agreed time and were positive. They talked about future plans, ideal places to vacation, politics, religion, gossip about the neighbors, experiences involving members of their family. They even had a talk exclusively devoted to exchanging jokes. The conversations were so enjoyable they started to last longer each day. "We are supposed to stop now," one would say. "But I just want to say this one thing," the other would say, and the conversation would continue. They told the therapist they were going beyond the time limit. The therapist explained the rationale again and stressed that they should stop after ten minutes. Al agreed, but Marian thought the restriction was unreasonable. "Why stop doing what we need and is good for us?" she asked, even though the answer had been given repeatedly. Soon there was a three-way argument about the rule, with the therapist referring to the original agreement, Marian asking for a change, and Al supporting the therapist in the office, but supporting Marian at home when the conversations were occurring.

The issue was resolved when Marian experienced the consequences of deviating from the agreement. The conversations got longer and she kept adding new material to them. She had her husband's attention and she would clarify a few problems. She would point out how he could improve. The conversations became more heated. Al and Marian finally told the therapist that the conversation assignment was not working out and should be discontinued. They felt the assignment itself was ineffective, not that it was being carried out improperly. The therapist pointed this out in supportive, positive terms. There was no "I told you so" response. The couple was reminded how enjoyable the experience was in its earlier phases because it had boundaries. Eventually they would extend the length and frequency of the conversations, the therapist said, but for now it was best to stay with the plan. Thereafter they were able to restrict the conversations to the plan, and the therapist's prediction of their future success was validated.

The therapist, as host or structure-provider, won't humiliate the client for violation of the norms. There will almost always be deviations from stated rules. Every time it happens, when the therapist knows about it, the couple is reminded of the importance of staying with the plan and using agreed-upon procedures whenever a change is required. When the therapist is accepting, but firm about the structure, the couple is more likely to acknowledge that deviations have occurred or are contemplated. If the therapist seems very punitive or rejecting about any violation, the couple may be more inclined to conform but certainly would be less inclined to reveal nonconformity. Experienced marital therapists find an acceptable and workable middle ground between being too punitively rigid about structure and being too lenient or vague about enforcement.

The host role also provides a frame of reference by which couples can measure their progress or lack thereof. Therapy is evolutionary and its progress is imperceptible to most, including clients. Like a plant whose growth is not visible, the growth of improvement in the marital relationship cannot be observed either. One notices growth in the plant by going away and returning later. Since couples cannot step away from themselves, they have to measure their progress against some objective standard; this is provided by reference to the explicated goals. It comes also from the therapist's reminder of what the couple once typically did in similar circumstances. The therapist notes what the progress is or what the direction appears to be and what additions to the relationship are needed to achieve stated goals.

The Engineer

An engineer is given a set of objectives and designs a plan to meet those goals. If the goal is to, say, get cars from one side of a river to another without using a ferry, the engineer might set about designing a bridge. He doesn't actually build the bridge, but shows others how it can effectively be accomplished.

The marital therapist also plays this part with most couples. The role is usually activated in the early stages of marital therapy, plays a diminished part in the middle phase, and has little part in the concluding phases. It is intrinsic to the goal delineation process, because many people need to know if there are reasonable and reachable ways they can achieve their goals before they can formally state them. Most people wouldn't even think about getting cars across rivers if they hadn't first conceived of bridges and ferries. Of course, the engineering role is closely related to the goal-determining process.

Basically, the role consists of designing methods for the couple which will efficiently help them reach their goals. The therapist is aware of different methods which could be used to reach the goal; he needs to show which of the possibilities will be most advantageous, least costly, and the most durable. It is basically a consultative function. The therapist-engineer shows the client what is to be done and how to do it.

Many of the designs are already well-established in marital therapy and require only slight modification to suit the individual needs of the clients. Established designs often consist of various communications techniques or experiential devices which therapists and couples have found helpful. Many of them will be described in Chapter Ten.

An example of the engineering role is seen in the following:

Bob and Sandra sought marital therapy after several separations in their ten-year marriage. They had violent fights, temper tantrums, anger, jealousy, suspiciousness, manipulation, and negative confrontation. They were separated when they entered therapy and wanted to decide if they should stay apart.

The therapist saw their problems were primarily due to inflexibility issues; the goal was to facilitate adaptability. Needed was a plan to help them be more open about their expectations of each other, more mutually accepting, and less inclined to want to mold the other into some preconceived notion of appropriate behavior.

The therapist recommended several techniques which had been well documented as to effectiveness. These included the "caring days" procedure devised by Stuart (1980). For several days they were to behave so that they could mark off a checklist of positive behaviors which the partner had wanted. (The process will be further discussed in Chapter Ten.) They also were asked to do some role playing. Each was to pretend to be the other partner for 30 minutes daily, during which time a problem would be discussed. The therapist explained both procedures and prescribed them as homework. Eventually, the therapist saw that the role playing was counterproductive since it stimulated some unwanted confrontations. But "caring days" seemed very useful; the therapist advised continuing with that, discontinuing the role playing, and adding another homework assignment. They were to write a love letter to each other. When the couple reported progress, it was apparent that both techniques were effective.

The Maintenance Person

Every structure requires maintenance. A large building has someone to repair the leaky pipes, fix the faulty electrical outlets, and replace broken glass and wooden frames. Problems develop and need to be fixed, or everything begins to deteriorate. This is also true with couples. Relationships are always in need of minor or major repair, patching, mending of broken hearts and frayed nerves. Couples make most repairs themselves; they develop better understandings and practice alternative ways of communicating or enhancing their closeness. But sometimes they need an expert to assist, the marital therapist who plays the role of maintenance person.

The maintenance role of the marital therapist is to keep the therapy process moving. It will move if it is properly designed, unless there are obstructions. The therapist is alert to these obstructions and seeks to remove them. For example, if the husband or wife perceives the partner in an inaccurate way, or attributes motives or characteristics to that person which are not actually there, the person might well behave as though it were so. This would lead to mixed messages, contradictory responses by the other, and reciprocal confusions.

Harry Stack Sullivan (1953) called this phenomenon the "parataxic distortion." It is similar to "transference" but encompasses a greater range of social phenomena. It is a parataxic distortion when a husband or wife relates to the other, not because of the other's actual attributes, but because of what is fantasized about the other. The distorted perception becomes self-perpetuating. The wife may see her husband as cold, rejecting, and hostile when to everyone else he seems a warm, loving, empathic person. She has selective inattention and doesn't notice those traits which show her husband's warmth. She is quick to notice the infrequent mannerisms which confirm her ideas. During the course of therapy it becomes apparent that a perceptual distortion exists and must be corrected.

Sullivan believed that most parataxic distortions can be changed through consensual validation. That is, in the above example, both partners could be made aware of their incongruent view of the husband. The wife would be shown that others perceive her husband differently. The therapist wonders aloud why such a divergence of opinion exists; eventually the wife notices the interpersonal distortion, and her perception of the husband's personality becomes more accurate. The therapist, in the role of maintenance person, is alert to these perceptual distortions and "repairs" the problem whenever it interferes with the healthy marital functioning.

One of the more common aspects of the therapist's maintenance person role is that of helping the couple keep balanced during the course of therapy. For example, an important marital therapy norm is that some evenhandedness occurs in each session. It would cause serious problems and prevent solutions to other problems if the therapist were consistently more attentive to one or the other partner. Both husband and wife usually are given approximately equal amounts of attention, opportunity for self-expression, and amounts of approbation and confrontation. This is true no matter which of the pair has the "most problems" or is mostly "to blame." It is also true when one is more articulate, psychologically sophisticated, attractive, assertive, or whatever. If the husband and wife were absolutely equal in all relevant traits, the therapist in playing the maintenance role might do nothing but keep track of the time devoted to each. But no two people are ever so evenly matched.

Usually there are imbalances which must be corrected or are not to be encouraged. Since either the husband or wife is likely to be more assertive, articulate, "right," or whatever, the therapist as maintenance person gives a little more coaching to the less assertive or articulate partner, or a little more encouragement to the other partner. Sometimes the role calls for the therapist to interrupt the more verbal person and ask for the views of the quieter one. Sometimes a less articulate person needs more help in clarifying certain points. Sometimes one has repressed more anger and is almost immobilized because of the emotional buildup; this person might need more support to let it come out in the therapist's office, where it will be dealt with more safely and objectively than could happen at home.

In this role, the therapist determines what the couple wants (a healthy, working, functional relationship), sees where they differ between actual and ideal functioning, and sees that the problem is corrected. This, of course, is always done with the consent of the couple. The therapist provides the couple with the means to achieve their goals, but does not do it for them. This is crucial to the durability of any improvement. If the couple were not instrumental in bringing about the changes, they might be grateful to the therapist, but would subsequently be unable to resolve similar problems. Therapy epitomizes the Chinese proverb which says, "Give someone a fish and he eats for a day; teach him how to fish and he eats for a lifetime."

The maintenance role does not occur in all marital therapies, and it never occurs throughout one entire therapy. If the partners find that they are already good at fixing those things which go wrong, and are not prone to perceptual distortions about one another, they rarely need the therapist as maintenance person. Most couples need some of it, but none who do should need or receive it throughout the course of treatment. The therapist does not continue to repair problems. It happens at first, so that the couple can get at other issues. The therapist will show what to look for and how they can make the repair.

Eventually, before therapy stops, the therapist pulls back from this role. The process of "weaning" from therapy is in part the process of letting clients take over this role from the therapist. The treatment sessions should continue for a while after the couple has assumed their own maintenance functions, to demonstrate that they are able to make the repairs properly.

> The case of Red and Linda illustrates how the therapist uses this role in treatment. They were a young couple, still in college and working evenings to support themselves and their continuing educations. Red was a mathematics student, while Linda majored in psychology. She planned to become a family therapist, and she said she initiated marital therapy for didactic purposes. Linda saw Red as a very mechanistic thinking person, who related better to machinery than to people. He was serious, quiet, and even-tempered. Linda misinterpreted his apparent passivity and his disinterest in psychology. She saw him as neurotic, as concealing his true feelings behind defense mechanisms, as suffering unresolved internal conflicts. She was frustrated in her efforts to get him to "open up" and cathartically expurgate emotional conflicts by talking with her.

The therapist soon realized that Red was a healthy person who was highly regarded by his many friends and professional associates. It happened that his interests were different from those of his wife. He found it easy to accept that she would have her own interests, but she was not similarly inclined to accept his orientation. Her wish to get the therapist to take her side and work together on "restoring him to healthy psychological functioning" was unsuccessful.

The therapist, instead, helped her see how her perceptions about her husband were imprecise and leading to problems. The therapist was able to do this in a way which was supportive of Linda without causing her to feel as though she was wrong or that her motivations for helping her husband were misguided.

The Focuser

One of the more common experiences of dysfunctioning marriages is that the husband's and wife's communication often roams sporadically, without direction, without resolution. A frequent complaint is that the couple doesn't stick to a subject long enough to resolve anything. An argument about who is to wash the dishes tonight leads to an argument about who does the most work altogether, who is more responsible in filling obligations, and so forth. Soon the discussion takes on cosmic proportions. The goal of such discussion is not to understand or clarify a point, or even to communicate; it is to win, to be officially declared the one who is "right," while the other is declared "wrong." When one starts to get an upper hand, the subject is changed to an area where the other is stronger. Such discussions end only when one or both are too tired to continue, or are interrupted by some other obligation they must meet.

This pattern is often reflected in the marital therapist's office. The couple can't focus long enough to settle something. The issue is related to other problems, which remind the husband or wife of other incidents, which in turn remind them of still other unrelated issues. Often, whether or not either spouse has the other's attention, they want to say everything they have stored for days.

The therapist who permits such behaviors, unless it is explicitly part of the treatment plan, obstructs progress or is colluding with the couple in their obstructionism. The therapist should remember the goals, the methods agreed to achieve them, and the subject at hand. When the couple deviates from any of these three, the therapist assumes the role of focuser. The couple is reminded about the goals, methods, and subject. The therapist shows the couple what subjects tend to lead to deviations and what speech patterns and gestures relate to their getting off the subject.

Therapists sometimes train clients to note and change this behavior. They recommend a homework assignment in which the couple discusses a preselected topic for 30 minutes, using an audio tape recorder. During the replay they check the number of times each deviated from the predetermined subject. They note the particular ideas which were expressed which led to the deviation. This helps the couple better understand some of their communication patterns and digressions. It also helps locate areas which are seemingly threatening and thus verbally avoided.

The therapist in the focuser role is like a specialized audio recorder, only the playback is immediate and activated when the deviation from the subject begins. The therapist is there to retain the focus, to remain goal oriented, to get back to the subject at hand. Therapists are sometimes reluctant to actively focus the subject, because it violates a theoretical premise of letting the subject go where it will to uncover more meaningful insights. Free association doesn't often happen in conjoint marital therapy, since two people influence the direction of everyone's attention. The following dialogue, taken from a videotape of a marital therapy session, illustrates some of the focuser role.

MARVIN: "Yes, it's true. I did stay out too late that night. I already told you that there was a bunch of us guys who wanted a beer after the meeting. We just lost track of the time, that's all."

RACHAEL: "Sure, if it was just one time, that would be okay, but it happens every few days, now."

MARVIN: "Oh, for God's sake, it does not. The last time I stayed out with those guys was two months ago, at least, and maybe. . . ."

RACHAEL: "You do, too, Marvin. You forget. How about last week? You didn't get home til after midnight, and you didn't call or let me know where you were, or, . . ."

MARVIN: "I don't either. Maybe every few days, but what's wrong with that? I don't do anything wrong. I'm no alkie or skirt chaser. You know that. I don't know why it makes you so up tight anyway, except that you're so jealous and. . . ."

RACHAEL: "I wasn't jealous til you starting acting funny that time. And I'm not jealous now either, just concerned."

MARVIN: "Oh, you are too. How come you always look in my wallet and glove compartment? You know damn good and well you are worried that I'm messing around."

RACHAEL: "I only looked in the glove compartment once, and I was looking for the state map. Why are you trying to make me look bad in front of the doctor? You're the one to blame, not me."

THERAPIST: "Hey. I thought we were talking about the amount of time you have to spend with each other."

MARVIN: "We were, weren't we?"

RACHAEL: "Well, I know I was, but Marvin kept trying to get out of it."

THERAPIST: "I think a lot of other issues got brought into the discussion, too. Let's get back to how much time you both think is reasonable to be together and to be apart. And let's not get into things like who did what last week. Okay?"

MARVIN: "Yeah, okay. You're right. We always do that. We can't ever seem to stay on track, so we never get anywhere."

RACHAEL: "Well, it's you who keeps changing the subject, Marvin. You're really good at it. It keeps you out of a lot of trouble most of. . . ."

THERAPIST: "Rachael, suppose you help Marvin stick to the subject better. The best way is to stay with the subject no matter what he wants to say. Don't talk at all when the subject digresses. You could do that, too, Marvin. You can help Rachael stick to the subject by not saying anything if she gets off the subject. Okay? Now, where were we?"

RACHAEL: "We were going to say how much time we should spend with each other and how much time we can have to ourselves."

The Catalyst

Marital problems are always painful, and for many couples it is even more painful to bring them to a helping professional. Baring one's soul, exposing skeletons in the closet, admitting to mistakes or deficiencies is never easy. Many find the pain so great they deny there is a problem, or that it is as severe as it is. Sometimes they tell themselves they can deal with it by ignoring it. Sometimes they blame the problem on their spouse, or their terrible childhoods, or the economic climate, or the bomb—anything to keep it from being too close. They avoid the real issues, close their eyes to the threat, bury their heads in the sand. Since it provides the appearance of immediate relief, they are encouraged to continue the denial. They try to encourage their partner to deny, also. Obviously, the long-term consequences are serious. The couple can't get more than symptomatic relief. Usually the problem will recur, continue, grow, and become ever more difficult to resolve as it becomes habitual and entrenched. When this occurs, as it often does, the therapist dons the cloak of catalyst.

The therapist's role as a catalyst is often active, verbal, and confrontative. However, the therapist can get the couple to reveal hidden fears and overcome resistance by being calm, accepting, and noncensorious. Sometimes the couple can be assured that the pain will reduce by disclosing the problem. Some couples respond better with therapists who gently cajole or supportively encourage their openness rather than by being confrontative (Wile, 1978). But other couples require active confrontation about emotionally disturbing patterns and thoughts which they had tried to obfuscate.

The astute marital therapist looks for signs which suggest what will be most effective with the particular couple. More confrontativeness might be indicated for couples who tend to resist through intellectualizations, denial, and withdrawal. If the husband and wife are verbal or volatile in their relationship, overt confrontation might be useful. Bound-up, passive, detached, or rigid couples might also do well with a confrontative manner. Couples who are already emotionally overloaded, who might be depressed or feel defeated, might be better served with a less confrontational tone. It is never safe to generalize about which couple needs what therapy behavior; there will always be exceptions. The skilled therapist learns that individualization is important.

The catalyst role, whether it is played in a softer, accepting manner or in an assertive, confrontational manner, is designed to energize the movement process. It is to stimulate overt action, to make explicit that which has been concealed but which covertly influences the relationship. Its most important and frequent use comes in responding to client resistance.

Clients resist in a variety of ways; the therapist sometimes may not even know it is happening. A common type of resistance is for the husband or wife to talk of their history rather than the "here and now" in their relationship (Luther and Loev, 1981). Many couples have a preconceived notion that the therapist's office is where you talk about your childhood, your traumatic past, your painful memories, the terrible things your spouse once did to you. If the goal is to help an individual uncover unconscious conflicts, then the focus on history is important. In marital therapy, however, it is more often of secondary importance, as an additional or supplementary aid to revealing current patterns and restructuring them.

What is usually more important is what is happening now, not why something might have happened then. Some clients want to spend an inordinate amount of their time detailing past events. They don't want to uncover unconscious conflicts, or understand the dynamics of the present relationship. They want to avoid a painful encounter with current situational and relationship problems. The therapist as catalyst often interrupts historical discourses with questions which relate it to the present.

The Educator

The educator imparts information to students, teaching about new, more effective ways of looking at and dealing with the world. More importantly, educators teach students how to get and use needed information. Much of the marital therapy process is an educational one; helping people to discover more satisfying and effective relationships between themselves and their spouses is, more than anything, an exercise in learning.

The therapist regularly provides information which tells the marital partners how to be more effective in relating to one another. The therapist sometimes provides a new vocabulary for the couple so they can explain themselves better to one another. They are taught the rationale behind methods which are used for more effective understanding, communication, and conflict resolution. They are instructed to look for patterns so that they might more efficiently deal with the causes of their problems. The therapist tells them how other couples have dealt with these conflicts and may show them experientially how to use similar approaches. They are taught to replay what they have learned in therapy in circumstances outside the sessions.

The therapist sometimes teaches about available resources which can be called upon for specific or situational problems. For example, problems about the care of a handicapped child contribute to a marital disturbance, and the parents are unaware of social agency services available to help the child. The therapist informs the parents of the resource, the knowledge of which achieves some of the therapy objectives.

The Reference Model

Reference or role modeling is closely related to the therapist's educator function. Essentially, role modeling is a means of teaching the couple alternative ways of interacting as they observe how the therapist relates to them. Many times couples have problems because they have not had sufficient exposure to alternative behavioral responses. They usually emulate the behaviors of their reference groups. Reference groups or reference individuals are those with whom the person identifies, wants to be like, wants to imitate. The individual sees these people as the "way to be."

Socialization is fundamentally a process of emulation of the reference group. If the behavior of that group has undesirable characteristics, the person who emulates them scarcely considers that the behavior may be ineffective or inappropriate in different situations. He probably will have difficulty making the distinction between behavior which is effective and appropriate for new and different situations and that which is not. This is the major reason why spouse or child abusers tend to come from families in which the same problem existed. This is why many couples whose parents were divorced or combative are more likely to be similarly inclined.

In such circumstances, husbands and wives are helped when they are exposed to new role models to emulate. The therapist relates to the husband knowing at all times that the wife is observing the interaction. When something positive, beneficial, or effective occurs, the wife may remember and eventually want to imitate it. Another husband tends to interrupt his wife and finish her sentences. Then he is frustrated that he never gets clear answers from her. The therapist demonstrates an alternative; he asks the wife the same question the husband just asked and waits for her response. The therapist makes sure the husband doesn't answer for his wife. This might be done with a finger to the lips when the husband begins to speak or a shake of the head. The therapist may have to interrupt the husband and say he really wants to give the wife a chance to speak for herself; then he listens to the wife intently, using body language to show that he is with her; he nods and is clearly on the same wave length. He is careful not to interrupt or finish the wife's sentences; he avoids responding as the husband generally does. After the wife has finished, the therapist says, in a non-sarcastic way, that he understands what the wife is saying and that the wife expresses herself clearly. He has provided a pattern for the husband to imitate.

The therapist's words and gestures are likely to be used as guides for emulation by the husband, wife, and both. It won't always happen, but there is no way to know which behaviors will and which won't be imitated. It is safer to operate as though everything will be. Keeping this in mind, he must be extremely careful about revealing his own personality characteristics. His personality might be commendable and suitable for emulation by some clients, but it might be harmful if emulated by this particular couple. In most instances, however, openness provides opportunity for couples to have positive influences for emulation (Miller, 1983).

The Mediator

The role of mediator is perhaps the most recognizable one which clients attribute to marital therapists. It is the activity of hearing both sides of a dispute and effecting agreement or reconciliation on the issue. Mediation, as used here, is not the same as the therapy specialization known as "divorce mediation." That will be discussed in Chapter Thirteen. Many husbands and wives expect to present their views to the therapist and receive a judgment about who is right; some expect that this will be the primary purpose of the sessions. They come wanting a neutral forum in which to present their grievances to the therapist and obtain a ruling in their favor. They want an objective person to decide whose side of the argument is accurate. They believe the therapist will see the wisdom of their position and finally show the spouse that they must yield on the issue. Often couples are disappointed to find that many therapists downplay this role; some therapists avoid playing it altogether. Mediation has a place in marital therapy, but not as important a place as many clients expect nor as unimportant as many therapists want it to be.

Many marital therapists downplay or attempt to avoid mediating because of its inherent problems. There are almost never unequivocal "right and wrong" solutions. Almost every client is partly right and partly wrong on the issue being debated. Even if one partner were absolutely right, the therapist would ill serve the therapeutic purpose by saying so. The therapist cannot stay a lifetime with the couple, resolving each dispute as it occurs. His job is to provide the couple with a means of resolving disputes so that they can do so on their own after therapy has concluded. The therapist is more properly concerned with facilitating an exchange and process whereby the couple can find ways to communicate, to compromise, to make decisions together. The role of mediator is essentially that of helping to enhance this interaction; it is not to make decisions.

One of the primary activities inherent in the therapist's mediation role is that of the "go-between" (Zuk, 1966). This behavior occurs when either the husband or wife can't express a particular message to the partner without misinterpretation. Or it occurs when the partners become stubborn with each other, pout, remain silent, or remain adamant in their refusal to listen to the words of the other. This is not to imply that the therapist is more articulate or persuasive than the spouse; it is possible because the aggrieved spouse has attributed a series of painful memories to the partner, but not to the therapist. It was the spouse who failed to understand or who was neglectful or cruel, not the therapist.

Ray and Diane provide an example of how mediation played a part in the treatment of one couple. They entered therapy so furious they didn't want to understand or help each other. Diane had grown suspicious with Ray's implausible excuses about his whereabouts: He had to work late, until 3:00 a.m. He had to attend a conference out of town on New Year's Eve. The lipstick on his collar came from the office retirement party when one of the elderly ladies must have kissed him there.

On several occasions, Diane accused him of having an affair. Ray's response was ridicule. He would laugh uproariously at her pathetic charges. He would tell her friends how paranoid or menopausal she seemed to be getting. Diane was humiliated by the ridicule and tried to suppress her concern. Then one day she received a letter. The envelope was addressed to her, but its content was addressed to Ray. This is what it said:

Dear Ray:
Since you have stopped seeing me and don't return my calls, I thought I should write. You told me never to contact you at work, so I'm sending this home to Diane. Remember how we used to lie in bed and talk about her? Remember how you said you wished her boobs were as big as mine? Remember how you said she was a bitch and no fun and always angry? Now I know why. She has a lot to be mad about with you. You really are a turd, you know.

I know why you are dumping me after all these years. They were lovely years, at first. Except on those many occasions when you couldn't get it up. You are letting me go because of your new sweetie. It's that slut Elizabeth Smith we met at the New Year's party, isn't it? I wasn't sure at first, so I found out where she lived. Last Thursday night I drove there. Guess whose car was there at 2:30 A.M.? It was yours. Well, Luv, I say good riddance. But I thought I'd better warn her about you, too. I sent her a copy of this letter. You'll probably talk her into believing that I'm a liar, but she'll find out soon enough. I hope your wife does too.

Love,
Vickie

Diane kept the letter two weeks before revealing its contents. She reread it almost hourly, and her rage grew to almost uncontrollable proportions during that time. She didn't confront her husband and said nothing to him, even when he continued making new excuses about his evening whereabouts. She also stopped speaking to him, having intercourse with him, or doing anything for him. Her unaccountable behavior was making

Ray nearly as angry as she was. Then the explosion came. Ray got home late, slightly drunk, looking sheepish. Diane was standing in the entry, holding out a copy of the letter. After she let him read it she began screaming, throwing things at him, scratching his face, pulling his hair, kicking him and smashing everything she could reach in the house.

The divorce proceedings were venomous. Both were adamant about making the courtroom hearing as messy as possible. Their lawyers tried to find places for compromise, but were unsuccessful. They were able to convince both Ray and Diane to see a marital therapist together to see if some common ground could be found. The couple finally consented to one therapy session together, mostly in order to help their case in court.

In the office they would barely acknowledge the other's presence. The therapist got each of them to talk directly to her, pretending that the other was absent from the room. She asked that the other remain silent, to facilitate the illusion. She had to repeat her admonition several times when Ray spoke, because Diane was so appalled at his apparent distortions that she wanted to correct him. After each had had a chance to describe their feelings, situations, and goals, the therapist asked for some positives. What is good about your spouse, she asked each. What are your happiest memories with your spouse? What makes you proud of your spouse? Only positives were allowed, even though both wanted to express otherwise.

Finally the therapist summed up the feelings and positions of both Ray and Diane. She turned first to Ray and explained how she was conveying his wife's viewpoint. "She is angry, Ray, and that is to be understood. She is frightened. She doesn't want to lose you and she doesn't want to be ridiculed. Perhaps you two can never again live together, but at least you can get out of the relationship in a more harmonious way. If you give her something to help restore her self-esteem, overcome her embarrassment, her feelings that you don't think she is worthwhile, it will make a difference." Then, before Ray had a chance to speak, the therapist turned to Diane and interpreted Ray's point of view. "It isn't you, Diane. He knows and regrets his dishonesty. He feels he has some need which couldn't get met at home. But now he knows he didn't allow you the chance to help meet those needs. He knows you're better for him than the other women. He knows the many nice things he said about you are true."

The therapist then asked Ray and Diane to talk to each other. She asked them to describe their thoughts about what the therapist had said to each. Of course, this didn't lead to an immediate reconciliation, but it was a beginning. They did begin talking and considering the other's viewpoint. They began showing other than the desire for revenge or vindication. The therapist as "go-between" or mediator had facilitated the beginning stages of this process.

The Side-Taker

In the role of side-taker (Zuk, 1976), the therapist exerts leverage to facilitate movement in the relationship. He overtly sides with the husband or wife against the other in a disagreement; sometimes he sides in favor of or against the couple when they are in a dispute with outsiders. For example, if in-laws, neighbors, or employers cause distress for the couple and it eventually manifests itself in conflicts between them, the therapist might effectively influence their perceptions of the situation by taking sides. He might speak in behalf of the neighbors or in-laws against the couple. The therapist might also role-play an advocacy position on behalf of the couple to the outsiders. This side-taking behavior is akin to the role-modeling behavior which provides a guideline for the couple to emulate.

The most common of the forms of side-taking is to endorse either the husband or wife on a given issue. It is sometimes useful to do this when any of the following events or situations are taking place: (a) when one of the partners has a valid viewpoint but is intimidated or somehow less capable of clearly expressing it; (b) when one partner is more sensitive to the subtleties or qualifications inherent in a dispute while the other continually "wins" through rigid or bullying behavior instead of through the merits of the dispute; (c) when the partners stubbornly refuse to budge on an issue and require an outsider to stimulate movement; (d) when the couple lacks energy or sufficient drive to pursue an argument, resulting in an apathetic stalemate; (e) when one partner is depressed or ill and cannot match the forcefulness, articulateness, or domination of the other; (f) when one is clearly and unequivocally "right" but the other won't accept it because of pride or ego problems; and (g) when one partner has given in to the other, not because of agreement with the viewpoint, but because of fearing the consequences of winning.

There are inherent dangers in taking sides. Some of the major risks include the alienation of the partner who is sided against, the loss of respect for or confidence in the therapist, the escalated efforts by the one who lost the therapist's support to regain the support, subsequent distrust of the therapist for taking sides not because of the merit of the argument but because of some nefarious motive. Consequently, some of the other therapist roles can be used to reach the same goal with less risk. For example, couples might not need someone to take sides if they are simply provided more information about a given issue. Rather than declaring that one or the other's position is preferred, the therapist states the relevant information so there is a face-saving way out for the one who was misperceiving the situation. Education, role modeling, and setting boundaries are often roles which might be used before taking sides. Still, there are instances when there seems to be no other effective way of generating movement from the rigid relationship pattern except through this role.

The Celebrant

The last of the ten marital therapy roles is the celebrant (Zuk, 1975). A celebrant oversees an important event and is respected by its participants. The celebrant gives the event the stature and public sanction which it deserves. People often don't feel married, or that their loved one is properly buried, or that they have really graduated, unless there are official ceremonies to document the event. The role of celebrant in most life situations helps people take the event seriously; it is meaningful and is not to be taken lightly. There are consequences to the event. It marks major points and changes in the participant's life.

The marital therapist plays the role of celebrant at various stages in the therapy. In the beginning there is a welcoming ceremony, in which the therapist acquaints the couple with the procedure to be followed. He conveys the importance of the therapy. The description and formal listing of goals is part of the celebrant role. When major breakthroughs take place during the therapy, when new insights or old goals are reached, or when specific methods have been specifically accomplished, the therapist as celebrant is there to attach proper importance to it.

When termination occurs, the celebrant recognizes the work the couple performed, the accomplishments they made, and the goals they have reached. The celebration and acknowledgment solidify gains made in therapy, improve its durability, and increase its applicability to non-therapy situations.

In sum, the therapist's roles are, of course, not mutually exclusive and not the only behaviors of the therapist. They are delineated here as a convenient way of encompassing some of the major activities which are part of the therapist's repertoire. It is unlikely that the therapist would use them all in the course of working with a given couple; only a few are performed in a given time, and fewer still occur at the same time with any couple. The therapist chooses to perform one role over another depending on the individual circumstances, needs, or assessment of the couple. Some roles are activated, then discarded, and then reactivated depending on the needs of the couple or their special circumstances. The therapist's developing skill will be instrumental in determining the appropriate time to use each of them.

Chapter Ten

Techniques in Marital Therapy

There is no single method in marital therapy which is best for all couples. Therapists find that interviewing skills and working relationships may be necessary, but these are often not sufficient to help certain couples reach their unique goals. Thus, the conscientious marital therapist develops a repertoire of techniques or specific methods to call upon when a couple or one of the spouses faces special problems.

This chapter provides an overview of some of these methods and techniques. The methods discussed are not to be considered mutually exclusive, discrete entities; by themselves they are not enough to meet all the couple's needs and reach all their goals. Simply knowing how to use them is not enough to provide competent marital therapy. Even more important is knowing when to use them, which ones to combine, which ones to use before others, and what style to employ in enacting them. This is part of the art of marital therapy—and experience, not books, is its most effective instructor. The techniques are organized here, not according to the theory base from which they are derived, but around the objectives which they are designed to help the couple reach. The major objectives are to enhance the couple's (1) decentering, (2) activeness or marital energy, (3) catharsis, (4) understanding, (5) role reequilibration, and (6) intimacy.

The Task of Decentering

Piaget formulated the concept of "decentering" partly to explain how children often focus on one aspect of a situation at a time and thus misinterpret the overall meaning (Piaget, 1962). In one classic study, he demonstrated that young children often are influenced to think the number of beads in a vase changes when they are poured into a vase of a different shape. The child focuses attention on the shape of the vase to the exclusion of other relevant information. As the child grows older, he decenters. That is, he is able to allow more than a single feature to determine how the overall event is perceived. He begins to notice that the number of beads stays the same if poured from one vase to another which is differently proportioned.

The concept has been extended into an understanding of family dynamics by several family therapy theorists, notably Feffer (1970) and Steinfeld (1978). It is posited that one or all members of a family often focus on a single characteristic or outstanding trait of one of the family members and project all the family troubles on that individual or that person's trait. If it is a couple, one person might believe that all the marital problems could be solved if only the other person would change that trait. Marital therapists see this pattern occur when one of the spouses focuses on the other's having an adulterous affair, or on the other's constant nagging, or on never spending enough time at home, or whatever. The single trait looms so large as to obfuscate the myriad of other problems, including those which might have contributed to the central problem. It is, of course, difficult to progress when a single item focus dominates the therapy process. The spouse says to the therapist, "How can you ask me to think about the way we talk with each other when he is involved with another woman?" To progress, it is incumbent upon the therapist to help the couple decenter so that they can have and act upon more accurate, relevant, and extensive information.

Toward this end, the therapist first determines the reasons the couple might focus on one trait in their partner and ignore others. Basically there are five overlapping reasons. First, it is because a spouse sometimes finds other relevant traits to be so painful that they are ignored in favor of one which is more palatable. For example, victims of spouse abuse sometimes return to their mates because they remember only the happy moments. Remaining focused on positive events, one might simply feel more comfortable. Secondly, one of the partners cannot understand a complex situation and so concentrates on a part which is understandable. Such a person feels capable of grasping the whole situation better by looking at one element at a time. Third, sometimes it is more fun to focus upon a given trait. Attending to it rather than something else often provides a kind of reward; many couples get in financial trouble by dwelling on things they want to buy rather than considering the bill for it. Fourth, sometimes the trait is so threatening that it is impossible to look elsewhere or at the big picture. An explorer in the Serengeti would find it difficult to concentrate on the terrain when being chased by a lion. In similar fashion, a spouse might not have the usual capacity for looking at all the relevant data when experiencing an immediate threat to personal or marital well-being.

The fifth possible cause of this orientation is becoming more prominent. One of the more difficult centering problems in working with many couples in today's "me-generation" is that of narcissism. Many want help because they think their marriage doesn't provide them with what they assume they deserve or "need." Their primary focus is on "What's in it for me?"; their sole criterion for marriage is that if it makes them happy it is worth keeping, but if it doesn't, it must end. Not only is the overall marriage viewed in this way, but so too are the day-to-day events which occur within it.

The narcissistic partner may give little attention to, or derive little gratification from, the overall happiness or security of the partner or the relationship. The happiness of the other person is given little emphasis. The partner keeps score: "How many times did my spouse do this or that for me today? How often did my partner give me what I need or want?" The narcissistic spouse quite often was initially attracted to the partner because of an outstanding but often transitory trait found in the other. Physical attractiveness, wealth, charismatic personality, political influence, and important connections are among the most common examples. The existence of one of these traits becomes so important that it conceals the absence of others; eventually the other characteristics are greatly missed.

One or several of these misperceptions may combine in the individual and lead to relational difficulties. The partners aren't aware of these problems and therefore cannot tell the therapist about them. The therapist notes their existence by observing the overt manifestations. Among the most common manifestations seen in the therapy interview are one spouse's attempts to speak or think for both, one spouse's attempts to form a coalition with the therapist, and one partner behaving as though the spouse's interests in the session are secondary.

The decentering objective is to redirect or enlarge the partner's direction or span of attention. The therapist does not necessarily show the partner where else to place the attention, but seeks to divert it. The decentering work may be implemented by the way the interview is conducted and by assigning the couple several tasks.

The interview itself provides a vehicle for decentering. Basically, the therapist shows major interest in important traits which are almost ignored by the client. When the therapist determines which of the five factors are behind the misdirected focus, it is possible to redirect. For example, if the partner is too threatened by a trait to focus on it, the therapist can talk about it so gently and with supportiveness that it can be faced. If it seems too complex, the therapist helps clarify the whole situation. If a wife dwells on her husband's lack of attentiveness to her, the therapist may eventually ignore her complaints and change the subject. This shows the wife that other concerns deserve attention.

If narcissism is behind it, the therapist rewards the partner who thinks about the spouse. For example, the husband describes his many needs and says how his wife fails to meet them. He wants the therapist to convince the wife that she should be more attentive to him, or give him "permission" to leave her and find a new partner who won't deprive him. For the therapist to confront the wife about not meeting her husband's need would affirm the husband's preoccupation. Instead, the therapist who seeks to decenter would turn the discussion to the wife's desires. "What has been done about her needs?", could be asked. Attention would be diverted to the gratification one can receive by giving to the other: "How did your wife look when you gave her that Christmas present?" "How do you feel when you please her?" The therapist also demonstrates that it is pleasurable or educational to give attention to the other. "Your wife really has a subtle sense of humor," the therapist says, laughing and nodding at the husband. The therapist rewards the narcissistic husband for having such a dynamic and clever wife. The husband then looks beyond himself at this person who has received a compliment from the therapist.

Decentering Coalitions

Human triads, such as those comprised of a husband, wife, and therapist, often attempt to form coalitions. Two members of the triad seek an alliance, an "inclusion," for their reciprocal benefit or power; this typically occurs at the expense or "exclusion" of the third person (Caplow, 1968). Effective marital therapy is vitiated when the therapist permits such alliances to exist for long, unless by design.

The coalition tendency has many forms. For example, each partner may attempt to convince the therapist that the partner is the one with the problem, the "identified patient," and work with the therapist as a colleague or consultant to improve the mate's emotional condition. The husband or wife attempts to win over the therapist and be declared the "innocent" party in the dysfunctional relationship. Some spouses attempt to monopolize discussion with the therapist and ignore the partner. They form alliances by talking to the therapist about their spouses rather than directly to the spouse. These and the other many variations of coalition-forming attempts have to be recognized and combatted by the therapist or the treatment will be hopelessly bogged down.

Therapists have several techniques for countering these attempts. For example, they do not permit either of the partners to speak about their values or opinions in the first person plural. When a husband says, "We don't think . . .," the therapist asks him to restate the point singularly. "Okay, I don't think . . .," says the husband.

Each partner in therapy should be spokesperson for his/her own values and opinions, but not for the other. When one of the partners receives this message from the therapist often enough, the tendency might be to express the values and opinions in neutral or impersonal terms, rather than as a referent to the spouse's thinking. One spouse might say, "Normal married couples spend at least a few hours a week talking with each other."

Such statements are value judgments rather than immutable laws, and are not necessarily shared by the partner or the therapist. If allowed to stand, they may thereafter be interpreted as cardinal principles which are not to be questioned. The therapist keeps the speakers from making such generalizations and encourages them to state everything in personal terms. "Are you saying that you don't get to talk with your partner as often as you want?", asks the therapist. "Tell us how you, not necessarily the rest of the world, think it should be."

When one partner attempts to exclude the mate by talking only to the therapist, the therapist brings the other person into the discussion. The speaker is told to talk *to* the spouse, rather than *about* the spouse. The therapist looks not at the speaker but at the partner when the speaker avoids looking at the spouse. The therapist moves physically closer to the excluded partner and talks more with that person than with the other until the equal balance is restored. Both partners are included in everything being said. For example:

> JOE: "She never wants to get together with other people."
> THERAPIST: "Say that to her instead of me, Joe."
> JOE: "Aw, she never listens to me. You tell her. I keep saying stuff like that and it don't do no good."
> THERAPIST: "Try again, Joe. Tell her what you think."
> JOE: "Okay. Kim, you never wanna do nothing. You're getting boring."
> THERAPIST: "How does that make you feel, Kim?"
> KIM: "Well, Joe, you hurt me a lot when you say stuff like that."
> THERAPIST: "Hurt?"
> JOE: "She always says she's hurt but really she's pissed."
> THERAPIST: "You're speaking for her and telling it to me instead of her."

The instruction of "speak to, not about" brings the interview into the here and now. It provides direct access to whatever conflicts might exist between the partners. Accordingly, it affords opportunity for direct intervention. It focuses attention on what happens between the partners rather than within one or the other.

Decentering "Mind Readers"

"Mind reading" is another problem in the marital therapy interview which is overcome with decentering activities. It happens when, for example, the husband speaks about his and his wife's feelings as being synonymous. He might say, "We don't think this should be the way to live." The wife tells the therapist that her husband "is always grumpy when he's worried about the bills."

"Mind reading" is making unsubstantiated descriptions of the partner's subjective states, as in, "She feels I shouldn't be saying this to you right now." They tell the therapist what their partner is thinking or feeling. Since many therapists encourage their individual clients to bring out what is on their own minds, they sometimes forget to prevent this from happening when the partner does it for them. The objective here basically consists of getting the mind-reading spouse to differentiate his/her own ideas from those of the partner (Bandler and Grinder, 1975).

When the spouse interprets the partner's thoughts, the therapist asks for confirmation by the other:

> THERAPIST: "Do you think what Joe said about you is correct, Kim?"

Or the speaker can be questioned:

JOE: "Kim hates it when I want to invite the neighbors over."
THERAPIST: "I won't ask yet if that's how you feel, Kim. Joe, how do you know Kim feels that way?"

To eliminate mind reading often necessitates untangling rigidified patterns between the couple. It helps to shatter previously held incorrect assumptions about the partner and permit more accurate understandings to take their place.

Assignments for Decentering

Decentering assignments basically ask each partner to look at the spouse from different vantage points. They begin by a demonstration in the office; the couple is requested to perform the activity at home at least once before the next appointment. In one assignment, the therapist asks the couple to state in a single brief sentence one problem which they think exists in the marriage. They take turns doing this until completing ten statements. They are asked not to elaborate, comment on the other's remark, give justifications for their accusations, give defenses, or to be concerned with who is right or wrong. This has the effect of expanding their range of concerns beyond the limited single item grievance. If the rules are followed, it precludes the discussion taking off into wide-ranging accusations. It puts limits on the respective statements, while at the same time permitting the couple to communicate beyond a single subject.

A variation of this assignment is to ask the partners to reverse their roles and take turns with single sentences about the marital problems from the partner's perspective. This exercise helps the couple decenter in several ways. Putting themselves in the shoes of their partner helps them look beyond their own needs to the needs of the partner. It gives the partners a chance to see how their complaints sound. It tells them that the partner is aware of what the complaints are. Couples frequently are helped to see the situation quite differently.

One wife reported she had not considered how her grievances sounded until she heard them repeated by her husband in a nonsarcastic way: "When Larry and I did that exercise at home it felt funny. I kept wanting to correct him when he was quoting my gripes pretty accurately. He was saying just what I always complain about in the same way I do it. It sounded different coming from him, so petty, or unimportant, or not serious or something. When we talked about it later, he said he had the same feeling. He said I recited his gripes accurately. But when he heard them coming from outside himself, they didn't seem the same."

Another form of reversed role playing also helps couples decenter. It asks each partner to assume the role of the spouse, but this time the discussion is more open and flexible than in the one-sentence exchanges. The partners engage in a discussion about one single problem in their relationship, from the other person's viewpoint. As always, the assignment is first played in the therapist's office to reduce possible misunderstandings.

The therapist might give the instruction in the following way: "Now Betty and Al, tomorrow night at 8:00 P.M. you've agreed to try the role reversal exercise. Betty, you imagine you are Al. Discuss one problem about the relationship, pretending you are Al. Think like he does, talk like he does, and even move as he does. Give Al's side of the argument. Try to win the argument for him. Al, you do the same. Pretend you are Betty and act just like she acts in a discussion. Give her point of view just as she would. I suggest you limit the exercise to ten minutes. Then take a few minutes to be apart. After a short wait, get together and talk over how it sounded to hear yourself from the other's viewpoint. Okay Al? Betty? Good. Now let's practice right here. Pick a subject. . . . Okay, the issue is, who should have to wash the dishes. Remember, you are now your spouse. You have the next five minutes to convince the other person your viewpoint is right."

Couples are often surprised by the degree to which their spouse can accurately present the other viewpoint. They are often surprised by the way their own logic and grievances sound when coming from the mouth of their spouse. They tend to feel more understood, more "objective," more decentered, with the completion of the assignment.

Another assignment is to ask the partners to describe their similarities and differences in one-sentence descriptions. After each statement, the partner offers a different sentence about the similarity or difference, but does not comment on the first person's statement. Each partner could make 20 statements every time the exercise is conducted. The first ten would cover similarities and the next ten the differences. A typical exchange might sound like this:

BETTY: "I think we both like Chinese food."
AL: "I think we both like living in the suburbs."
BETTY: "We both are Methodists, but we agree we don't go to church much."

AL: "Neither of us likes to wash the dishes."

BETTY: "Okay, now it's time for some differences. Let's see. I think Al likes to be alone a lot, and I like to be around people."

AL: "No, I don't think you've . . . what? Oh yeah, don't comment about what she says. Uhmm. Betty wants to see those romance movies and I like action pictures instead."

The exercise allows couples, in a less threatening way, to understand their healthy differences from one another. Marriage can be stimulated or invigorated when the differences are recognized and accepted and when there is no perceived obligation by either partner to get the other to change or conform. Married people who appreciate differences in their spouses are far more likely to grow as individuals, and their individual growth enriches the relationship (Rogers, 1970). Conversely, couples who can't tolerate differentness devote some energies toward becoming identical. They might subordinate their unique aspects to those of the other or manipulate the other into conforming to their wishes. Ironically, if they achieve a goal of absolute agreement, they are more likely to be bored and uninterested in the other; they are married to a mirror and find nothing new to discuss.

The decentering assignment known as "looking," which was popularized in the human potential movement (Schutz, 1967) also has applications to marital therapy. The therapist asks the partners to spend ten minutes simply looking at each other with no verbal or physical contact. They are not asked to stare eyeball-to-eyeball, but rather to look at all parts of the partner's face and body. They are to do this from all imaginable angles, distances, and positions. The therapist may recommend that the partners first stand about 20 feet apart for a few minutes, then look at each other from ten feet apart, then only a few inches. Then one might lie on the floor and watch the other or do so while standing on a chair. The assignment literally asks each partner to observe the other from a different viewpoint. It often causes the person to be understood differently.

Couples in marital crisis often stop really looking at the partner or don't see what they are looking at. Their view has become routinized, programmed, and rigidified. This assignment helps change that; it also helps the partner feel more important, more recognized and more attended to by the other.

Other assignments to help couples see their partners from different perspectives come from group therapy psychodrama techniques (Moreno, 1953). The therapist might ask each of the partners to imagine being a new person, either someone who is admired or who may be repulsive. The imaginary person is given a different name and background. Then the couple engages in a "get acquainted" conversation. This enables the partners to "unlock" some of the rigidified role patterns and expand the way they relate with each other. A variation is for the partners to imagine they divorced, went their separate ways, and accidentally met at a party 20 years hence. They pretend to tell each other what they have done with their lives for the past two decades. They are essentially saying how they imagine they would be if unfettered by the other person. The assignment gives the couple a chance to share ideals, aspirations, and goals. Often spouses find that their desires for the future are compatible.

A challenge for the marital therapist is to get couples to participate in some of these assignments. Many people are extremely discomforted when they step out of their traditional roles. Some are anxious when the therapist doesn't conform to their stereotyped expectations. Some might promise to do the assignments at home, but never seem to get around to them. Knowing this, the therapist can try to get the couple to perform the activity in the therapy office, but some couples find it even more threatening to behave this way in front of another person. Experienced therapists find that, as they become more comfortable with these assignments themselves, they are presented so matter-of-factly that the couple is more comfortable about performing them, either at home or in the therapist's office. When the couple is more comfortable about performing the decentering assignments, the results go far in helping them to focus not on minutia or diversions, but on those issues which must be dealt with to solve basic marital dysfunctions.

Apathy or Mutual Withdrawal

Motivation is a necessary ingredient which a client must bring into therapy. Non-motivated couples or even non-motivated individuals in a marital dyad make the prognosis for goal achievement limited. Dealing with undermotivated institutionalized clients, for example, has always had discouraging results (Stanton and Todd, 1981). Even in settings where the client is only mildly interested in the potential benefits of therapy, the value of therapy is questionable. Marital therapists find that apparent indifference, diminished energy, and will to work toward improvements in the marriage are commonplace.

Many couples are in "mutual withdrawal" (Wile, 1979). They seem to have no feeling for each other, are indifferent to the partner or to the marriage. They feel bored with their partner, find nothing to talk about, sense a barrier between them. They start the therapy with the words, "We are drifting apart," or "The old flame just isn't there anymore." They rarely say anything to each other except the bare essentials. They watch TV during meals and devote themselves to activities which exclude the partner. They fantasize about how much fun it would be if they had a more exciting mate. They rarely fight because they apparently don't care enough to bother convincing the other of the merit of their argument. They seem to have low libidos or at least express sexual desires indirectly rather than with their partner. Behavior, at least in the presence of their partner, is that of "placating" and "distracting" to avoid any disturbing or disruptive actions (Satir, 1972).

Apathy is possibly the most difficult of all marital dysfunction problems to overcome. When couples fight or even express frustration toward each other it is more workable; then their energies can be redirected into more constructive areas. But if they simply don't care, it isn't possible to go on in therapy until this problem is addressed.

Fortunately, most couples who enter marital therapy are not completely apathetic or they would not have had the motivation to make the appointment. And couples don't just happen to lose their interest—something caused it. Their apparent apathy developed during the course of the relationship, or they would have lacked the energy and motivation to marry in the first place. Thus, therapy is able to do something about apparent apathy. The therapist doesn't actually instill motivation but creates an environment and uses techniques to reverse the factors which led to the behavior. The first step, then, is to determine why the apathy or withdrawal exists.

There are two common elements related to apathy or "mutual withdrawal" which are amenable to marital treatment. One is that the partners have stored so many grievances, so many frustrating and bitter experiences with each other that they fear the consequences of further discussion (Bach and Wyden, 1969). Perhaps past confrontations were too painful, and possibly inconclusive as well. Perhaps they learned the hard way that bringing up emotional issues with their partner would inevitably result in physical or emotional harm. They have given up trying to change or improve the relationship; the best they can now hope for is "getting along," or accommodation. They live the illusion of having some consensus with the partner, or some "pseudomutuality" of marital goals (Wynne et al., 1958).

The other common reason for apparent apathy is that the couple has suffered so much disappointment in their expectations for the marriage that they have given up (Frank and Kupfer, 1976). The classic scenario in which this occurs has the husband coming home after a hard day at the office. He envisions returning to a wife who prepares his drink and meal, comforts him, is sensuous but nondemanding, who is there when he wants her but is unobtrusive when he wants solitude. The wife, on the other hand, wants her husband to rescue her from the drudgery of her life. She wants a mate who provides her with interesting adult conversation, perhaps a night out, one who dotes on her as he did in the days of their courtship. Instead she encounters a man who wants to get away from the hectic pace of his workday world. He is greeted by someone who tells him the toilet is leaking, the children need to be disciplined, and the mother-in-law is coming over for a visit. The couple experiences frustrated fantasies; they cope with the disappointment by barricading themselves behind emotional walls of indifference.

Techniques for Coping with Apathy

To cope with apathy, therapists attempt to precipitate movement, any movement, which gets the couple away from rigid positions. The techniques are designed to compel the spouses to come out of their "safe" hiding places. It is often done by "shaking up" the couple's style of relating. Sometimes it occurs through legal pressure, bribery, persuasion, or fear of worse consequences. For example, some couples visit therapists as a condition of a decision in a court of law (Johnson, 1974). Some families are paid to participate (Stanton, Steir, and Todd,1982). Many reluctant clients enter couple therapy because of manipulation by the spouse or because they just don't want to divorce, even though they don't want therapy either.

Sometimes the therapist can overcome this apprehension by the assurance that the interview will be noncensorious, and perhaps not even painful for the client. But all these factors are at best only helpful as short-term inducements.

Therapists sometimes destabilize an inert, withdrawn, relationship by changing the structure of the sessions. This is often done by assuming the "side-taker role," or by bringing other family members into the meetings. In playing the side-taker, as described in Chapter Seven, the therapist overtly agrees with or supports one partner against the other. Many couples will not react to this by further withdrawal. Instead the partner whose side is taken is often stimulated to come to the aid of the spouse. The spouse who is sided against may also fight back more enthusiastically. He or she may say things to the therapist which couldn't or wouldn't be said to the spouse. The partners may form a new alliance with each other to cope with the therapist.

If side-taking is used with withdrawn people, however, the therapist must be exceedingly cautious. If one or both partners are too dispirited to muster the energy for an argument, having the therapist apparently turn against them may be more than they will tolerate. They could easily withdraw from therapy as they have withdrawn from the spouse.

Bringing into the session additional members of the family or relevant others who care about the couple can also generate movement. Children, in-laws, other relatives, and close friends can sometimes unveil issues which were previously obscure. The others can reveal dimensions or set off confrontations which had been previously concealed. Couples can sometimes become quite moved when relatives and friends attend a session to show how the marriage relationship has adversely affected others (Speck and Attneave, 1972). Sometimes one parent will speak up to protect the children against the spouse, when nothing else can change the apathetic response. He or she might remain silent during the partner's diatribes, but feel compelled to interject ideas when the children seem confused or frightened.

The therapy techniques which seem to address the underlying causes of apathy or withdrawal may have the most potential for enduring results. These techniques are designed to minimize the risk of openness and reduce the fears of caring. They also address the disappointment at the spouse's failure to live up to expectations. To cope with the fear of openness, the basic techniques are designed to maintain boundaries. To cope with disappointed hopes, the techniques are designed to clarify expectations.

Maintaining Boundaries: The Marriage Conference

The inability to maintain boundaries causes problems for many couples. It finally causes them to give up because there is no other acceptable resolution. For example, many, if not most, troubled couples argue that they find it hard to stick to one subject; they often can't place limits on the amount of time or effort they will spend on a given issue. Every discussion potentially leads to violence, interminable bickering, and getting all the dirty linen brought into it. Finally, it just doesn't appear to be worth the effort. So they remain silent no matter what the partner says. The therapist counters this apparent apathy by facilitating more openness, by helping the partners focus, stick to one subject, avoid diversions, and by placing time limits on the discussion. The therapist's presence itself is a partial boundary-maintainer. There is less likelihood of physical violence or devastating verbal abuse with the therapist present. The therapy interview itself will place some limits on the discussion, especially when the therapist is careful to help the couple maintain those boundaries.

One assignment to facilitate the boundary-maintaining effort is called the "marriage conference." The therapist might prescribe the activity in the following way:

> "The assignment takes one hour. It is called for by whichever of you feels the need to open things up and clarify matters in a relatively safe way. Whoever calls for it is the 'host' and suggests where and when it is to take place. This person arranges for the meeting place to be comfortable and distraction free. This means no music, no TV playing, no reading matter or children nearby.
>
> "This person is also the first one to do the talking. He/she has the floor and the other person's undivided, uninterrupted attention for one-half hour. You can say anything. You can talk about problems, or you can talk about your goals, hopes, plans, or anything that interests you. But this won't be a conversation. You do all the talking. Your partner will stay silent, saying nothing, but looking at you for the entire half hour. If you run out of things to say, then both of you stay put and keep silent. Then the other speaks for a half hour, also without interruption. He/she can also talk about anything. He/she doesn't have to respond to what the first person said, but may do so.
>
> "At the end of this hour, both of you go away from one another for about half an hour to let things settle. Then you do whatever you normally would do. But you don't bring up anything that was discussed by either of you during the conference for at least 12 hours. You can have as many of these conferences as you want or have time for before our next session.
>
> "There are some important rules to follow about time. Whenever one of you calls for the conference, both of you should agree then and there when to have it. But you can't have it right away. It should be held no sooner than 12 hours or later than 48 hours after it is called for. This gives you both the same amount of time to pull your ideas together and plan what you are going to say. When you agree to the time, stick to it. Consider it an important appointment which you must prepare for and keep. Do you have any questions?"

This assignment reduces the likelihood that the couple will get into an endless or violent confrontation. It facilitates an exchange of ideas and feelings but in a way which does not lead to vitriolic exchanges, or "I did not, yes you did" type talks. It puts both on a fair and equal footing, minimizing problems which occur when one is more articulate than the other. More often than not, couples who use the marriage conference find that they run out of things to say before the half hour is over. They find it difficult to go on without feedback or responses to their charges or admonitions. They have been used to having their statements disputed, and often feel they never really are heard or understood. It is, of course, crucial that all the rules of this assignment be followed. Otherwise the couple will not benefit from the essence of the prescription, which is to enhance communication within safer boundaries.

There is a purpose to each rule; sometimes it is necessary to explain these purposes to assure compliance. Keeping to the time limits is important to conveniently prevent endless controversy. Waiting for some time before the conference is important to give both partners an equal chance to collect their thoughts. Sticking to two consecutive monologues rather than dialogue exchanges is important as a way of getting all one's ideas out without being influenced by the partner. Having a time after the conference for cooling off permits some consolidation of the ideas gleaned from the encounter. It also allows each partner to cool off from any angry provocations in the encounter.

Techniques to Clarify Expectations

Mutual withdrawal which comes from disappointment in one's mate may be dealt with by reexamining expectations more realistically. Some have given up because they no longer believe their spouse has the ability or interest in meeting their needs. The therapist combats this feeling by helping the couple to understand and modify their expectations. It is done in the interview by frequently asking each partner what they want, expect, look for, hope for, seek from the partner. Therapists get couples to consider this from many perspectives: what was expected in the past; what was expected during courtship; what one sees other spouses doing to meet similar expectations; what is to be expected under certain specific conditions; what is to be expected from the spouse in the future.

The therapy interview usually brings such expectations into greater consciousness when the therapist asks each of the spouses, in many ways, what it is they want from their partner. Often when the spouse outwardly states what the expectations are, without sarcasm or veiled threats, the expectations acquire a different, more workable meaning. Sometimes the expectations sound unreachable or unreasonable to the one making them. Sometimes they sound reasonable but were not previously understood or recognized by the partner.

When people don't know what to expect or what is expected of them, they often act passively, guardedly, and apathetically. If the partners are not sure what the other expects, their response is almost preordained to appear apathetic. The therapist helps fight apathy in part by clarifying the expectations. Reciprocal expectations which are unclear, contradictory, unreachable, or implicit are to be explicitly delineated. Much of the ongoing work in the interview is devoted to this task; it is usually achieved as the therapist asks each partner to specifically state what is expected.

Every couple in the therapist's office is trained, to a small extent at least, to be more overt and direct about their wishes with one another. Both husbands and wives very often suggest that their mate "should know" or "should do" certain things without being asked. The therapist immediately demonstrates that such assumptions are unhealthy for the relationship. They must make their wants overt.

When apparent apathy seems to derive from this circumstance, the therapist may assign one of three activities for the couple to use at home or in the therapist's office. Each is designed to clarify and explicate expectations. They were originated primarily by marital therapists oriented to gestalt psychology, or to encounter techniques and the human potential movement (Smith, 1973). They are called "I expect," "needs-wants," and "marriage models."

In the "I expect" activity, the couple sits facing each other for about five minutes. Each takes turns delivering one sentence which begins with the words "I expect you." The other person listens, does not concur or dissent or express any other response. Instead, the second person does the same thing as the first, completing one sentence which begins "I expect you." They continue trading statements for 20 exchanges. If this occurs in the therapist's office, there is an opportunity for the couple to safely discuss what was learned from the task, what was seen as reasonable and unreachable, do-able and impossible, desirable or repugnant about the other's expectations. If the couple does the exchange, each is asked to refrain from comment on the other's expectations for a 30-minute "cooling off" period.

Couples often find it surprising how little they actually know of what the other wants and are surprised, when not cornered or provoked, to learn that most of the expectations are in fact do-able and desirable. When a partner utters an expectation which is not considered do-able, making it explicit in this safe context often allows it to be revealed for what it is. Then it can be withdrawn and replaced with more appropriate expectations.

The "needs-wants" activity is a way of prioritizing the expectations or distinguishing the very most important wishes from those which are less so. When partners are subjected to a single continuous barrage of demands, all expected simultaneously, the recipient is likely to feel so overwhelmed as to avoid doing anything. It is helpful, therefore, for the couple to learn how to parcel out their wishes and expectations into segments which are manageable enough to be more readily accomplished. The "needs-wants" exercise facilitates this. The couple is again asked to face each other and uninterruptedly exchange single sentences without commenting on what the other is saying. They start each statement with "I want" or "I need." The partners are encouraged to be very parsimonious about the "I need" statements. The spouse will pay more attention to the "I need" statements than to the "I want" ones. Both are asked to understand that their obligation to each other is to meet the needs and to fulfill only those wants which the provider chooses to fulfill. Eventually, the partners will find it easier to meet an increasing number of the other's wants when it is understood that they are "extras."

A third task, called "marriage-models," encourages the spouses to share with each other their impressions of how marriages should be. This is based on their respective impressions of couples they have observed. The therapist asks each partner to think about the one marriage which has had the greatest influence in his/her life in showing how marriages are "supposed to be." Most people will select their parents' marriage, but they may also choose grandparents, uncles and aunts, close neighbors, and so on.

If the exercise takes place in the therapy office, each partner is asked relevant questions about this marriage model: "What did the man do best and worst for the marriage?" "Who was in charge of the relationship?" "How did he/she stay in charge?" "How did they say 'no' to each other?" "How did they have and resolve conflicts?" "How did they avoid or assume responsibility for the conflicts?" "What was their style for being affectionate?" "How could their communications have been improved?" Then each spouse is asked how he/she resembles this model, what are the similarities and differences, and how should he/she be different.

The exercise can take a considerable amount of time; the marital therapist who prefers short-term treatment approaches usually suggests how the couple can do it when they are alone. Sometimes this can be facilitated when the therapist writes out the questions which each person might consider in comparing his own marriage with that of the model. The exercise helps couples understand the origins of their mate's expectations, especially those which seem unwarranted or unreachable. The activity is useful in helping couples better state their expectations, their wants and needs, and to meet those in their partner which are important.

There are, of course, other techniques for generating involvement and energy toward working on the marital problems. It is reiterated that the therapist does not instill motivation, but at best removes some of the obstacles installed by the couple as protection. With real apathy, the couple and therapist would probably find better ways of spending their time than trying to end marital dysfunction.

Techniques to Encourage Talking

Talking is important to the well-being of most marriages. It is almost essential in communication and a vital ingredient in the expression of many feelings. When it stops, for whatever reason, marriages usually become troubled. When couples know how to talk well, they seem able to overcome most of other relationship obstacles. Accordingly, the therapist's repertoire includes techniques designed to facilitate constructive talking.

The interview itself is inherently valuable as a talk facilitator. The therapist asks questions and the spouses respond verbally. The atmosphere is conducive to talk because the therapist maintains boundaries, is a go-between and referee. The therapist keeps the couple on one subject at a time, encourages them to express their feelings, and keeps the situation from becoming too threatening. However, for many couples, special additional efforts must be made to encourage their talking.

One effort involves showing the couple that talk can be pleasant. Many couples find that all their conversations seem to lead to problems or arguments; to avoid unpleasantness, they avoid talking altogether. The therapist helps such couples distinguish between the pleasantness of talking and the unpleasantness of arguing. If the two are not perceived as inextricably associated, then the couple can enjoy one without the consequences of the other. The therapist does this by encouraging the couple to confine some talking only to "positive" subjects. The method may be assigned as follows:

> "Kim and Joe, let's try this homework every day this coming week. Pick the same time each day to have a 'fun talk.' Allow fifteen minutes for the talk. Make sure there will be no interruptions or distractions. Talk together about anything you want, except problems. No problems about your relationship, or none about anything else. You have plenty of time for problem talks, but this is reserved just for fun, for learning again how nice it is to just talk with each other. Be prepared to say things which are interesting and upbeat. Talk about funny experiences, happy goals, tell jokes, whatever. But if either of you start to veer off into something which is unpleasant, just raise your hand. That will be a signal to change the subject, no questions asked. No one has to justify if the subject should cause a problem. Please do this every day this week. Okay, Kim? Okay, Joe?"

Sometimes couples are reluctant to do this because they see the exercise as contrived. The therapist affirms that it is contrived and describes the benefit of stepping out of the "normal" behavioral relationships, for the time being at least. Then this exercise is seen as being pleasurable. It encourages more fun talk at different times. It doesn't preclude ample opportunity for arguments, of course, but it adds another, more positive dimension to the verbal communications.

Not all talking is pleasant, however. Therapy must also help the couple learn to better express the unpleasant parts of the relationship. Couples often need help in sharing their grievances, in expressing their frustrations and bitter feelings. Some of this occurs in the therapist's office, even though it has to be limited. If the therapist doesn't permit any of it to go on, there is the risk that it will happen in the couple's home where it cannot be given direct attention. The arguments permitted in the office teach the couple how to argue more effectively. The therapist teaches them to stay with one issue at a time. The couple is taught to look at the issues from different perspectives and to avoid power plays or manipulations.

There is some debate among marital therapists about the value of encouraging couples to express their anger to each other. On one side are those who say it is needed to air things out. They point out that couples can become so angry, so loaded with apparently pent-up emotions, or so emotionally suppressed that they seem unable to communicate clearly or relevantly to their spouse. Often the feelings have not been caused by the spouse, but are directed to the spouse because it seems safer and more convenient to do so. These therapists want to help each spouse let off steam, to help them safely express what is on their minds, to openly and directly show their emotions.

Once they learn to do this more effectively, the partners can achieve better emotional self-control and understanding. They learn to use each other as a sounding board. Each partner is an object on whom to release feelings directly, so these emotions are not subsequently released covertly and even more harmfully (Bach and Wyden, 1969).

The opposing viewpoint says more harm than good often comes from encouraging couples to ventilate their frustrations on their partners (Ellis, 1978). Even though the partner has trouble coping with his/her own and the spouse's anger, it doesn't follow that it is healthy to express it whenever it is felt. Such behavior might be appropriate if the individual were unconcerned about the effects of the vituperation on its recipient. There may be no problem if there is no possibility of future retribution; but this is rare between partners.

Some therapists also challenge the notion that one must release stored up emotional pressures in order to avoid emotional harm. They question the validity of this "hydraulic theory" (Fromm, 1975), or the necessity of releasing pent-up emotions to prevent a psychic explosion (Hokanson, 1970). But whether the idea has merit or not, most therapists agree that they must devote less attention to helping couples express negative, hostile, angry emotions and commensurately more to showing them how to avoid taking them out on the spouse (Mace, 1976).

There are several effective assignments for having couples argue and confront one another in relative safety. One is to let them pick one issue for debate and stick to that topic only, and for only a specific period of time. The therapist might suggest the topic and the time limit, based on the major concerns and needs of the couple. The time limit, usually an hour, causes the couple to focus, collect their thoughts, and deliver them more systematically. This still gives them time to actually ventilate about their frustrations on the matter. Most couples find that one hour is ample time if the subject stays on one topic. If it is not, of course they can select the same topic for discussion on a different day.

Another method is called the "hold back encounter." When one partner feels something needs to be expressed he/she says, "There is something I am holding back from you." If the second person is in the mood to hear it and is not inclined to get defensive or justificatory, he/she says, "Would you tell me about it?" The first person then states in one sentence, without elaboration of any kind, what was being held back. The partner might say something like, "I have not liked the way your breath has been smelling lately," or, "I feel you have been getting more distanced from me this week." After the sentence has been spoken, the second person says, "Thank you." The "thank you" is important. It conveys that the overall message has been received. The verbal response suggests a positive appreciation for calling it to one's attention. The first person is not threatened with counterattacks and an opportunity to do something about it is provided. Naturally, they are able to discuss the issue in more detail at a later time if they want; they have been alerted to it beforehand, and a nonthreatening opportunity to do something about it has been made. It provides the recipient the opportunity to hear or not hear what is of concern. It allows both a chance to select a more opportune time to discuss the matter.

In talk facilitation the spouses may also be asked to pretend they have a disagreement about something which is completely imaginary. It is best to find a topic which is contrived so that the exercise will not spill over into real issues in their relationship. For example, they might "disagree" about how to discipline a teenaged son, when they are childless. Or they might disagree about whether their trip to Europe was more fun than their trip to Asia was, even though they have never traveled. The point is that they go through the mechanics of arguing without suffering the consequences; it enables them to see more objectively how they argue. It gives them much the same emotional release as in a real argument—without having to endure lasting antipathy, because they have little at stake in who wins or loses.

Methods to Foster Understanding

Most therapists start sessions by trying to understand what is wrong with the marriage. They gather information from each spouse. They listen as these new or differently stated facts are revealed. Greater understanding often takes place. But for many other couples, this isn't enough; they have already heard all these facts. What they need now is something which gives them new ideas, a new way of looking at the situation, presented with such impact that it will shake loose their rigidly maintained impressions. Generally, couples have already diagnosed their marital problems before they started therapy. They understand what's wrong. Now they want the therapist to fix it.

Major techniques to achieve these objectives include relabeling, paradoxical instigation, and redefining family myths. Basically, the techniques require the therapist to react unpredictably to the client.

Then they are designed to get each partner to respond unpredictably as well. The routine has been scrambled and the communication is changed. This provides an opportunity to replace the unhealthy rigid relationship patterns with those which are potentially more healthy.

To relabel, the therapist changes the individual's frame of reference used to describe the problem. For example, when one of the partners attributes negative behavior or feelings to the other, the therapist redefines the attribute positively as follows:

WIFE: "My husband never takes me out."
THERAPIST: "He must really love to be home alone with you."

Or the therapist renames the feeling a spouse identifies:

WIFE: "I was hurt when he came home late."
THERAPIST: "You were angry when he came home late."

The feeling is looked at differently by the couple. The feeling is interpreted without changing the feeling itself. Sometimes the therapist may underplay the presentation of a symptom by one partner:

HUSBAND: "My wife never wants to have intercourse."
THERAPIST: "Your wife has been pretty busy lately."

Relabeling does not make it go away (Haley, 1977), nor does it mean to trivialize or minimize the actual feeling. It is simply to view it differently.

Paradoxical interventions take many forms and often are devised on the spot by the therapist to alter an unhealthy aspect of the relationship. This occurs when the therapist asks one of the marital partners to react differently than usual whenever a certain event occurs. And it takes place when the therapist defines events or steps leading to those events which the couple had not previously considered. Some examples illustrate how such interventions might take place:

Suppose a couple agree that the husband is the victimizer and the wife is the victim, because he has a violent temper and often abuses her. Movement cannot occur because both are firm in their conviction that he is the wrongdoer, but just can't seem to stop. After the couple demonstrates that they are locked in this pattern, the therapist paradoxically compliments the husband for the way his behavior is helping his wife: "Joe, it really is thoughtful of you to do that for your wife. She seems to benefit a lot by your anger and violence. It keeps her on her toes, keeps her mind alert and active. And it takes a lot of effort for you to do that, so obviously you must love her a lot."

Usually in paradoxical instigations, "complimenting the symptom" is just the first step toward helping the couple get rid of troubling behaviors. What comes next depends on the goal and the situation. In one technique the therapist verbally reverses the roles of "innocent victim" and "malevolent perpetrator." The wife might be encouraged to act mean and unreasonable like the husband does, while allowing the husband to remain as before. Or the couple might be encouraged to search farther back for the emergence of the causes of the present problem. In this case, the individual defined as the victim may be revealed as doing something to provoke the victimizer.

As Bateson (1972) has shown, there are rarely any definite origins to a sequence of events, even though the couple comes to believe there is. Every exchange of communication is both stimulus and response. The therapist helps look at the communication by relocating the origin, from wherever the couple has decided to place it.

Techniques to Enhance Intimacy

Ultimately, the objective of marital therapy includes helping couples get together. The techniques described are not designed to bring couples into a more harmonic, intimate bonding, but they are often necessary preliminary steps toward that objective. Often the other techniques are all that is necessary to permit functional intimacy because they have removed barriers to it. Without the obstacles, many couples can become as intimate as they ever were or even imagined they could be; but many couples cannot. Even when the barriers are removed some cannot achieve the closeness, the emotional and physical openness, and reciprocal responsiveness which they seek.

Many couples have not learned to demonstrate intimate caring for their spouse, at least not in the way the spouse wants. Some know how to show it, but feel uncomfortable doing so, as though it is contrary to their style or values. But very few, if any, couples dislike its manifestations when they engage in it, get used to it, and become habituated to it (Allen and Martin, 1971). The therapist has the pleasant task of helping the couple to break down the inhibitory barriers and prescribe activities which give them practice in sharing intimacy; through repetition of these activities the couple becomes more familiar with intimacy.

Richard Stuart's (1980) "caring days" procedure is one of the most systematic of these techniques. The therapist asks each partner to list behaviors desired from the other person which demonstrate caring. Both partners put an equal number of items on the list. They are told that the items must be positive, specific, "small" enough to accomplish daily, and must not be the focus of a recent sharp conflict. The therapist encourages each to write at least 18 items to begin. Several new ones are added every week thereafter. It is important that the items be specific and stated in positive, do-able terms. The therapist may suggest some items and may write and edit them as they are stated by the spouses. After the list has been composed, the therapist goes over each one with the couple to clarify and eliminate misunderstanding. The therapist asks each spouse to state specifically how he/she would like to implement it and to respond. The couple takes the list home and indicates with checkmarks or dates whenever an item has been accomplished.

If the partners are unwilling to participate, some additional explanation may be in order. The therapist justifies the activity by stressing that change takes place when one spouse desires it, regardless of the partner's willingness to work for it. One may participate even if the other doesn't. But preferably both can participate whether they actually care or not. They can act as if they care, whether they do or not. Usually the more reluctant spouse will participate either when it is shown that this is a low cost way of assessing the possibilities about the future of the marriage or when the partner is actively participating. The result is that the couple receives the benefit of each partner doing what he/she wants. If one partner knows the importance of these behaviors regardless of the other's activity, it often encourages the other to follow suit.

Couples are also encouraged to be more expressive physically with each other; they generally feel more positive about doing so in private than in the therapist's office. Thus, techniques to enhance the physical relationship are assigned as homework. In one exercise the therapist asks the partners to exchange statements saying what they like about the sexuality or physical intimacies originated by the partner: "I like the way you lick your lips when you are about to kiss me"; "I like the way you always seem to touch my navel as a signal that you want sex." The couple exchanges these items for a limited, specified amount of time, usually five to ten minutes. The idea is to build up a list of recognized positive behaviors and actions both partners see as beneficial to the relationship and to the other person. Often these items were not previously known by the partner who is being complimented. Doing this alerts both partners to all the good that exists between them. It also sets a more positive stage for the next part of the assignment, that of saying what behaviors are disliked or not appreciated. The format is repeated, but this time the couple exchanges sentences about how they don't like something and wish the partner would change the behavior: "I wish you would fondle my nipples more when we are getting ready for sex"; "I don't like it when your arms go limp when we kiss." It is important that the couple makes these statements simple and without elaboration or defense.

These exercises encourage the couple to talk about the intimate details of their lives, without embarrassing the partner or making the partner angry. Many couples, who can readily talk about other aspects of their lives, find this most difficult. The method emphasizes positives and it permits limited time and elaboration for negatives; this makes the activity easier to accept and possibly correct. Of course, the couple later will have an opportunity for more free-form discussion about all the matters concerned in this chapter, but these techniques set the stage for a more constructive interaction.

Chapter Eleven

The Diagnosis of Marital Dysfunction

The concept of diagnosis has become a troublesome one for marital therapists in recent years. It is a word and concept which many therapists consider inappropriate for the kind of work they do; but those related to marital therapists expect them to use it and sometimes insist on it. They may be illustrated in the following dialogue:

> "Dr. Jones, this is the insurance company again. We need more information about your patient who submitted a claim to us. Did he give you permission to answer our questions yet?"
>
> "Yes, he has. What do you want to know?"
>
> "Well, Doctor, we aren't sure about his diagnosis and treatment. He wrote on his form he had marital problems. Does he have a clinical diagnosis?"
>
> "Yes, ma'am. My diagnosis was 'generalized anxiety disorder' and 'marital disturbance.' The treatment plan was to treat the man and his wife together once a week in one-hour sessions."
>
> "Okay, Doctor. Let me write this down. Let's see . . . generalized anxiety disorder is coded 300.02 in the diagnostic manual. Now, you said you treated him together with his wife?"
>
> "That's right. He was always fighting with her and that made him anxious. So the treatment for his anxiety was to treat the marriage. The

treatment helped them get along better and that relieved his nervousness."

"I see. Now how much of the time was spent just treating his problem?"

"I can't break it down like that. They were always seen together."

"Well, I'm sorry, Doctor, but all we can cover is your work with him. We're a health insurance company and that means paying for sicknesses, not marriages."

"But I just said the cause of the man's problem was his marriage. He wouldn't have had a sickness if his marriage were okay!"

"We have our rules, sir. But maybe we can work this out. You said you always saw his wife with him. Well, we cover her, too. What was her diagnosis?"

"She was pretty healthy. Mildly depressed, perhaps. We could call it 'depressive neurosis.' Or I guess the new term for it is 'dysthymic disorder.' "

"Okay, how much time did you spend treating her for this?"

"I can't tell you that, either. Remember, I just saw her with her husband. I can't separate the time spent on each. It was a back and forth kind of thing."

"This is getting complicated. I don't know what we can do when you work with two people together."

"Listen, ma'am. I have an idea. How about this? I saw him a half hour each week to treat his anxiety. I saw her a half hour weekly to treat her depression. They were just two individuals. Separate claims. Is that okay?"

"Yes, Doctor. That makes sense to me. Why didn't you just say so in the first place?"

Does Diagnosis Belong in Marital Therapy?

The trouble with diagnosis in marital therapy is that meanings have been ascribed to it which are contrary to the way marital therapists tend to think. To a great extent, medicine has co-opted the word to connote the identification of diseases by their observable symptoms. To marital therapists, this relation to disease implies something which goes on within an individual. Since marital therapists are concerned with problems between people rather than within a person, they question the appropriateness of the word in their work. Many therapists avoid the word and use "assessment" in its place. Others (e.g., Haley, 1975) say diagnosis has no place whatsoever in marital or family interventions.

Reflecting this dilemma is the American Psychiatric Association's Diagnostic and Statistical Manual (1980), or DSM-III. This manual represents the official way emotional disturbances are diagnosed in the United States. It includes all internal psychic disorders but specifically excludes those pertaining to relationships between people. The DSM-III gives marital problems a code number (V61.10) among those categories of problems which are explicitly outside the province of psychiatric diagnoses. It is a position emulated by private insurance companies and other third-party financing organizations which rarely help pay for the treatment of situational or relationship problems.

Nevertheless, the word "diagnosis" is appropriate for use in marital therapy; it encompasses more than a clinical or individual phenomenon. It is derived from the Greek words, dia (through) and gnosko (to know). The word originally suggested a process of knowing through something, or seeing it deeply, understanding it and its causes through observing its external phenomena. As such its meaning is as appropriate to social, environmental, ecological, and mechanical systems as to physical ones. It is at least as applicable to marital therapy in considering the dynamics of processes between people as to any other situation in which it is commonly used. Its meaning is to distinguish, to recognize what is wrong and consider why, to tell the difference between what is dysfunctional or unhealthy and functional or healthy. Diagnosis is an integral part of the treatment in which the marital therapist brings together all the information at his disposal in order to plan for achieving stated goals. It is out of this process of synthesizing, understanding, focusing, and organizing that the treatment plan is developed (Turner, 1978).

Moreover, others expect marital therapists to use the word. Most marital therapists are closely related to medicine, either as physicians or as mental health professionals who often work with physicians. The American health care system is organized with mental health and psychotherapy fields being closely related to medicine. The term is a common part of the medical nomenclature; others will assume marital therapists think in "diagnostic" terms, no matter what they themselves might want. It is a word imposed on the field from without, if not from within.

This is fortunate. Abandoning the term or process would diminish the idea that problems of interrelationships are also a unit of treatment attention. It would be another step away from the principle that health and mental health have to do with social factors as well as individual ones. As pointed out in Chapter Two, there is a significant correlation between the physical and emotional health of the population and its marital health. If pathology is seen as residing exclusively within individuals and not within relationships, then a disproportionate amount of our limited resources expended on emotional health care needs is diverted from prevention, primary care, and improved social amenities. It is placed in tertiary care, to restore individuals who have already become sick. If funding is more available for these more expensive intrapsychic forms of treatment than for the less expensive social forms of treatment, the whole health care system is more costly and less effective (Enoch and Sigel, 1979). As marital therapist and psychiatrist Harold Lief (1982) has indicated, the DSM-III contributes to this unsatisfactory state. He recommends that the next edition of the manual categorize marital problems as diagnostic entities in their own right. At best this will not occur for years, as the DSM-IV is not scheduled for release until after 1990.

Diagnostic Classification of Marital Dysfunctions

Contemporary marital therapists have considerable difficulty summarizing all the information they glean from a troubled couple and organizing it into a usable, coherent entity. Those who support the notion that diagnosis is appropriate in marital therapy would like a system similar to that in the DSM-III. They sometimes envy the diagnostic systems readily available to other helpers, such as physicians, lawyers, and auto mechanics. Such specialists can label a group of symptoms and thereafter refer to that label when thinking about the problem. When a computer service person tells others what the machine's problem is, he might say, "The anode chip causes too much resistance and needs replacing." He doesn't have to explain the entire electronic system.

The marital therapist doesn't have an accessible and uniform list of words or diagnostic symptoms which apply to complex relationships. Instead, he is sometimes forced to write voluminous summaries about the couple. His thoughts have to encompass the entire constellation of relevant components. Because there are few words or concepts which succinctly describe interrelationship problems, he sometimes feels compelled to label the respective personality characteristics of the two individuals. This, of course, is insufficient because relationships are always more than the composite of the individual personalities.

There have been few diagnostic "labels" which have had particular applicability to disordered marriages. These include such terms as "folie

a deux" (marital partners sharing a delusion); "sado-masochistic relationships" (one partner deriving pleasure through physically or emotionally hurting the other and the other deriving pleasure from being
hurt); "role complementarity discrepancy" (failure to understand or
conform to the partner's appropriate or inappropriate expectations);
"enmeshment" (insufficient autonomy between the marital partners to
allow for independent thought or action); "mutual withdrawal" (marital partners indifferent to one another); and so on. But, for the most
part, marital therapists do not yet use single terms to symbolize particular aspects of the disturbed relationship. The marital diagnostic statement is more likely to be a short paragraph describing the couple's
more common relationship problems. Almost every issue of the good
marital and family journals, such as the *Journal of Marital and Family
Therapy, Family Process,* and the *Family Coordinator*, contains clinical articles with current examples of such diagnostic statements.

Lacking a concise, abbreviated diagnostic nomenclature has made it
very difficult for therapists to communicate with one another about
problem syndromes. It has retarded efficient teaching, effective research, and systematic conceptual development. As philosophers and
philologists point out, without a language or a word to symbolize a
concept, thinking about that concept remains very primitive. So too, in
marital therapy, the lack of one or a few words to encompass a marriage problem, with all its unique characteristics, idiosyncracies, and
subtle nuances, has prevented such advancement by the field.

It is clearly a formidable assignment to delineate mutually exclusive
descriptive categories of dysfunctions which are comprehensive enough
to cover the range of possible marital problems. It is even more challenging to develop a list of diagnostic entities which is short enough to
be workable and readily accessible, and yet remain long enough to provide for distinctions between different types of disorders. The dilemma
is to avoid oversimplification on the one hand and too much obfuscating detail on the other.

The lack of a diagnostic classification system is not for lack of interest or effort, however. There are several dozen different classification
systems, and their numbers continue to proliferate. Most have been
well thought out; many have been subjected to intense empirical analysis with some positive outcomes (Fine, 1974). However, there has been
little movement toward consensus or uniformity of the use of any of
these systems. To date none seems to be becoming popular with more
than a few marital therapists at a time.

Systems of Diagnostic Classification

When Lawrence Fisher (1976) pulled together and evaluated the dozens of major diagnostic typologies, he said it is not yet possible to integrate the different types of diagnostic systems into a single entity. They were simply too diffuse and emphasized too many different areas of interest. He was, however, able to place the different strategies of assessment into four groups. The first, single concept notions, attempts to build a diagnostic typology around the notion that a broad range of dimensions can be seen as varieties of a single concept. Those typologists who use this approach primarily focus on the single concepts of power, conflict, and conflict resolution. They might, for example, diagnose a couple as having one of several types of conflict; because of certain typical power balances the conflict is perpetuated. The second kind of assessment strategy is based on theoretical orientations, such as role theory (Parsons and Bales, 1955) or social learning theory. Here a couple might be considered unable to accurately perceive or respond to the partner's expectations. This approach has not been satisfactory to all because there is not, as yet, a single integrated theory of marital or family behavior, and certainly no single theory to which all marital therapists could subscribe. Therapists have had to develop assessments around bits and pieces of theories, accounting for some of the popularity of the so-called eclectic approach. The third strategy is to empirically analyze different variables to find ones which are discrete and clustered. This approach has led to a huge variety of variables which haven't always demonstrated generalizability across clinical or general populations. The fourth strategy for developing a typology comes from the practitioner's clinical experiences and observations, and are often developed for applicability to specific settings. For example, the Family Service Association (1965) and the GAP Report (Group for the Advancement of Psychiatry, 1970) have accumulated lists of variables to look for in assessing each family or couple. These lists are simply based on the reports of practitioners; they provide a format for organizing and communicating data without the added complication of theoretical formulations.

The fact that none of the myriad of typologies or assessment strategies has achieved widespread usage is, in one sense, a testament to the high integrity of marital therapists. They often avoid such categories because they believe classifications are too confining. The range of variables to consider in making a worthwhile diagnosis is limitless; to do justice to any typology would probably require a huge multidimensional list.

Most marital therapists will, for the time being, continue to describe dysfunctional marriages with short descriptive statements rather than with single-word diagnostic labels. But it seems probable that a uniform diagnostic terminology will soon have to be established. If this doesn't come about through a dramatic discovery or new way of conceptualizing, it must be done arbitrarily as a political expediency. If the field itself doesn't develop and become consistent about a typology, others will. Already, the World Health Organization has designated committees to study the inclusion of relational and social problems in its International Classification of Diseases. Third-party financing organizations, computer specialists, government bodies, and health organizations may be among those to impose it on the field. Until the diagnostic classification system has been formulated, marital therapists must continue to use the present system of diagnostic summaries. This system, while not as efficient as desired, can be very useful in formulating the treatment plan.

The Nature of Marital Diagnosis

The diagnosis of disordered marriages is more complex than that of two separate individuals with problems. It encompasses clinical diagnoses of the husband and wife as individuals and includes an assessment of the unique social constellation of which they are a part. It consists of fact gathering, synthesizing information, integrating the data with goals, and a plan for treatment. It has both static and dynamic aspects. It is, in other words, a process and a conclusion.

As a process, marital diagnosis is an ongoing activity between the therapist and couple. It is not something the therapist does *to* the couple; they arrive at it together. It begins with the first bit of information exchanged between them and continues until the relationship has ended. Preliminary impressions begin immediately and are thereafter modified. The age of the individuals, the way they talk, their manner of dress and physical carriage, the fact that they appear in good or ill health, all are observed and used to formulate this assessment. As additional information is acquired, the diagnosis becomes more focused and refined. It begins to distinguish between what is wrong and what is not wrong. This process never ends, because the exchange of information is continual and the facts keep changing as the unique circumstances of the marital dyad continue to change.

The aspect of the marital diagnosis which is static, the diagnostic conclusion, is equally important. It is the summation, the shorthand way of explaining complex phenomena to ourselves, our colleagues, our clients, and all those to whom we are accountable. If the field had its uniform diagnostic typology, this would be the single word, few words, series of numbers, or entity which succinctly symbolizes the complex of interacting events. Without the typology, it would be the short paragraph description of the troubled relationship.

Diagnosing problems carries certain risks, no matter what the field in which it occurs, and marital therapy is no exception. Diagnosis can lead to stereotyping of clients and can preclude individualizing treatment. And of course, the greatest risk is that of misdiagnosis.

No two people or couples are identical, but to subsume them under a single diagnostic statement implies to some that they are. If someone were to assume that all sado-masochistic partners are identical in every respect, it would be a gross distortion and oversimplification. It is usually understood by the professional person that diagnostic categories do not hinder individualizations, and may enhance them. Categorizing makes it possible for the therapist to mentally set aside the major similarities which are suggested by the diagnostic description, in order to focus on the unique and special differences which exist within it.

However, there is a problem of stereotyping in diagnosing marital problems, just as there is in diagnosing intrapsychic ones. Every experienced therapist has heard a husband or wife complain that, because they have a diagnosis of some emotional disturbance in their record, they are sometimes seen by their physician or hospital as malingering or hypochondriacal when they subsequently present a physical symptom. So too are marital therapists vulnerable to this process, even when they themselves have first provided this diagnosis. When they see, for example, someone diagnosed as "obsessive-compulsive personality," a self-fulfilling prophecy is often the result. Therapists might then expect such a person to be rather perfectionistic, to be rigid, to have a strongly developed sense of rules and conformity, and highly structured superego traits. For example, psychodynamically oriented therapists assume that many people with this diagnostic appellation have come from childhoods in which there was strict parental upbringing, with uncompromising toilet training and conditional love. So they ask questions about the childhood, particularly about the pre-oedipal or anal phases of development, getting more information about that stage until the impressions are confirmed. It might well have been that this particular person had only an average amount of this experience, but the diagnosis leads to a conclusion that it was much more.

Another hazard of diagnosis, of course, is the possibility of an incorrect one. Diagnosis is a subjective process. It is influenced by the therapist's values, understandings of human nature, conceptual orientation, and the specific information obtained from the couple from the vast amount of potential information which might have been provided. The danger of misdiagnosis is that it can result in improper treatment. However, the way to avoid the risk is not to avoid diagnosis; *no* diagnosis is also a misdiagnosis. Something is amiss with the couple or the therapist wouldn't be treating them. To use no differential diagnosis is to imply that all couples have identical problems, identical causes, or no problems at all. To minimize the risks inherent in diagnosis is not to avoid it, but to do it well. This means understanding how to go about it, knowing what causes or correlations to identify, determining what patterns go together, what the appropriate diagnostic terminology is, and relating the different diagnostic possibilities to specific treatment plans. To reduce the risk of misdiagnosis, therapists gather as much relevant and accurate information as possible and analyze it objectively and systematically. It is especially important that this information come from more than one source. Moreover, the therapist must be very careful not to overextend any generalizations he makes about the couple based on their behavior in his office.

Marital problems are inherently the result of conflicting priorities and are thus based on divergent viewpoints. Information which comes from a single source, such as the husband or wife alone, would only reflect one of those viewpoints; this is not sufficient. The therapist needs input from both individuals and, to make an accurate assessment, he must also observe first hand how they interact. Many marital therapists have no choice but to see one partner, because of the other's resistance (Luther and Loev, 1981). Work with the participating spouse does not lead to accurate diagnosis or treatment of the marital problem but of an individual who has a marital problem.

Therapists further reduce their risk of misdiagnosis by refraining from generalizing too broadly about the behavior of their clients. It is easy to assume that, because a husband or wife behaves a certain way with others, they do the same with their partner. Or conversely, it is risky to assume that the way the couple relates to one another in the therapist's office is indicative of how they relate outside. It is possible for a husband to suffer some clinically diagnosed emotional disorder but never exhibit this trait with his wife. Or a wife might be excessively suspicious of her husband; her behavior might be diagnosed as "paranoid" if it applied to others, but not if confined to her husband. The point is that the diagnosis of marital problems is unique to that relationship and does not inevitably mirror any other type of diagnosis.

Ingredients in Useful Diagnoses

To avoid these hazards and to be useful in marital therapy, diagnoses must contain four important attributes. They are (a) specifically relevant to the problem addressed, (b) lead to differentiated treatment plans, (c) are concise, and (d) are useful for the couple as well as the professional.

It is pointless to collect information for a diagnostic statement if it is not relevant. It is not relevant if the same procedures follow no matter what information is obtained. For example, most states in the nation (36) require blood samples before permitting people to obtain marriage licenses. This requirement was instituted in most jurisdictions in the mid 1930s when it was learned that a high percentage of the population had syphilis. The premise was that the diagnosis would help eliminate the problem. It may have been inherently interesting and it might have been useful for some purposes, but it was irrelevant to the licensed marriage. Most of the states did not forbid people who had syphilis from marrying. The diagnosis was irrelevant since the outcome was the same with or without the information. Incidentally, this is also an inefficient way to eradicate syphilis. It was learned that the cost of finding those afflicted using the marriage license procedure costs states over $100,000 for every diseased person found (Trainer, 1979).

This illustrates a potential problem in marital diagnosis. Marital therapists find it difficult to focus their diagnostic effort on that which is relevant to the problem for which help is sought. After all, what isn't relevant to the causes of marital disorder? One can easily argue that anything that could possibly be included in a diagnostic summary has some connection. Therapists who appreciate all the factors which may be important don't want to exclude anything which might later prove to have some applicability. This often results in diagnostic statements becoming as extensive as the narrative they are intended to summarize. There is no sharp line of demarcation between that which is and is not relevant; rather, there is a continuum of relevance. The therapist must make choices about which is most important in understanding the couple's problem, rather than including everything which has a possible connection. The criteria for making this choice comes from the second ingredient in useful diagnosis.

This second ingredient is that the diagnosis is linked to differential treatment. If a profession had only two possible services for its clients, the diagnostic purpose would be limited to determining which of the two to offer. Efficient information gathering would simply try to answer that question. Information which doesn't contribute to that answer may be interesting, or its acquisition may give the partner an opportunity to express conflict, but it is not relevant to the diagnosis. If a profession had but a single type of treatment for everyone, no matter what their problem, then all information gathering would be irrelevant. The treatment could start immediately with no exchange of information whatsoever. If the field had thousands of different possibilities, the information would have to be quite specific and meticulous. Marital therapy has a multitude of different possible treatments; the diagnosis is designed to determine which of those to use for each couple treated.

Third, the diagnostic statement is concise. A description of the marital problem which goes on for many pages is not a useful diagnosis but a report of a group of facts and impressions. The diagnostic statement is to synthesize these facts and impressions and make them communicable; it is to provide a focus and direction. It is not to unsystematically repeat what the couple has told the therapist. If the therapist or others have to read an extensive amount of material to get an overview of the particular marital problem, they probably won't. They might skim the pages instead, and thus notice only certain facts and impressions.

How do diagnostic statements get so long? Usually it happens when the therapist sees the diagnostic process as an end in itself rather than as a means to an end. Some therapists ask questions and collect information as a matter of course, not to formulate the diagnosis, but to treat the problem. All problems, they are assuming, are treated through this procedure. Then, having collected so much information and knowing that all of it has some relevance, no matter how remote, they are loathe to exclude it from the diagnostic statement.

The last ingredient in useful marital diagnosis is that it be worthwhile for the couple as well as for the therapist. Diagnosis can be useful to the husband and wife if shared with them. Diagnosis is also useful if the couple has helped to develop it, if it is communicated in language which is understandable and agreeable to them, and if it is presented in positive terms. Every client has the right to participate fully in the development of the diagnosis and to know what labels or diagnostic statements are being ascribed to them. Moreover, it is against the ethical codes of most marital therapy–delivering professions to impose treatment procedures without the clients' informed consent (Bernstein, 1978). The only possible way to achieve informed consent is for the couple to understand what the diagnosis and treatment plan are to be.

To be assured of informed consent, increasing numbers of marital therapists are preparing their diagnostic statements with the couple's full participation (Houghkirk, 1977). The therapist lets the couple read any notes he has written about them. Then, if they agree with the therapist's assessment, they can so indicate with a notation in the record. If they have additional relevant information, they are invited to record it next to the therapist's remarks. If they disagree, or feel that there were factual or perceptual errors, this becomes part of the discussion. If some written part is demonstrably in error, the statement is deleted. If it is a disputed perception, the client is invited to write his or her own view next to that of the therapist. If disputes occur as a result of the open record, the resulting discussion becomes a valued part of the treatment as well as of the diagnostic process. This means that the diagnostic statement is a dynamic document but still concrete enough to be used as a point of reference. It involves the couple throughout the assessment process.

Information Sources in Marital Diagnosis

The diagnostic statement can be no better than the data from which it is derived. So the skilled diagnostician is skilled in obtaining accurate and relevant information. Since the main objective is to learn about the dynamics of the interaction, most of the focus is on the marital relationship rather than on the individual characteristics of the partners. Of course, the primary source of information for this comes from observing the husband and wife as they interact with one another in the therapist's office. There are many other sources as well, including the therapist's review of the possible goals and resources available, questioning the marital partners separately, written questionnaires, medical records, information from referral sources (Selvini-Palazzoli et al., 1980), psychological tests and personality inventories, and contacts with the children or other interested parties. Marital therapists usually seek additional information from only a few outside sources, depending on how confident they are in the information provided by the couple. The therapist may be more confident about the diagnostic accuracy if the various sources of information were relatively consistent in their depiction of the situation. If there is great inconsistency, the therapist must acquire increased amounts of information before finalizing the diagnosis and treatment plan.

The first information obtained does not come from the couple. It comes from determining the goals toward which the therapist is prepared to work and the treatment techniques available to achieve these goals. Available techniques consist of all the tools to which the therapist has access; this includes his knowledge of different methods, his ability and willingness to use them, and his awareness of other resources which are needed but beyond his expertise.

The ethical and conscientious therapist always keeps in mind that the couple might need a different kind of help than he is prepared to provide. One of the therapist's most frequent ethical problems comes from violation of this professional standard. The failure of a therapist to refer a client to a specialist for needed services has led to many malpractice claims against marital and other therapists (Green and Cox, 1978). For example, a couple entered treatment with a marital therapist because the husband was excessively irritable and violent with his wife. The therapist's usual repertoire of intervention techniques was to no avail. After three months without improvement in the husband's symptoms, the couple dropped out of treatment. Subsequently their violent conflicts culminated in a fight which resulted in the wife's hospitalization. She told her physician that her husband's increasingly hostile behavior and physical abuse was very much out of character. The physician recommended a thorough physical and neurological examination, which revealed that, for many months, the man suffered a degenerative neurological disease. Had it been detected and treated earlier, it was ascertained that the severity of the illness would have been mitigated, the wife would not have been harmed, and the treatment would have been easier and less costly. The couple won a substantial malpractice suit against the therapist for his failure to refer the husband to someone who could have properly diagnosed and treated the malady (Barker, 1982).

Obviously, marital therapists must, as a part of their diagnostic effort, rule out the possibility of physical problems. It is always advisable for a marital therapist, even if he is a physician himself, to recommend that the husband and wife get a physical examination at the onset of marital therapy. Acting on this recommendation is essential if somatic complains are even a remote factor in the marital dynamics.

Conjoint Interview Assessment Strategies

After the therapist has considered the available resources and goals which can be sought, he is able to turn to the primary source of information for diagnosing marital problems: the observable patterns of interaction between the marital partners. He usually develops a way of asking questions of the couple which does more than obtain objective facts. The questions also are catalysts to encourage the interaction in the therapist's office. When the therapist asks only about factual data which could be answered with straightforward and concrete answers, the husband and wife are more likely to respond concretely and factually. Since the therapist is looking for information beyond the partners' perception of dates and events, the questions would be more effective if they brought out some of the tension that exists between them. For example, if the marital therapist asks the couple when they had their last argument and what it was about, he is getting only isolated facts. But if he asks why they argued, something else begins to happen. He is triggering memories about their respective perceptions of a tense event.

Marital therapists ask many questions which are designed to elicit this type of exchanged emotion. The following are examples: "Why do you think (s)he always wins the arguments here?" "How come you seem to do more of the talking than your partner?" "Why do you seem to move away from your husband whenever he gets closer to you?" "What other things does your wife say that make you interrupt and change the subject?" "What are you disliking about one another right now?" "Whose side do you think I am on right now, and why do you think so?" "What do you think your facial expression tells your partner right now as you say that?" "What thoughts do you think are going through your husband's mind now?" "What do you think your wife is going to do after you leave my office?"

The purpose of questions like these are not only to obtain the obvious responses to the questions, but also to see how the other partner responds. Do they correct one another? Do they protect or encourage difficulty for the partner? Are they in relative agreement about these issues or far apart? The information thus learned about the partners' interaction is more important in marital therapy than facts about either as individuals.

The therapists who find it useful to periodically interview the husband and wife separately believe that this provides important additional information. The husband and wife may think or act differently when in the other's presence. If they are never seen separately, this fact may not be learned. Furthermore, it may be diagnostically worthwhile to see various of the family members separately and in various combinations. Their respective influences on one another can be more easily noted when there are frames of reference with which to make the comparisons.

Written Sources of Diagnostic Data

Of course, diagnostic information gathering is not restricted to question/answer sessions with the family members, although it is certainly the most important way. Written questions requiring written answers can also be helpful; this helps the therapist obtain data and helps many couples by permitting them more time to formulate their thoughts and responses. Written questions and answers are often intimidating to many clients, so they are generally used as a supplement, not a replacement for the oral interview. Many therapists arrange to have clients fill out questionnaires at the beginning of the treatment. While there are many standardized questionnaires available, most therapists prefer to design their own, which can be more compatible with the therapist's own focus of interest and skill than could a generic questionnaire. They usually include "face sheet" information, as well as objective and open-ended questions. The face sheet questions are the general facts, i.e., the individuals' names, addresses, family history, health history, and so forth. The objective questions, i.e., 'true/false' and multiple choice, help the partners pin-point their specific beliefs about their own and their spouse's personality and behavioral traits. What is particularly relevant about these responses is the way the partners diverge in their views of many of these traits. When a great disparity exists in the way the partners perceive one another, a probable treatment will focus on bringing their perceptions closer together. Other objective questions ask about the presenting marital problems, the history of the marital situation, sexual data, nature of disputes, previous separations, previous marriages, and general feelings about the spouse.

The subjective or open-ended questions give the partners the opportunity to describe in writing their hopes, goals, worries, and beliefs in a general way. Some such questions are "projective" and often take the form of sentence completion items. Examples of such questions include the following: "When we have an argument, I try to _____."

"What I want out of this marriage is to _____." "More than anything I wish my spouse would _____." "When we make love, I get
the most pleasure when _____". "When we have intercourse, I wish
my partner would _____." "I get most upset with myself
when I _____." "What I like about my partner's looks is _____."
"What I don't like about myself is _____."

Questions such as these can be tailored for the specific couple quite
easily after the therapy has been underway awhile. They can also be developed in advance of any initial interview when the therapist expects
to be working on a known set of considerations with every client. Because some clients are reluctant to speak about some issues, either to
their spouse or to the therapist, or both, the questionnaire can be most
useful; conversely, writing some things can be distasteful for some clients. The therapist has to use professional judgment in deciding when
or whether to use them and how much emphasis to give them.

Generally the same questionnaire is given to each marital partner.
They are asked to write their answers as honestly as possible and to not
change anything once their answer has been given. They are asked not
to complete the questionnaire in the presence of their spouse; this is to
enable them to express their own thoughts without the influence of the
partner. However, they are then permitted to compare their answers,
either upon completion of the questionnaire, or later in the therapist's
office. The information thus obtained is used as a catalyst for further
questions during the marital treatment.

Proper diagnosis of dysfunctional marriages depends on much
more than information derived from the couple. These problems do
not occur in a vacuum but in a social-cultural-biological context; the
complete diagnosis, then, also depends on knowledge about this context. One needs to know about the inevitable pressures and stresses to
which every couple is subject. A framework for looking at this context
is found in crisis theory and the developmental stages of the marital life
cycle.

Chapter Twelve

Crises of the Marital Life Cycle

The word "crisis" is used here, as in the title of this book, not for dramatic effect but because it provides a valuable context for further understanding marital diagnosis and treatment. It helps explain why some marriages become dysfunctional and suggests additional ways therapists can help them improve. It is a framework for considering the pressures to which all couples are subject. It helps expand the therapist's diagnostic frame of reference from deficiencies of the marital partners to the stresses with which they must cope.

Some people think of crisis only as a calamity, a horrible threat or chaotic circumstance. But such a view is too simple. What seems horrible to one person may be routine to another. What actually distinguishes crisis from noncrisis is not its inherent "badness" but one's capacity to deal with a change. Successful coping usually involves experience. A grizzled combat veteran might not see death and destruction as extraordinary, because it is within his common experience. But compel him to conduct a Sunday School class before a group of prim socialites and his ordeal may seem overwhelming.

A crisis is, in fact, an opportunity as well as a problem. It is a turning point, a catalyst which disrupts old behavior patterns, evokes new responses and becomes a major determinant for new directions. A crisis is a summons to adapt, a provocation to develop new coping mechanisms, and a stimulus to strengthen one's healthy resources and discard those which may be ineffective. As such, understanding its nature and effect can be vital to effective marital therapy.

Marriage and Crisis

Caplan (1960) defined crisis simply as "an upset in a steady state"; it is any deviation from the status quo. Every marriage or individual, indeed every living system, seeks to maintain a state of equilibrium called morphostasis. But living things cannot remain static. They must continually move to higher levels of complexity and organization, a process called morphogenesis. What makes the crisis tolerable or intolerable is not the degree of deviation from the steady state but the capacity of the organism to adapt to required change.

All crises have some characteristics in common. They never last indefinitely; some solution to the upset, whether healthy or not, is eventually found. The individual may try the old problem-solving behaviors for awhile but, if they do not work, he will experiment with new ones until equilibrium is achieved once again. The new behavior may not be healthy in the long run but at least it becomes familiar, comfortable, and then static. The individual or system seeks to end the tension by solving whatever problem caused the change. Eventually the problem-solving behavior causes one of three things to happen: (1) the problem is solved and a new steady state is achieved; (2) the problem is perceived differently and accepted, resulting in an alleviation of the tension; or (3) there is withdrawal, regression, and avoidance of the problem.

Overcoming the crisis is more likely achieved when the individual has previously experienced and solved a similar problem. If he has not directly experienced that problem, he may still be able to solve it because he has been exposed to similar ones. For example, when a husband and wife have a first child, childbearing and rearing are outside their direct experience. However, they may have seen how others raise children. Watching others is surely different from doing it oneself, but there is sufficient similarity so that some of the information is transferable. The crisis is not as stressful as it would be to someone who has disregarded all previous information about it. If the change had never been previously experienced, the individual has to experiment with unaccustomed responses; new, untried behaviors must then be used. Since they had not been tried before they are stressful, risky, and less likely to succeed. If they do succeed, the tension is reduced and the information is retained for future application. The individuals thus acquire greater capacity for coping and adapting to the inevitable changes of the future.

To a considerable degree, couples enjoy functional marriages by learning to cope with crises (Freeman, 1982). The marital partners do not avoid change but acquire experience in adapting to it. Thus, when change occurs, they can call upon behaviors which have already worked for them, or which they have seen work for others. They don't have to deal with the crisis by experimenting with untested responses. If a couple does not or cannot adapt to change, one or both of them tends to get stuck at a level of coping that is ineffective and inappropriate for the next crisis.

For example, when a young married couple has their first child, the coping behaviors appropriate to the new circumstance may be alien to one of them. If it is the husband, he may feel uncomfortable with the father role and its demands. He may try to behave as he has seen fathers behave, but he still feels uncomfortable. He tries another behavior; he begins to imitate his child, playing a role with which he has had experience. Or he regresses to adolescent mannerisms, avoiding his wife and child, hanging around in bars and video game parlors with his unmarried buddies. He is no longer in the state of crisis, having solved the problem to his immediate satisfaction. Of course it doesn't stop there. He has precipitated yet another crisis. He must cope with a wife who is now unhappy with him, and he has no experience with that, either. His wife faces the dual crises of coping with a regressed husband without previous experience, and coping with the unfamiliar mother role. One or both marital partners are thus locked into a maladaptive response to crisis. They can't successfully resolve one crisis without developing new ones. They need to expand their range of coping skills so that they can effectively respond to the next stressful event.

The marital therapist treats dysfunctioning couples by focusing on the crisis points and facilitating movement toward a new balance. Much of marital therapy is to guide the couple in coping with change. It is to expose them to the new roles which they will have to face. The therapist gives them controlled practice in facing change. Therapy is a guide for couples who find themselves in unfamiliar terrains; it shows the partners what the terrain will be, equips them for the journey, tells them what they might see as they go along, helps them avoid danger, keeps them from getting irretrievably lost, and encourages progress.

Naturally the couples will often resist. At first the husband and/or wife may only reluctantly participate. The therapist recognizes this resistance as the product of still another crisis. It is that of encountering the unfamiliar experience of marital therapy. This crisis is, itself, an experience which adds to the couple's range of coping skills. The therapist alleviates it by clarifying what is to come in the treatment, and what will be asked of each spouse.

Even though each marriage faces its unique set of crises, there are some which almost all marriages have in common. A marriage, like an individual, goes through specific and rather predictable stages during the course of its existence. Since each stage represents a change with which the individual or marital partners have had little direct experience, it is a crisis. There are certain points along the marital life cycle where these crises are more likely to occur. The last three sections of this chapter will focus on this phenomenon. The life cycle of one marriage will be described first, followed by a discussion of how various theorists delineate the predictable crisis and tasks faced by couples through the cycle. Finally there is a discussion of a typology of marital crises.

A Love Story

"Where did Hap go?"

"Shh. Keep it down. He went to bed to get away from all this fuss. Don't bother him."

"Oh, sure. Okay. I've gotta go and wanted to tell him how sorry I am. We're going to miss Vi. But maybe it's a relief. These last two years have been rough on him. Well, I'll see him soon. 'Bye, everyone."

The bedroom was dark. Hap was sitting on his bed, staring into nothingness, hearing but not listening to the somber conversations in the adjoining crowded living room. He wished everyone would leave. He wanted time alone, to think, to remember, to relive the years. He wanted to savor his marriage, not to be reminded of its end. Sixty-three years were gone, except in his memory.

It wasn't supposed to happen like this. He thought she would outlive him. She had never been sick before. Now he was the one left alone. What would he do? He had to look ahead, not back. But he couldn't. For now he could only remember. It's just as well, he thought. After all, how much future does an 83-year-old man have? The only thing to look forward to was his own end, to be with Vi again. Who was it, Dylan Thomas maybe, who wrote, "Do not go gentle into that good night." Why not? It's time. It's been a good life, a good marriage.

The 63 years were better than most people experience. Sure, there were fights. Occasionally he thought of leaving her. Sometimes he imagined what it would be like with another woman. But he would never do that to Vi. Their lives had been filled with problems, but full of happiness, too. The ups and downs are to be expected. It would have been boring otherwise.

They had known one another since they were young children. They grew up on nearby farms in the Nebraska sand hills. She was so popular, so outgoing, a beautiful young girl, much in demand by all the single men of the county. But everyone knew she would marry Hap. Everyone knew they would move away. There were too many other youngsters and the farms couldn't support them all as it was. Hap had wanted to be an automobile repairman since he was 12 and saw his first car. A school in North Platte, the closest town of any size, trained mechanics. Throughout his adolescence he saved every penny by helping the blacksmith, helping ranchers with their cattle, working wherever there was a job to do. Finally he had the $175 it would take for school and the three months' living costs.

It was 1917 and Hap was 18. He was two weeks into his training when she told him. She would have said something sooner, but wanted to be sure, didn't want him to give up his dream because of a false alarm. But now there was no question. They had to marry immediately. Of course she had to move away from their community. Hap was discouraged. All his planning, saving, working to build a future for them had been futile, he thought. It wasn't fair. They only had intercourse a few times. He shouldn't have been so persistent. Vi had wanted to wait. Now he was going to pay the price.

The first years of the marriage were the hardest. They were both 20 with an infant daughter when they took the train to the Pacific Northwest. Hap heard about jobs that were available in the paper mills there. But he insisted that Vi would never work. No wife of his would ever have to do such a thing. Besides, little Virginia needed her mother to be home. That's how everyone who was any kind of man thought in the 1920s.

Hap hated to think about the many arguments during those years. He had two jobs most of that time. He worked in the paper mills all day and delivered ice all evening. He came home exhausted and irritable every night. Vi wanted him to slow down. But they had to buy the house. The arguments grew heated. She nagged about how little time he spent with her and Virginia. He complained about her nagging. They talked of divorce. But normal people didn't do things like that. It was only those Hollywood Jazz Age types who divorced. Hap and Vi could fight continually if they had to, but they knew that whatever they did or said, their marriage would remain intact.

After several years of struggle they bought the house. It was a little four-room place in the blue collar neighborhood of their friends. It was modest, but they didn't know of anyone who had better. Now the problem was to pay for it. More struggles. The Great Depression. Lay-offs. Months with no work. Little food on the table. More arguments with Vi. Constant fear of destitution, or of losing the house to the bankers. The only consolation was that everyone else seemed to be in the same situation. The house became an emergency relief shelter for relatives, friends, and distant acquaintances. The visitors sometimes stayed for months. Hap got lucky. He was rehired at the ice plant and soon became its foreman. Their financial struggles seemed over. They became more affluent than most of their friends.

Virginia, their only child, grew up, married, moved, had two children, divorced, remarried, had two more. Then, at the age of 39, Virginia died. Heart failure, the hospital said. Her four young children moved into Hap and Vi's small house. The childrearing cycle began anew. So did their economic struggle. The ice plant closed. No one needed ice anymore. They were getting refrigerators. More searching for work. Employers weren't enthused about hiring 55-year-olds. Eventually Hap was hired at a hospital heating plant. The pay was low, but it meant security—hospitals don't close.

Finally the grandchildren matured, married, and moved off to disparate lives. The house, the only one Hap and Vi ever owned, was quiet at last. Now there was retirement, the chance to take it easy, make the lawn nice, work on the car, visit neighbors, attend an increasing number of funerals. Happily there were still many friends, despite the funerals. The little house was filled with them for Hap and Vi's sixtieth wedding anniversary.

The stroke happened on Thanksgiving Day. Vi was fixing the turkey while supervising three of the nine great-grandchildren who were setting the table. Twenty-five people were expected soon and everything must be just right. "Hap, Hap, help me, Happy," she screamed. Hap heard a crash in the kitchen. He found her crumpled on the floor, conscious but mumbling incoherently. It was the beginning of the most painful two years of Hap's life, and its memory will not go away even now: the ambulance, the hospital, the doctors, and then the nursing home. There were his daily visits to the home, his vain attempts to get Vi to talk, to comprehend, to convince her she would soon be well.

Then, four days ago, the phone rang. "Sir, you'd better come to the center right away." Hap knew it was over then. She would never return home. Sixty-three years. It wasn't supposed to end this way. Please go home, everyone.

Developmental Phases in Marriage

The marriage of Hap and Vi, the author's grandparents, was by no means extraordinary. Nor was it representative; no marriage can represent or typify all marriages. The tasks which Hap and Vi had to accomplish, the problems they had to overcome, the norms which influenced their thinking, goals, and behavior were unique. But one thing that was not unique was the inevitability of change, of crises, of the need to adapt to unexpected developments, of movement from one stage of life to another. Every marriage goes through these experiences at rather predictable phases; every phase requires a sequence of tasks to be performed in order to work through the crises. The typical way couples cope with these inevitable transitions, the way they move from one stage to another throughout their lives together, will largely determine whether their marriages will be healthy or dysfunctional.

Couples face marital problems, but they are not evenly distributed through the span of the marriage. They are more likely to occur at certain points along this continuum. For example, demographic statistics show that divorces tend to occur in disproportionately high numbers among couples married less than four years, and again among couples married between 15 and 20 years (Department of HHS, 1980). Couples report that marital satisfaction diminishes after the first child is born and diminishes thereafter until the last child leaves home, at which time there is a reported improvement (Schram, 1979). Higher risks of divorce and marital dysfunction seem to occur among those couples who marry at younger ages and to those who begin child-rearing responsibilities sooner after they marry (Norton and Glick, 1976). Couples who have been married longer than twelve years are less likely to benefit from marital therapy than are couples with shorter marriages (Beck and Jones, 1973). Other studies show correlations between the duration of marriages and the likely onset of problems such as infidelity, spouse abuse, separations, abandonment, and individual emotional disturbance (Fields, 1983). They make it clear that time is significant and that couples face increased stresses and pressures at predictable times in their marriage.

Speculating about crises occurring at predictable times during the life of an individual or marriage is not new. Ancient Greek physicians discussed it at length. It is at the heart of psychoanalytic theory which focuses on early psychic growth through the oral-anal-oedipal stages of development. More recently, there has been increased attention to extending and refining the understanding about these developmental processes. Among the most influential is the work concerning children done by Margaret S. Mahler and others (1975), and Daniel J. Levinson and associates (1978) concerning adults.

Mahler concluded that the human infant progresses through three stages. In the first phase, called the autistic stage, the newborn is unable to distinguish self from others. But because of the parents' tension-reducing care, a foundation is built for emerging autonomy. The infantile awareness of dependency on parental nurturing occurs in phase two, called the symbiotic stage. This provides a basis for the growing baby's sense of object-constancy, trust, recognition of and positive regard for others. Finally, in the separation-individuation stage, the infant becomes gradually aware of his/her distinctiveness, autonomy, and reciprocal relationship with relevant others.

Many marital therapists have extended Mahler's ideas to concepts about marriage (Startz and Evans, 1981). They suggest that a couple's prognosis for marital success is largely influenced by the resolution of the separation-individuation process in infancy. With the inevitable changes in every marriage, each partner sometimes feels the need for more intimacy and at other times seeks more autonomy. It would be exceedingly unusual for the needs of any two marital partners to occur in perfect synchrony. Thus each partner must understand and accept this variability in the other. The degree to which acceptance will occur, it is posited, is profoundly influenced by the partner's infantile separation-individuation experience. If he or she successfully resolved the process during infancy, there is much greater likelihood of ability to accept the vicissitudes along the marital intimacy-autonomy continuum.

Levinson life-stage theory describes a sequence of four overlapping eras, each lasting about 25 years in adult males. The first era, childhood and adolescence, concludes at about age 22. The second, early adulthood, commences at about age 17 and goes on to approximately age 45. Middle adulthood, covering the years 40 to 65, is followed by the past 60 phase, late adulthood. Each era is separated by transition periods, known as early adult transition (17–22), the mid-life transition

(40–45), the late adult transition (60–65), and sometimes another transition when entering the 80s. Each era and each transition is characterized by a unique set of biological, social, and circumstantial events which influence the individual. The person changes in personality, in values, in typical behavior patterns, and in the way the environment and relevant others are perceived (Levinson, 1978).

Of course, many other conceptualizers have also delineated various phases in the life cycle. Most prominent among these are Erik Erikson (1963), Carl Jung (1964), Bernice Neugarten (1964), Roger Gould (1972) and Sonya Rhodes (1977). These and many other writers have proposed their distinctive typologies to explain what the particular stages are and what are the tasks peculiar to each phase. Unfortunately, the proliferation of typologies may cause more confusion than clarification. When each theorist says individuals go through stages that no other theorist has described, the validity of any of them has to be questioned. Other than for pedantic exercise, it may not be as important to segment individual life stages and give each of them a catchy title, as to recognize that there are gradually evolving personality and situational changes in each person and each marriage.

It is certainly important, however, from the perspective of marital therapy, to recognize that couples do not evolve through these phases on a single timetable. Couples are often not the same age, and even so, their maturational development is never identical. As is quite evident in male and female children, the biological and psychological development of men and women has considerable time variance. Furthermore, social and normative influences generally have quite different impacts and expectations for husbands and for wives. Thus it might be helpful for marital therapists to look, not at the evolving phases of married individuals, but at the developmental phases of the marriage itself.

Typologies in the Marital Life Cycle

There is proliferation of typologies about the marital life cycle to rival those of the individual stages. For example, Bernard L. Greene (1980) suggests that there are four major phases of marital development. The first occurs in the pre-childrearing years of marriage when couples form new family systems distinct from their families of origin. The second phase, childbearing and childrearing, is often a catalyst for considerable marital distress. The third phase, the "empty nest" syndrome, occurs when children leave home and the marital partners must meet mutual needs which are no longer fulfilled through the performance of parental roles. The major tasks of the final phase are facing problems of the aging process and adjusting to the death of one partner.

Berman and Lief (1975) also point out that marriages are more vulnerable to stress at points of transition; their typology is of seven stages in the marital cycle. They delineate the major conflict and task at each of the transitional stages, beginning with people who marry in their 20s. At stage one (18–21 years), the task is to shift from the family of origin to the new commitment. The major conflict involves original family ties versus the new orientation. In stage two (22–28 years) the task is to achieve a provisional commitment to the marriage. The basic conflict involves uncertainty about choice of marital partner. The stage three (29–31 years) task is to resolve the question about commitment and cope with feelings of restlessness. The conflict centers around feelings of doubt, parenting problems, and divergent rates of growth. The task of stage four (32–39 years) is to maximize productivity with work, children, and other associates. The conflict is in disagreements about how to achieve the productivity. In stage five (40–42 years) the task is to sum up successes and failures, but the conflict is the different perceptions of success by husband and wife. Stage six (43–59 years) has the task of resolving conflicts and stabilizing the marriage, while the conflict is aging and different rates of growth. Finally, the stage seven (over 60 years) task is to achieve mutual support, and the major conflict concerns aging and death.

Typologies similar to this have been proposed by many other family therapists including Haley (1968), Tamashiro (1978), Vines (1979), Singer (1980), Startz and Evans (1981), and Levant (1982).

Ronald Levant's concept is of particular interest. He sees married couples as evolving systems of functioning based on their mutual judgment and perspective taking. Marital partners look at one another differently as they move through these phases. The four nondiscrete stages are called egoistic, reciprocal, conventional, and subjective. Both of the marital partners in the egoistic stage seems generally self-preoccupied, rather than interested in the other person. Each spouse is concerned with satisfying his or her own needs through the relationship and by some grandiose expectations of the marriage. They are sometimes more interested in impressing friends and family with their "catch" than with the needs of their mate. The second or reciprocal stage emphasizes the growing awareness of the concerns of the partner. Negotiations are established to determine equal or specific exchanges of mutually supportive behaviors. The third or conventional stage is more expansive; it includes the influence of third parties on the relationship. It emphasizes the establishment of the marital rules and conventions and of "getting along." The fourth or subjective stage sees couples learning to expect and tolerate ambiguity and individuality in their partners.

The orientation used here has a similar idea. It is that marriages commonly experience six major crises during the span of their existence. These crisis points are transitions in which the marital partners are particularly vulnerable; they are more prone to marital dysfunction during these times but are also more amenable to the positive influences of marital therapy. The crises are known here as the crises of complementarity-seeking; dyad to triad; the disequilibrium phase; the discrepant years; dyad revisited; and marital terminations. This is not to suggest that all couples experience all these crises or that there are no other transitions to which some couples are also vulnerable. The myriad of possibilities among marital partners precludes such an oversimplification. But if the therapist includes in the marital diagnosis a clear notion of the transition to which the couple is currently vulnerable, the resulting treatment is immeasurably enhanced.

Crisis One: The Quest for Complementarity

The first crisis in the developmental process of marriage is that of complementarity-seeking. It begins before marriage, when the man and woman first seriously consider the mutual commitment and lifetime relationship. It approximately concludes with the birth of the first child. During this phase the man and woman assess one another to determine whether the other's attributes will fulfill one's own needs and goals. It is a narcissistic time; each is often more concerned with the rewards of the relationship than with its obligations. The partners both magnify their mate's positive attributes and overlook the liabilities. They form mental pictures about what the marriage is to be. But the picture is often too static; the idea of change is annoying. They generally don't contemplate the inevitable extension of their present circumstance. They overlook the probability that they will be eventually married to the elderly, possibly sick, probably very different personality, which their spouse will become. They often dismiss such thoughts with jokes or kidding threats to find ever younger partners. Or they deny, by telling themselves no one can predict the future anyway, so why try.

Complementarity between two people can only be partially realized at best. To achieve and maintain perfect complementarity would be to overcome impossible obstacles. Each partner would have to be completely honest with the other so that all traits are actually as advertised. Yet couples are inclined to portray themselves to the partner in the most flattering light. Even if they could find traits which reciprocally fit, they can't be sure they will remain so. Each partner must be willing and able to look objectively at the partner's actual, not fantasized attributes and deficiencies. Yet couples are more inclined to overlook negative attributes. They think more about meeting their own short-range interests than the partner's ability to adequately fulfill them. To achieve perfect complementarity requires that nothing will dramatically alter the existing needs, values, personality characteristics, physical appearance, or social circumstances of the partner. If change is tolerated, perfect complementarity requires that they occur in predictable, well-rehearsed sequential ways and that both partners will make the adaptations simultaneously. It would require that each change will also be complementary, or that each person would accommodate to the new needs of the other. Obviously this can never happen, no matter how well suited for one another the partners might seem to be in the beginning.

Achieving complementarity is illusory, too, partly because early attraction between couples may be based on unconscious needs, hidden motivations, or concealed expectations. Dicks (1967) points out that the potential partner seems to represent or promise a rediscovery of an important lost aspect of the individual's own personality which, because of earlier conditioning, has been recast as an object for attack or denial. The positive side of this is what we call "chemistry" and is the prevailing explanation for the phenomenon of "love at first sight." It is the obvious way to explain how two people who have little in common can be attracted to one another. Dicks calls this "projective identification." Therapists often see it in the way one partner attempts to influence changes in the other so that the other conforms more to one's ideals (Feldman, 1982).

It must be remembered that, as the marital relationship goes through this first stage, the two individuals who comprise it are also experiencing personal transitions. Most partners are individually going through what Levinson and associates (1978) called the "early adult transition," or what Sheehy (1976) called the "pulling up roots" phase. The fundamental task for people of this age is to psychologically disengage from their family or origin. They do so through the traditional vehicles of military service, college, moving into apartments with one's contemporaries, and marriage. Overriding these activities is the contradictory compulsion to be separate from parents, but simultaneously belong to someone. Being alone for them is a crisis, and a young person who has never been independent isn't sure he can cope. Attachment to another, either a peer group or a marital partner, is an apparent way to achieve the best of both. During this phase, the husband and/or wife often retain attachments to the parents or friends; rather than talk with their spouses, they frequently discuss their feelings, their marriage, and the relationship with the parent or a friend.

During this first phase, the couple also establishes its "contract." It is the couple's establishment of the rules to follow, the agreement about what each wants and is willing to give to the marriage (Clifford Sager, 1976). It is almost never a written document, but is just as emotionally binding for the couple. These are unspoken agreements which continue to change as the couple advances through the stages of their marriage. Couples invariably outgrow the original contract, so it has to be periodically renewed. Each renewal is itself a potential crisis.

The marital therapist who works with couples in this phase of the marriage cycle deals with the contradictory expectations and needs. Therapy exposes the fantasy, and shows the couple that complementarity is an unrealistic goal. Often the focus of therapy here is on clarifying expectations, teaching about the future, and helping the couple become more comfortable with change and accommodation. They are shown that discrepancies between expectation and realization are normal, and not a reflection of inadequacy in the marriage or the partner. When couples seek marital therapy at this early stage, they have a much better chance of learning the adaptive skills which will be sorely needed during the next few years of their relationship.

Crisis Two: Dyad to Triad

Another crisis occurs when the couple has the first child. More often than not, the transition from dyad to triad takes place even before the couple has satisfactorily resolved their own expectations. But whether they have or not, the new addition changes everything. Parenthood is a crisis (Lidz, 1968). The expectations change again. The roles of mother and father are quite different from the roles of wife and husband. Now both parents have to accommodate to the needs and expectations of the child as well as of the spouse.

The expectations made by spouse and child are often competitive, inconsistent, and incompatible. The new parent is faced with the task of accommodating to inconsistencies and fitting them in with meeting his/her own needs or wishes. All this occurs with little or no experience for adequately performing the roles or fulfilling the expectations. Thus, the baby is more than an addition; it is a catalyst for a basic shift in the nature of that relationship, and it irrevocably alters the way the marital partners will relate to one another (Scherz, 1971).

In coping with the demands of parenthood, many ill-prepared couples have marital problems. They have difficulty with a triad where they might have adapted successfully to the dyad. Murray Bowen's discussion of "triangles" (1978) has been instructive in understanding this change. Triangles are three-person emotional configurations which have the potential for instability and tension in relationships. Unless each member of the triangle achieves a satisfactory degree of differentiation of self, they remain in the unstable situation and possibly pass it on to succeeding generations. This happens when one spouse allies with the child against the other parent. Coalition-forming patterns (Minuchin, 1974) can be healthy when the parents have compatible expectations of the child; it can be unhealthy when parents do not. It is worse yet when the child is made the scapegoat (Bell and Vogel, 1960). Couples in conflict sometimes use their child to divert blame; the infant is viewed as the cause of the problem, so the parents feel no need to do something about their relationship.

The marital therapist helps couples in this crisis in several ways. Making explicit the expectations about the changed relationship is important. So too is helping them define their parental roles to one another. Therapy may inform them and provide resources about the responsibilities of child rearing during the pre-birth months to smooth the transition into the parental role. They are encouraged to get direct experience with parental obligations by closer associations with other couples in similar circumstances. The therapist may alert them to potential problems with triangles, coalitions, and scapegoats before and after the birth. Gradual familiarization with the upcoming responsibilities facilitates the adaptation and reduces the problems of the crisis.

Crisis Three: The Discrepant Years

Those couples who do not have children directly enter the third crisis phase, called the discrepant years. This is the time the partners face the fact that their fantasies and their expectations of the marriage are different from the reality. The crisis is not as time-bound as the previous stages and may overlap them. It also may last for many years if one or

both partners fail to face the realistic demands of their lives and seek
refuge in their idealizations. Many couples find this adjustment difficult
because they fail to recognize the origin of the dissatisfaction. They attribute their disappointment to some failure by the spouse, rather than
to their own unrealistic expectations of the marriage. They feel they
made the wrong choice; if only they had married a more suitable partner they would not be disappointed. When a marriage breaks up during this phase, the spouse who attributes the separation to some fault in
the partner may avoid potential marriage mates who have similar
"faults." They find in a second marriage that they are still dissatisfied,
and still attribute it to characteristics of the new spouse rather than to
unrealistic expectations.

The discrepant years constitute a crisis, even among those couples
who understand that marriage and the spouse cannot fulfill all their
needs. This is because of the contradictory expectations imposed on
marriages by society, as discussed previously. For example, most Americans still think of the traditional nuclear family as their ideal, yet less
than one-fourth of all marriages fit this model. Only seven percent of
American families have the prototypical circumstance of a working
husband, stay-at-home wife, and two or three children. But whether or
not they conform to this model, they are sometimes considered "different." The partners themselves realize they are living differently than
they expected, differently than the lifestyle for which they prepared
themselves. If the couple skipped the second phase and chose a child-
free lifestyle, they are still confronted with some disapproval, especially
among some subcultural groups (Burgwyn, 1981). Trying to fulfill all
social expectations is futile. Even in the relatively few marriages which
conform to some idealization of the nuclear family, spouses feel themselves at odds with some segments of society. Traditional families and
their advocates have often felt compelled to defensively justify preserving the tradition (Peck and Senderowitz, 1974). It is increasingly difficult for wives to remain home with their young children. There are few
neighbor women with whom they can coffee-klatch (Bird, 1979). Staying home subjects them to the risk of feeling that there is a gap between
themselves and their husbands, brought about by their different expo-
sures and worldly pressures (Lee and Casebeir, 1971). If she remains
home, she is more likely to overinvest in the children and exclude the
husband.

If the wife works, as do more than 65 percent of American wives
now, there are going to be other discrepancy problems. She has to be
"supermom" if she is going to meet her children's emotional needs. If
the family cannot afford child care, there is the conflict about not fulfill-

ing the needs of any of the family members. Even if child care can be afforded, the children's emotional parenting needs are going to be shortchanged in most instances. It is becoming common to see fathers assuming more of this concern, but when they do another discrepancy occurs. Society still looks questioningly at "househusbands" and puts greater pressures on women to fulfill parental roles than it does on fathers. So regardless of the couple's willingness to accommodate to the realities of their situation, they have to cope with contradictory expectations of society.

One important way the marital therapist facilitates the transition through this stage is to help the couple clarify boundaries. As Minuchin (1974) theorizes, healthy marriages must have clear boundaries to ensure that the partners are defined as separate entities to be protected from outside subsystems, including children, in-laws, and relevant others. The boundaries between the couple and the other subsystems must not be so rigid that they prevent interaction with the outside world or between the husband and wife. But this is becoming increasingly difficult for couples; they are faced with increasing pressures and attractions from the outside world. Whether they want to or not, they no longer can live as if they only have eyes for one another. They are part of a larger system.

There are three general types of boundaries. Minuchin calls them "disengaged," "enmeshed," and "clear" boundaries. When disengagement occurs, the marital partners may be even more narcissistic than in phase one, and are little involved with the marriage; the partners maintain some boundary between themselves and are much more open to outside influences. At the other extreme are the enmeshed couples. Here the boundary encompasses the couple and excludes other subsystems such as the children. At the center of the boundary continuum of disengagement-enmeshment are the clear boundaries. These are flexible, penetrable, and readily apparent. The therapist helps couples deal with the discrepant phase by helping them to define their boundaries. They are helped to become more flexible and inclusive when appropriate, and to move away from extreme enmeshment or disengagement responses.

Crisis Four: The Adult Marriage

Eventually functional marriages achieve more durability and stability. The couple has completed the process of negotiating rules. Each has come to know the partner. They find that they can accept their partner's individuality. They no longer blame their partner for their own unrealized hopes. They have become less narcissistic and derive pleasure from what they give to the marriage and the partner. They have weathered the storm caused by the addition of new family members and have outgrown any wish to form alliances with the children. Their expectations are more realistic; while they might feel disappointment that their ideals won't always be achieved in this partnership, they learn they can live with it. This is the stage, perhaps, when healthy marriages truly experience mutual love and respect. The marriage partners have been able to establish awareness of their own identities, both as individuals and as spouses. Individually, they are often entering what Levinson calls the "settling down" stage, which typically follows the "age 30 transition" and precedes the mid-life crisis transition.

Of course, there are problems during this most "adjusted" of marital phases. As often as not, the problems come from outside the marital relationship. Trouble may come from economic difficulty, from physical illness, problems with the increasingly independent children, in-laws, and careers. Marital problems happen when the outside frustrations are taken out on one's spouse. The crises of this stage are due to the understandable lack of preparation for dealing with unpredictable events. In the adult marriage, each partner may feel helpless to deal with the external threat, and seeks mutual support.

The role of the marital therapist in this phase centers around facilitating the couple's ability to support one another in their efforts to cope with the stress event. Therapy helps the couple see the benefits of their reciprocally supportive endeavors and helps them cope with the external event as a team. If they successfully grow out of this crisis, they will greatly add to their capacities for coping with all their subsequent crises.

Crisis Five: Dyad Revisited

Much has been written of the "empty nest syndrome" in recent years. Not long ago, this experience was unusual. Now, with earlier marriages, fewer children, and increased longevity, a couple may have more years without the children in the home than with them. When the last child becomes independent, the roles between the marital partners once again are renegotiated. A central purpose of their lives for 20 to 30 years is gone; for some there is a devastating sense of emptiness and purposelessness. The father and mother no longer feel needed, though typically in rather different ways. The change is most difficult for the homemaker mother. Even mothers who had outside careers have difficulty, though, since it presents a greater deviation from her expected role than from her husband's. The father's adjustment is less radical, but he is often faced with different needs and expectations from his wife.

In any event, the married partners now face one another in a new light. They realize their partner is different than when fulfilling the parental role. Sometimes they face each other without the children as intermediaries and move toward emotional or physical disengagement. A common, unhealthy manifestation of this phase is to hold onto the children, emotionally if not physically. Another is to throw oneself into a career at the expense of the needs of the marital relationship (Henton, 1983). This phase often happens during the partners' individual life-stages known by Levinson as the "mid-life transition," a time when one questions his future, seeks new roles, and attempts to affirm that (s)he is still of some value (Kerckhoff, 1976). Biological and emotional changes of the climacteric must also be faced. Couples who can adapt to the empty nest have the potential for considerably more satisfaction in their relationship after they have made the adjustment (Harry, 1976; Rollins and Cannon, 1974).

The marital therapist sees a disproportionate number of couples during this crisis. There are a disproportionate number of divorces between couples soon after their last child has become independent. Many have postponed a wish to be apart from their spouse until the responsibilities of child-rearing have been fulfilled. Many others have been so preoccupied with such obligations that they didn't notice how little they still had in common with their partner; the relationship had grown stale. Therapy can be most helpful in such instances. Couples are taught to revitalize the relationship, to achieve more realistic expectations of their partner, to appreciate independence from former responsibilities. The relationship can be fulfilling if they can maintain their individual identities and learn to tolerate the independence of their spouse (Farley, 1979). Again, the therapist sees a major concern of the treatment process as adaptability.

Crisis Six: Marital Terminations

Relatively little has been written about how the aging process affects marriage, especially when compared to the profusion of material now available about middle-aged marriage. Most of the studies which do exist suggest that the final years of marriage can be very satisfying if the couple prepared for it in advance (Appleton, 1981). When the partners are beyond age 60, they are often more concerned about companionship and friendship than with the less stable and more transitory vicissitudes of earlier years. By the time the couple has reached these advanced years, they generally have come to recognize and accept their needs and obligations with one another. Both partners appreciate that there is room for the relationship as a unit and for individuality, too (Karson and Karson, 1978). The major tasks facing the marriage during this final phase are the psychological processes of individuation and refocusing. The couple can experiment with different patterns of life and cultivate new interests unburdened by duties to children or work. There is, as Bernice Neugarten (1973) discussed, a movement of energy from an outer world to an inner world in the elderly, a "the process of disengagement." For the married couple this process may consist of pulling back from others, but not necessarily from the marital relationship.

Therapists who work with older couples find that their effort is largely to facilitate the couple's interest in one another, even when they seek to withdraw from others. The therapist also seeks to prepare them for the probable outcome of the marriage, that one will outlive the other (Thompson and Spanier, 1983). The resources available to the survivor to cope with this crisis are limited. If each partner remains physically healthy, the task might center around helping them remain as involved in their community, their peers, and children as their energies permit. Much of what needs to be done for those in this phase goes beyond the clinical role of the marital therapist. Working to improve the American treatment of the elderly, improving facilities for the care of the single elderly, widows and widowers, and raising public consciousness about the need for mutual involvement between the elderly and younger people would be important contributions. Therapists may also specialize in work with the marital problems of the elderly to better meet their unique needs.

Chapter Thirteen

Specializations in Marital Therapy

Specialization within any profession is a result of growing knowledge. As the field expands, its practitioners have an increasingly difficult time keeping current; human limitations on time and energy are finite, whereas there is no commensurate limit on knowledge. Professionals begin to focus their attention so they can at least keep pace within a concentration. They communicate with colleagues who share their special interest; eventually their profession formally or informally recognizes the uniqueness of this group. Those in the speciality have less to do with those outside it, and the field experiences some fragmentation. Specialization is often lamented by both practitioners and consumers, but it means the field is progressing, improving in its knowledge base and ability to provide service.

Marital therapy has enjoyed dramatic expansion in its knowledge base in the past decade. This has been accompanied by the trend toward specialization. It was once reasonable for the conscientious marital therapist to keep abreast of the latest developments in the field and to treat every type of marital problem. The specific therapy literature was sparse, and one could easily read it all. This is no longer remotely possible; there are hundreds of journals and dozens of books which discuss various aspects of couples' relationship problems. Now it is challenging to remain current even in some concentrations. Practitioners within the marital therapy field have begun to coalesce around certain areas of interest which are becoming the marital therapy specializations. These interests have not all been granted formal recognition as specialities in the field, but the trend is clearly in that direction.

The emerging specializations of marital therapy include premarital counseling, sex therapy, divorce counseling, divorce mediation, advocacy and prevention, marital therapy education, and research. This chapter provides an overview of some of these specialties; it does not provide a detailed summary of all the knowledge relevant to each specialty. But the books and articles cited provide the interested marital therapist with a wealth of detailed information.

Premarital Counseling

The oldest marital therapy specialization is premarital counseling. Helping couples get ready for lifetime commitments predates efforts to treat dysfunctional marriages by centuries. It has existed in every culture which has sanctioned marriage, though its forms and practitioners have been diverse. It is in the province of the clergy in most societies, but it is also practiced extensively by physicians, relatives of the couple, village leaders and assorted keepers of the cultural institutions. Its practice has taken such forms as informal private talks, group lectures, social isolation for weeks, practicing at sex with village elders, and very formal indoctrinations. In many cultures premarital counseling is required in order for the marriage to achieve legal or religious sanction.

Formal marital preparation efforts are of four types in the United States. The largest are the generalized education programs. These are primarily conducted in classrooms, often sexually segregated, and provide general information. The focus is on sex and conception, with less attention given to the social relationship and nonspecific household issues. The programs are offered in many junior and senior high schools and, to a lesser extent, in some religious and recreational programs. The programs are highly controversial in many communities, so that they tend to be exceedingly cautious in their presentation. The teachers have widely varying levels of training, experience, and motivation for the job. Such programs are not accessible for most of those who will marry; many school districts have never authorized such instruction while others have discontinued it in the face of community opposition.

Those who oppose it in public education insist that such instruction should be provided in the young person's home or church. Obviously many who will marry cannot or will not obtain information this way.

The second form of marital preparation is personalized instructional counseling. This is more specific, individually designed to meet the needs of a particular couple; it has been traditionally conducted by physicians and clergy. The usual procedure is for the counselor to describe the possible problems and benefits of marriage, instruct the couple about human sexuality, and discuss their mutual obligations. The counselor answers specific questions and sometimes gives them written materials to inform them about their particular concerns. Advice is given about how other couples face various problems (Ellzey, 1968). Sometimes the couple is given written tests which purport to determine the couple's compatibility or potential problems, though the worth of such devices is dubious. While couples are more often counseled privately in this model, group discussions are also becoming increasingly common (Gleason and Prescott, 1977).

A third approach to premarital preparation is marital enrichment. Marriage enrichment programs, such as those under the auspices of ACME, the Association of Couples for Marriage Enrichment, usually consist of groups of four to seven couples. Its goals are not to locate and treat specific problems, either actual or potential, but to help couples reach the positive potential of their marriage. It seeks to enhance the couple's communication, strengthen their commitment to the partner, and improve conflict-resolving skills. Marriage enrichment has some similarities with group therapy, human potential encounters, and classroom education, but is more focused on the marriage theme and individualized for the couple's needs.

Finally, the fourth approach, the one of greatest involvement by marital therapists, is that of therapeutic counseling of the premarried couple. Couples who partake of this service usually have identified some problem or at least have questions about the future of their relationship. They may have been referred to the therapist by others who have seen evidence of a potential difficulty. The goal is to locate the potential problem, isolate it, show how to keep it from spreading into other areas of the couple's lives, and show how to reduce or eliminate it. As the goals of premarital counseling have broadened, most therapists have been scheduling more sessions before the wedding. The average number of visits by premarried couples is three (Wright, 1976). Before 1960 the typical number of sessions with clerical marital therapists was only one (Wiser, 1959).

Therapists usually devote the first meeting to getting acquainted and to discussing the couple's expectations of the marriage and one another. In subsequent sessions, the therapist determines each partner's assets and potential liabilities and instructs the couple in ways to overcome the potential problems. When the therapist ascertains that more serious potential problems exist, the number of premarital sessions might be increased. The format might then become identical to post-nuptial marital therapy.

Sometimes couples see their family physicians for premarital examinations and find that the doctor is also a skilled marital therapist. The physician-therapist is able to combine the physical exam with an emotional and situational assessment. Joseph Trainer, M.D. (1979) provides a thorough description of the way physician-therapists can provide such service. His method consists of four premarital sessions, with the second and third devoted to the health examination and the first and last focused on marital roles and problem solving. His model calls for a fifth session after the wedding, to recheck the couple's progress.

The post-wedding follow-up is increasingly viewed as an integral part of this specialization (Guildner, 1977). The therapist sees the couple at least once after the wedding, usually eight to 12 weeks later. In relatively healthy new marriages, there is no predetermined agenda but the therapist often encourages the couple to discuss the discrepancies between their expectations and what is actually happening. David Mace (1948) has long advocated extending premarital sessions into post-wedding visits. He suggests that couples may not get much from premarital counsel because they have so many unrealistic, idealized expectations. But after they have been married several months, when they have become more reality-oriented and objective, they are more amenable to the service. Mace hypothesizes that a most important goal of premarital therapy is to establish a good working relationship between the couple and the therapist so that everyone will be better prepared to deal with problems after the honeymoon is over.

Despite a widespread belief in its importance, premarital counseling remains a peripheral activity for most marital therapists. Its practitioners spend relatively little time at it, have little training for it, and aren't sure if it is effective. For example, most clergymen conduct fewer than a dozen weddings annually, suggesting that their premarital counseling work is not substantial (Wright, 1976). It probably constitutes an even smaller proportion of the typical physician's time. And since other marital therapists spend much of their work in individual psychotherapy, they also do relatively little premarital work. Thus, it is not easy to learn how to do it on the job.

Nevertheless, the formal training program in premarital therapy, like the literature, is on the increase. Although even today rarely offered as a separate course in most seminaries, medical schools, and other professional institutions, it is now part of many marital therapy courses. For years Purdue University has had a program which centers around premarital therapy. Similarly, there are a few textbooks devoted entirely to the subject. Rutledge's *Premarital Therapy* (1966) and Wright's *Premarital Counseling* (1977) are currently among the most influential, particularly among pastoral counselors. But many books on family therapy include sections on the topic. The marital and family therapy journals devote much more attention to premarital interventions, and the literature is becoming much richer. The field is knowledgeable enough to necessitate its own subspecialties. Articles concentrate on the theory and practice of premarital therapy with special client populations. These groups include premarital therapy with adolescents (Reiner and Edwards, 1974), alcoholics (Hertzman and Hertzman, 1981), elderly couples (Masters and Johnson, 1981), and couples who live together (Clatworthy, 1975) to name but a few.

Despite the growing interest and specialization, many therapists and researchers wonder whether premarital work is effective. Emily Mudd, who developed a premarital guidance program in 1941, questioned its premises. Could it really prevent future marital problems? Could it dissuade people from marrying unsuitable partners? Could it help prepare people for roles for which they have no experience? The questions have yet to be satisfactorily answered.

Research to determine if premarital therapy does any lasting good is inconclusive (Schumm and Denton, 1979). Many earlier studies were enthusiastically positive but used dubious methodology. They rarely used control groups to compare the long-term outcomes of couples with and without premarital therapy. Their positive results were based on the couple's self-report of satisfaction with premarital counsel. They were often conducted soon after the wedding, when the couple is most likely to be favorable about the prognosis of the marriage and the worth of counseling. The more recent studies are methodologically improved, using combinations of self-reports, objective criteria, independent observers, and controls (Gurman and Kniskern, 1977). Their findings suggest that only limited success, if any, is achieved in premarital intervention. Considerable investigation is under way to determine how to make premarital work more effective. The speciality needs to know what techniques, skills, and therapist traits are appropriate (Curtis and Miller, 1976). As it continues to develop, more of this information will be obtained.

Sex Therapy

As often as not, marital problems are caused by or are the cause of sexual problems. Sexual and marital problems are almost inextricably intertwined (Sager, 1976). So it is not possible to be a proficient marital therapist without also possessing knowledge and skill in the treatment of at least some forms of sexual dysfunction.

However, the skills of marital and sexual therapists are no longer synonymous. To be competent at each requires different types of knowledge, personality traits, training, values, and physical facilities. This distinction was not so great in past decades; the treatment of sexual dysfunction was not very different from the treatment of other marital problems before 1970. The dominant premise in both was basically to understand the unconscious conflicts which contribute to the symptoms, allow the client to bring such conflicts to the consciousness, and thus presumably be freed of the problem. The approach was consistent with the skills and facilities of most marital therapists. Unfortunately, its results were not very good (Polansky and Nadelson, 1982).

The monumental achievement of Masters and Johnson (1970) revolutionized the treatment of human sexual dysfunction. Their "direct sex therapy" did not seek to uncover unconscious conflicts; instead it looked at objectifiable physiological changes and measured efficacy by observable changes in sexual responses. The approach used male-female therapy teams to teach couples how to eliminate specific sexual dysfunction. It required extensive medical and physiological involvement and special physical settings. The results have been systematically documented and relatively successful in short time periods.

Sex therapy clinics modeled after that of Masters and Johnson have since proliferated. This has followed an explosion of information about sexuality, as well as a heightened public consciousness about the benefits of sex therapy. More couples than ever have come to believe all their marital problems are caused by sexual problems. They sometimes expect all marital therapists to provide the same sex therapy. Many couples feel they will be instructed in an easy, foolproof, short-term therapy which will not only solve their sexual problems but all their other relational problems as well.

The training to become a qualified sex therapist, particularly in the use of Masters and Johnson inspired techniques, is extensive. Only a small percentage of all marriage therapists obtain the training to provide this service in more than a peripheral sense. Others study it independently or take courses in methods of sex therapy such as those offered

by the American Association of Sex Educators, Counselors and Therapists. They read some of the texts and articles about sexual therapy
such as those by Kaplan (1974), Read (1979), Meyer (1976), and many
articles, particularly those found in the *Journal of Sex Education and
Therapy.*

Levels of Sex Therapy Skill

The ethical marital therapist who works with sexually distressed couples must assess his or her own level of preparedness for such intervention. Not all sex therapists can competently perform all forms of marital therapy, and not all marital therapists can treat all types of sexual
problems. Therapists who are aware of realistic limitations will be able
to refer some couples to competent specialists and perhaps work closely
with them on the case.

This does not imply that most couples with sex problems will have
to be referred by marital therapists, however. The decision to refer or
treat is based on the type of sexual problem which exists, the cause of
the problem, and the treatment of choice for it, as well as the background of the therapist (Kentsmith et al., 1981). Annon (1976) has developed a hierarchy of sexual problems which provides useful criteria
for determining whether to refer or treat. There are four levels of intervention in Annon's model. These are to provide (1) permission, (2) limited information, (3) specific suggestions, and (4) intensive therapy. A
highly specialized form of training is usually required only for the
fourth of these levels.

The first level, "providing permission," is for couples whose sexual
difficulties stem from misunderstanding or misinformation. Many people believe certain sexual practices are abnormal; some feel that if they
like or dislike some expression of sexuality they are deviant. They don't
know what is "normal" or acceptable and become restricted or inhibited because of their uncertainty. A major reason for sexual dysfunction
is the couple's inability to just relax and pay attention to their physical
sensations rather than their preconceived ideas about how sex should
be. The therapist reassures the couple that they have the sole right to
determine what is normal for themselves. The therapist essentially
"gives them permission." Often this frees them from the constraints
which previously precluded fulfillment in their sexual experience. Therapists who provide this level of treatment must be knowledgeable about
human sexuality, be accepting of individual differences, and be fairly
free of their own personality or sexual conflicts. Most marital therapists

can provide sex therapy at this level or they would not be marital therapists.

The second level of intervention, that of providing limited information, is for couples who are basically knowledgeable and not particularly inhibited, but who have specific concerns about their sexuality.
Many couples become preoccupied with sex-related issues and develop
other marital problems as a result. Sometimes they might be concerned
about penis or breast size, intercourse during pregnancy or menstrua-
tion, masturbation, birth control, or sex-health problems (Jackman,
1980). The marital therapist provides specific information designed for
this couple's unique needs. Therapists providing this level of service often use anatomical models and audiovisual equipment to provide the
couple with the answers they seek. Of course, to provide this sex therapy, the therapist must possess the sufficient knowledge, freedom from
sex-related conflicts, and acceptance, as well as the needed facilities or
equipment.

The third level of sex therapy intervention is for couples who seek
advice about how to correct specific sexual problems. The therapist determines the problem, provides specific suggestions, and monitors subsequent progress. If the results are satisfactory, it is not necessary to
provide intensive therapy. Sometimes therapists provide suggestions
about how to revive couples' flagging interests in sex, alternative coital
positions, how to engage in sexual activity even though the husband is
impotent, or how to prevent premature ejaculation. Most couples who
eventually require intensive sex therapy begin at this level. Therapists
must exercise caution about offering suggestions which the couple cannot fulfill outside of intensive therapy. If they experience traumatic failure at this stage, it will be far more difficult for them to benefit from
subsequent intensive therapy. Thus, therapists who provide specific
suggestions must not only possess the traits previously described, but
also must be adept at assessing the potential for the couple to use intensive therapy.

The fourth level of sex therapy intervention has become highly
technical and requires extensive training, facilities, and predisposition
from the therapist. Since marital and sexual problems are intertwined,
it is possible for a sex therapist and a different marital therapist to work
with a couple simultaneously. There is no evidence that simultaneous
sex therapy and marital therapy, conducted by different therapists, im-
pedes the work of either (Sager, 1976). However, it seems advantageous for the sex therapist and the marital therapist to have some working relationship with one another during the course of the therapy.

It is, of course, beyond the scope of this volume to provide sufficient information for the marital therapist to provide intensive sex therapy. Many of the texts cited in this section have provided extensive detail about intensive therapy. What follows here is an outline of some of the techniques sex therapists use. The marital therapist who doesn't provide intensive sex therapy is at least advised to have some familiarity with these techniques.

Intensive Sex Therapy

Therapists provide intensive sex therapy primarily by treating six diagnostic categories of sexual dysfunction. These are orgasmic dysfunction, erectile dysfunction, premature ejaculation, ejaculatory inhibition, vaginismus, and inhibited desire. Of course, treatment of any one of these does not preclude simultaneous treatment of others and often includes treatment of the emotional relationship as well. Intensive therapy begins with assessment and attempts to isolate the sexual problem to the extent possible. Assessment includes personality inventories, conjoint interviews, individual interviews, and round-table discussions in which the goals are specified and the treatment plan is developed. Physical exams are usually necessary to rule out physical origins of the identified problems.

Most intensive sex therapy uses sensate focusing to facilitate the treatment. It is designed to help the couple experience sensual pleasure without the pressure of having to perform or even to experience sexual arousal. Couples suffering sexual problems are often in emotional pain about actual or perceived inadequate sexual performance. The resulting anxiety causes them to want to avoid further contact with their partners. They presume contact will lead to another unpleasant experience with intercourse. A vicious circle results. They no longer derive pleasure from simple touching or caressing; they fear it will lead to intercourse, and intercourse has become threatening. Because they feel they must perform, they force themselves, feel inadequate, and are again upset. In the sensate focus the goal is to separate physical pleasure from the fear of sexual failure. The couple is specifically asked to refrain from intercourse for the time being. Then they are asked to set aside enough time to be alone together without other obligations. The partners are asked to caress, hold one another, massage, take turns touching the other's bodies except for genitals, and merely to experience unpressured sensuality. Therapists might give fairly specific instructions for what to do or how often to do it, but it is important that it not be directly associated with intercourse or performance. Couples begin this experience feeling somewhat awkward but eventually come to enjoy it for its own sake. This sets a positive stage for the couple; it reduces anxiety so that treatment of any one of the six major sexual disturbances can be more readily facilitated.

One of the six sexual disturbances, orgasmic dysfunction, can be of two types. Primary orgasmic dysfunction occurs in those who never experience orgasms; secondary dysfunction occurs to those who have been orgasmic in the past. Masters and Johnson (1970) reported success of 83.4 percent with a 2.6 percent relapse rate after five years among primary orgasmic dysfunctional women, and a success rate of 72.2 percent in secondary anorgasmic women. Their method has been adopted or modified by different therapists, but there are several common characteristics in all the formats. After all possible physical reasons for orgasmic impairment have been ruled out, the therapist spends hours with the couple providing them with information about the nature of the difficulty. Often when they are instructed in knowing "what to look for," they have greater success. Next, sensate focus activities are assigned to the couple. Finally, work on the target behavior occurs. Masturbation training, use of vibrators, and erotic media are used to heighten the woman's arousal. The couple is given the task of learning masturbation, in gradual steps, from the woman's visual self examination of the genitals to masturbation, sometimes using a vibrator and sometimes using the husband's hand or penis. In some women Kegel exercises have been helpful. Women with weak perivaginal musculature have higher rates of orgasmic dysfunction, said Kegel (1952), so sexual feeling in the vagina is enhanced by improved muscle tone. Kegel muscle contraction exercises have thus been prescribed in many of these treatments. The woman is instructed in regularly contracting perivaginal muscles, often around her own finger.

Kaplan (1974) prescribes two types of coital contact designed to encourage the woman toward arousal and subsequent orgasm, the stop-start method and the bridge maneuver. In stop-start the man inserts his penis and thrusts for brief periods in a slow, teasing manner. Periodically he briefly withdraws and reenters. There is no effort to encourage orgasm at first. During interruptions of intercourse, clitoral stimulation is also helpful. When orgasm appears imminent, the man quickly penetrates after stimulating her to the edge of orgasm. The bridge maneuver combines penis thrusts with fantasy and clitoral stimulation. The woman, while fantasizing, is stimulated by her partner, a vibrator, or herself. This is interspersed with penile thrusting. It is found that when orgasm occurs, most women subsequently become more easily aroused and orgasmic. Some who become orgasmic continue to require additional clitoral stimulation. Other women become orgasmic with intercourse alone.

Treatments for erectile dysfunction, premature ejaculation, and ejaculatory inhibition treatments also have several common elements. Here again it is important to first rule out any physical basis for the symptoms. Urologists and researchers are now saying that 40 to 60 percent of impotence cases are organic (Scott et al., 1983). These problems can be associated with many physical health problems including alcoholism, high blood pressure treatment, diabetes, and hormonal imbalances. Premature ejaculation is the absence of voluntary control of ejaculation before the partner reaches orgasm. It is often treated by the stop-start technique and squeeze method following education and sensate focus work. In stop-start, the female stimulates her partner's penis almost to ejaculation before stopping. This process is repeated until the man begins to achieve greater control. In the squeeze technique, the woman is instructed to place her thumb on the frenulum, on the underside of the penis, and her first and second fingers on the opposite side, at the coronal ridge. She squeezes for about four seconds before release, just before ejaculation seems imminent. The likelihood of ejaculation is greatly diminished. This is often followed by intercourse with the female on top. She occasionally starts-stops, squeezes at his signal until the partners together are more comfortable that they are in control.

Ejaculatory inhibition occurs when the man becomes aroused and erect but has difficulty ejaculating intravaginally, sometimes not even after an hour of continuous thrusting. While the etiology of this disorder is still conjectural, the predominant treatment is systematic desensitization with a gradual shaping of ejaculatory behavior. For example, if the man is able to ejaculate while masturbating in private, he is encouraged to masturbate with his wife's awareness and eventual participation. First he will caress his wife and then go to another room and masturbate. After he ejaculates, he returns to caress his wife. Next, he will masturbate in her presence. Eventually this leads to ejaculation through partner stimulation and finally through intercourse.

Systematic desensitization is also a major factor in the treatment of erectile dysfunction or psychogenic impotence, when a high level of sexual anxiety is related to it. Much of the desensitization process occurs in instructing the partners about gradually coming to enjoy one another regardless of whether they have satisfactory intercourse. Sensate-focus pleasuring and fondling the partner to orgasm without erection takes away much of the discomfort and anxiety. It frees the partners to eventually experience unpressured intercourse. Of course, all these techniques include a considerable amount of discussion, instruction, education with visual aids, experimentation and, more than anything else, reciprocal sensate focus pleasuring.

Vaginismus occurs when the muscles surrounding the vaginal introitus involuntarily contract during attempted penetration, making intercourse impossible. Often women who experience this condition have an aversion to anything being inserted in the vagina. The treatment includes systematic desensitization and sometimes Kegal or dilation exercises. The woman is provided with demonstrations and visual aids to answer any questions about anatomy. Some therapists prescribe dilators which are inserted by the women and gradually kept in place for increasingly longer periods of time. Eventually the husband participates, by holding the dilator as his wife inserts it. Then he inserts it, and so on. This is accompanied by sensate focusing. Eventually penile penetration occurs but at the woman's initiative and in her general control, until her inhibitions are resolved.

Problems of sexual desire, ranging from mild apathy to extreme aversion, have a complicated and still unknown etiology. Studies have correlated them with physical and psychological factors, hormone imbalances, medications, emotional stress, depression, and fear. Assessment is difficult but very important in its treatment. The prognosis for recovery is less optimistic than in the other dysfunctions (Kaplan, 1979). Sensate focusing, desensitization, long term psychotherapy, and enhancement of communication skills are utilized in the treatment of such disorders, usually with modest results.

Sexual therapy has made considerable advances, but the interrelatedness of sexual problems with many of the other problems between couples suggests that a variety of approaches will always be used. Competent sex therapists must be able to select methods of intervention which fit the unique circumstances of each couple (Lief, 1980).

Divorce Counseling

Divorce, if constructively handled, can be positive. It can lead to emotional strengthening and to the ultimate growth of both individuals (Krantzler, 1975). If it is properly orchestrated by a marital therapy specialist divorce can be a liberating experience that promotes rather than undermines family solidarity. The goal of this specialty is to improve the odds that this will be the outcome.

Divorce counseling is not the same as divorce mediation. Each has different goals, methods, and client groups. The divorce mediator often sees the couple after they have separated and seeks to provide them with alternatives to the legal adversary system in marital dissolution. The mediator helps couples find ways to compromise and work out agreements about their respective futures. The divorce counselor, on the other hand, usually works with couples who are still together but considering whether or not to separate.

Do marital therapists ever advise couples to divorce? If so, under what circumstances should it be done? Answers to these questions depend upon how one views the role of the marital therapist and the institution of marriage. The divorce counselor usually views his role as enabling individuals to achieve their potential for fulfillment and happiness regardless of the marriage (Kressler and Deutsch, 1977). As Arnold Lazarus has written, "If chronic unhappiness results from an unsatisfactory marriage, and all efforts to rectify the situation have failed, I do not hesitate to advise and aid my clients toward divorce. For me, the worth of a marriage is weighed solely in terms of human happiness. Marriage is not a sacred entity to be preserved for its own sake" (Lazarus, 1981, page 20).

Marriage is better than divorce. But divorce is better than the extreme pain, depression, sickness, and ill health that sometimes result from a disturbed marriage. If the marital therapist realizes that therapy will not change the fundamental problem faced by the individual couple, they should be so informed. The therapist is treading on questionable ethics if the couple is manipulated into divorcing, but it is appropriate to point out the merits and demerits of their possible decision. Marital therapists often see couples who have nothing in common, are truly unhappy with one another, are emotionally and physically capable of being divorced, and yet who remain married. Many marriages of this type are based primarily on neurotic interactions, sado-masochistic unions, exploitative-parasitical relationships, and emotional blackmail (Fisher, 1973). Some are afraid to separate. Some don't want to lose custody of their children. Some fear the economic or social consequences of a decision to divorce. The divorce counselor specializes in resolving such dilemmas.

The divorce counselor is a facilitator. Couples are helped to realize what their actual opportunities are and what obstacles might be in store for them if they decide to divorce or remain married. Sometimes the divorce counselor acts as a go-between for the couple during their process of disengagement and monitors their mutual efforts to extricate themselves from the marriage in a fair and positive way. Once a decision has been made, the therapist may change roles. If the decision is to remain married, marital therapy may be used. If the decision is to divorce, the divorce mediator role may be assumed.

Divorce Mediation

Another rapidly developing specialization in marital therapy is that of divorce mediation, a way of settling marital dissolution disputes, usually outside the litigation process. It is designed as an alternative to the adversary system of divorce, in which both husband and wife obtain different attorneys and have their cases presented in court in such a way that one is declared the winner and the other the loser. This procedure has long been the predominant format for divorce in the United States. It has, however, been subject to growing disenchantment from many sectors, including the legal profession itself. As Conciliation Court Judge Norman Fenton has written, "The filing for a divorce often intensifies family conflict and the adversarial approach tends to polarize the parties as it automatically places litigants at opposite ends of the domestic ring. It makes then unnecessary combatants, prolongs the conflicts, interferes with future relationships between the parties, and even worse, between the parents and their children" (Fenton, 1980).

As an alternative to adversarial divorce, divorce mediation uses the neutral third party who represents the interests of both husband and wife as well as the children. Divorce mediation, above all, never pits one party against the other. Rather, its goal is to help the couple make mutually acceptable compromises. Mutual agreement is the goal; when it is achieved, neither party has won or lost. The mediator helps the couple arrive at voluntary settlements but is also concerned with their emotional and material well-being. Mediation helps assure that the possessions are disbursed fairly. It is also a therapeutic process which includes helping the couple understand their marital problems and their respective contibutions to these problems. It facilitates their ability to disengage emotionally from the unhealthy parts of the relationship. The procedure is similar to the way marital therapists treat other couples. When resolution occurs, the probability of future legal or emotional dispute is vitiated because decisions were not forced on either party.

Divorce mediation operates under the auspices of family courts in many large American cities; the movement is spreading nationwide.

Most court-affiliated mediators trace their origins to the Los Angeles County Conciliation Court which started in 1939. Professional counselors, salaried at public expense, see couples who request the service. At this point the goal is to determine if reconciliation is possible and, if so, to facilitate the emotional and practical terms of the reunion. Often this means referral to a marital therapist. The mediator also helps the couple write a marriage agreement defining the nature of their dispute and possible solutions. The agreement is not legally binding but is useful as a guide in helping reconcile couples so that there is no further need of legal intervention.

When it is ascertained that divorce is the only available option, the mediator outlines the possible ways to dissolve the marriage. All options are weighed along with their various consequences. The mediator might help the couple choose among the options. Their agreement may be presented to the family court judge, whose decision to follow the agreement makes it legally enforceable.

The entire mediation process is generally short term, often consisting of a few meetings at most. In the first session the mediator usually allows the husband and wife to ventilate, to express their respective understandings of what went wrong and why they feel as they do. The mediator then meets with each person individually. In the second phase, the couple is helped to negotiate their respective goals and demands. Here the mediator helps the couple go beyond recitation of problems and into their dynamics. The mediator reframes the respective understandings of the conflict so that both can see it in a new light. In the final phase, agreements are reached about how to resolve the disputes. The mediator combines labor relations techniques with traditional marital therapy to reach the agreements.

Couples are not required to go to divorce mediators. If they want one, they many choose a private mediator instead of a court-employed one, even in those jurisdictions where the court has such services. During the mediation it is neither necessary or desirable for individual lawyers to take legal actions. However, if one or both parties have retained counsel, the mediator must discuss the mediation role with the attorneys. Specially trained lawyers often assume the mediation role themselves, but not as representatives of one or the other party. The absence of legal representation for each party at this point helps avoid litigation and lowers the expense of the divorce process (Irving, 1980).

Divorce mediation does not purport to do away with the legal profession's involvement in divorce matters. Contested divorce will always exist; the rights of some parties need protection, and sometimes this is only possible through the adversary system. But divorce mediation can provide a needed service for many other divorcing couples who are ill-served adversarially.

While many attorneys and judges are at the forefront of the movement, and while an increasing number of courts follow mediators' recommendations, there is considerable resistance by many lawyers. They argue that the rights of one or the other spouse may be mitigated without the adversary process or without a lawyer to act as one's advocate. They point out that the mediator's recommendations have no legal merit, so it is a needless expense to the couple or the taxpayer. And they imply that mediation may reduce the lawyers' revenues. Sometimes lawyers will advise their clients not to give information to the mediator; they fear that any disclosures will be used against their client. Some lawyers also attempt to subpoena mediators and compel them to disclose information in court. Mediators who serve under court auspices can usually avoid this, but it is more difficult for those in private practice. Accordingly, one of the cardinal tenets of divorce mediation is that all disclosures are considered confidential and that mediators are not available for court proceedings. Both parties need to know that they can discuss their situations in honesty and without fear that the mediator will be required to reveal the information in court. Thus, the mediator requires as a precondition of working with the couple that they or their representatives will not call the mediator to testify. Most mediators have their clients sign an agreement to this effect.

When agreements are reached, the details are written down, signed by the husband and wife, and shown to their respective lawyers. The agreement is then shown to the court and may be used as the basis of the divorce decree. If agreements cannot be mediated, then the couple has to settle things through the adversarial court battle. This will happen with some couples no matter how sensible the mediation process is, and no matter how ultimately harmful the litigation process will be. Some couples don't want reason to prevail; they only want their day in court to expose to the world the burdens which have been placed on them by an unreasonable spouse. Divorce mediators have been quite successful in dissuading many from such actions, but they will never succeed with everyone.

Advocacy and Preventative Intervention

Without question, the most important of the marital therapy specialties, the one with the greatest potential for achieving the goals of the field, is that of advocacy and prevention. This is environmental intervention, working to change cultural and social norms to improve the prospects of marital well-being. It is finding and implementing ways of keeping marital problems from happening, and influencing social change toward conditions which enhance healthy marriage. Prevention of marital problems is analogous to preventative medicine in which members of the population are protected through improved sanitation facilities, inoculations, and education about good nutrition. It would be unimaginable to assume that physicians and nurses, using such post-hoc methods as surgery and medicine, could have great impact on the nation's health without such preventative measures. So too, is it unrealistic to assume that marital therapists could have great influence on the health of marriage in this culture without effort toward problem prevention and the development of marital health factors. The most couples a full-time therapist could serve clinically in a year, seeing them an average of ten visits per couple, would be fewer than 200; there wouldn't be time for many more. There are only a few thousand marital therapists nationwide, most of whom do not work with maritally distressed couples full time (Barker, 1982). So obviously, only a small percentage of the millions of couples in marital crisis can be reached clinically with existing resources. If marital therapists are going to have a significant impact, it will come through their involvement in more than clinical intervention.

There are many obstacles, however, for the marital therapist participating in this form of intervention. One is that most marital therapists are still not adequately trained for prevention, environmental work, advocacy, or making institutional changes designed to facilitate better marriages. This is being remedied to some extent; therapists, educators, and educational institutions are emphasizing it more than they had in previous years. Most master's level and doctoral courses for marital therapists have at least one course on environmental or preventative involvement. But the courses are not always required, and the demand for them is not extensive. Another obstacle is that most marital therapists tend to think, and want to work, clinically. They want to leave the social issues to the politicians and social institutions and to devote their energies to improving the interviewing, assessment, and treatment skills. But more are seeing the futility of such clinical involvement as an effort to improve the health of the marriage institution.

The greatest of the obstacles, however, is the one with the least likelihood of being surmounted. There is little consensus about what marital therapists should advocate. Individuals and different marital therapists have widely divergent views as to what constitutes healthiness in marriage. Thus some therapists engaged in advocacy would be working at cross-purposes with others, depending on their values and goals. This can be an additional problem or stimulus for creativity in the field.

There are other specializations within marital therapy, and additional ones are certain to emerge in the next decades. Specialization will not be the only avenue open to marital therapists of the future, however, as there will probably always be room for the equivalent of "general practitioner" marital therapists as well. In any event, the field which already is rich with diverse approaches, goals, and methods will become even more so.

Chapter Fourteen

Values and Ethics in Marital Therapy

Marital therapists now help people make some of the most important decisions of their lives. They are consulted about who the best type of marital partner might be, about whether personality differences between mates and potential mates can be overcome, and about the consequences of separation, divorce, conception, and termination of new human life. Their opinions are sought in increasing numbers because the public acknowledges their special expertise. The following episode is one such example:

An "Expert" Opinion

They had done everything possible to make it work. They had seen a therapist for the past several months, and even she came to agree with their decision. They tried everything the therapist suggested. Before that, they had followed the suggestions of their families and friends. They had spent hours talking to find ways to reconcile their differences, but nothing seemed to work. The fights, the tension, the wholly disparate interests, the different backgrounds, and the essentially incompatible personalities were all too great for them to overcome.

He wanted to stay in the town where they had lived all their lives; she wanted to move to the city to accept the promotion she had coveted. He wanted another child; she didn't. She enjoyed people and wanted to be with them more often; he preferred quiet evenings at home with the family. They disagreed about how to allocate their budget, how to discipline the boys, religion, politics, in-laws, and lifestyle. They only agreed that their marriage was constricting them and keeping them from being the kind of people they knew they could be.

The decision to divorce was a relief, because it meant freedom. They would no longer impose their values on the other or have to make a daily choice between arguing or suppressing their feelings. Now they had to make one final decision. It was to be a terrible, gut-wrenching decision, one so painful they could barely allow themselves to think about it. Who would have custody of the children?

Both had been devoted, loving parents. Their two boys were five and seven and seemed to be healthy, happy children. THEY couldn't be asked to decide; all they knew was that they wanted their mom and dad to stay together. But how could the parents decide? Both wanted the boys, yet both knew the children would be in good hands with the other parent.

The mother was more ambivalent than the father. Her career was going places and she vaguely hoped to take the boys to the city. But she wondered if that would be good for them. With her new job, could she give them the attention they needed? She knew the boys wouldn't be so disrupted if they remained with their father. But she would miss them terribly. What would they think of her if she left them? What would her family and their friends think? Everyone she knew believed it wasn't right for a woman to leave her kids. Everyone would think she was an unfit mother, a person who didn't love her family, a selfish person who thought more of her own career than of her children's needs. She needed to discuss it with someone who could be objective. Maybe the therapist could help.

The father wasn't ambivalent at all—only scared. He thought he would do anything to keep them. He would go back to teaching so he could duplicate their school hours. If necessary, he would even take them where no one could ever take them from him. It was a desperate thought, because he knew he would have trouble winning custody. The judges in his county apparently hadn't yet heard about equal rights for fathers. He would try to convince the judge that he should get custody. Maybe the therapist would testify. She said he was very good with the boys.

The therapist had been impressed with this couple. She seldom saw people who were so basically equal in their abilities to provide emotionally stable homes for the children. She knew, as they did, that the boys would do well in either home. Their lives would be different depending on who won custody. With the father, they would probably grow up with a strong interest in athletics, in being small town businessmen with families of their own. With the mother, they might be more inclined toward academics or the fine arts.

The therapist suspected that the mother would be relieved if the boys lived with the father. But pride is powerful; if it was usual for children to live with fathers, then it would be easier for mothers to relinquish them. But that is not the way of the world. Not yet. Maybe in another generation or two, fathers will have as much chance at obtaining custody as mothers. For it to happen now, the mother would have to say, "I agree to give them to their father." But how could a loving mother say such a thing, even if part of her really wants that and feels it is best for all? The therapist, however, could give the mother a face-saving way out. Perhaps she could convince the mother that the children would remain mentally healthier by staying in the small town, with the father. She could say the boys need the parent of the same sex as their role model. Perhaps she could convince the whole family that the mother was doing a noble and loving thing by giving up custody.

Did the therapist know this as fact? Could she really know who would be best? Who can be sure what type of life or home is healthier? These are value judgments, not expert opinions. Who has the right to make decisions about people which will determine the course of their futures? The therapist only knew that she was no less able to offer such an opinion than was the judge. Yet, unless she was convincing about a choice which had no right answer, it would become the judge's decision.

The judge looked down from his bench. He looked first at the mother, then the father, then at the marital therapist. They waited for his decision. Shared custody or splitting the boys was out of the question. Neither parent believed that would work. He contemplated. Both parents had put up a spirited fight to retain custody of their children. Each had employed good lawyers. Both spoke persuasively on the witness stand, justifying with appealing logic why they should get custody. The therapist was good, too. She seemed so convinced that the boys would do better with the father. She had gracefully withstood the mother's lawyer's cross-examination, too. He had challenged her authority, her knowledge, her credentials, her ethics, her ability to make such judgments without equivocation. But she held firm. How could she be so sure?

The judge wondered why the mother didn't seem more antipathetic toward the therapist. She almost seemed to be agreeing with what the therapist was saying. But her lawyer brought in another expert, a therapist who showed how the children's "tender years" necessitated that they continue to live with the mother. Was the expert stating scientific fact? Or was this just a reflection another person's values? Oh, well, it was time for the decision.

"The children's custody is awarded to their mother," the judge said firmly. He was surprised at the response. The father began sobbing. The mother ran to her former husband to comfort him. "Don't worry. I'll come back often. You can see them whenever you want," she said patting the man on his back and looking contemptuously at the judge. The two of them embraced and then cried together as they slowly made their way from the courtroom. At the door they were greeted by their therapist, who joined the tearful embrace. The judge watched the three people hug one another comfortingly. He wished he worked instead in criminal court, on far less Solomonic cases.

The Credibility Gap

What is the basis for a professional person's "expertise?" Why does the consumer consider the opinions of the marital therapist to have value? The general belief that mental health care providers, including marital therapists, have worthwhile opinions and expertise derives from the presumption that their knowledge is both scientific and objective. But both of these premises are being challenged with increasing intensity.

Is the opinion based on scientific knowledge? Scientists who analyze psychotherapy conclude that these fields actually do not use the same kind of systematic rigor needed to remotely qualify as science (Thomas, 1981). Some say therapy is not a science because it only deals with hermeneutics rather than explanation. They say it is humanistic rather than mechanistic, that it attempts to obtain internal, private knowledge rather than observable replicable public knowledge. It is said to be an art, a body of knowledge with a unique status which frees it from the obligations of the true sciences (Jacobs and Williams, 1983).

The theory bases of the psychotherapies, including marital therapy, are rarely tested or testable in a scientific sense. The implications that derive from them have no more scientific validity than do the moral adjurations of religion. They are predictions based on values rather than fact (London, 1969). A therapeutic technique is scientific only insofar as it predicts specific outcomes of particular activities. But most therapies, including marital therapy, cannot incisively specify what the expected outcomes are to be. Those which have specified outcomes have tended to avoid testing their predictions. Most of the few tests that are conducted produce rather unimpressive or ambiguous results. The results that initially appear impressive often turn out to be dubious (U.S. Congress, 1980).

If not scientific, then, is the "expert" opinion valuable because it is objective? To be objective implies that the therapist is free of the biases, human idiosyncracies, illogical conclusions, and value-laden prescriptions which guide others. The objective professional hopes to make judgments about human conflicts based on what is inherently right or wrong. The judgments are not supposed to be based on subjective considerations such as who has the most "healthy" standards of conduct, who has the most noble ideals, who is least internally conflicted, or who is best able to adjust to some socially contrived standard (Karasu, 1980).

Few therapists can or do claim to be neutral beings who avoid imposing any of their values on their clients (Erikson, 1976). Value-free therapy is a myth (Strupp, 1974). Every suggestion, goal assessment, and treatment plan has to be made within a context of values. To think otherwise is to believe there is some universal, static, social norm which can be observed and to which people can be guided. The conscientious marital therapist is not value free and therefore cannot be considered objective.

If not objective and not scientific, then why should the opinions of the marital therapist or other helping professional be considered important? There are several reasons: The therapist's values are explicit and made known to the potential client. The values are compatible with those of the consumer. The therapist is professionally bound to serve within the context of explicated values. The obligation is also met through the therapist's adherence to the professional code of ethics which helps regulate the professional practice. Each factor deserves consideration.

Manifest and Latent Values

It is not always easy for a marital therapist to be aware of his/her own values, much less make them known to others. A distinction must be made between different kinds of values (Merton, 1957). Manifest values are those which are readily apparent to the observer as well as to the person who experiences them. They are what they appear to be. The manifest values of an industrious person might include the desire for hard work rather than taking it easy, perseverance rather than impatience, and economical use of resources rather than the proclivity for squandering impulsively.

Latent values are those not so readily apparent, not to the observer or even to the individual who possesses them. They may be unconscious and are often analogous to defense mechanisms. The latent values of an industrious person might include greed rather than generosity, intolerance rather than forbearance, obsessive-compulsiveness rather than flexibility. The latent value is often not acceptable in the subculture with which the individual identifies, so it is disguised behind something which has more approbation. Thus, the individual can maintain the value which is hidden from those whose approval he seeks. He can have his cake and eat it, too. For example, a person who covertly values the excitement and risk of gambling might devote his attentions to the church bingo game because it is a good way to raise funds for a worthy purpose. Or someone who secretly values efforts to maintain social dominance of one ethnic group over another could manifestly value the legalization of addictive drugs whose use might be popular in the community of that minority group.

Everyone has both kinds of values, and there is nothing inherently wrong with their occurrence. But sometimes a latent value provides justification for beliefs or actions which might not otherwise be taken. A marital therapist, for example, might covertly believe that sexual infidelity is an unforgivable act for which there is no justification or forgiveness. But if his profession tends to advocate open-mindedness, understanding, and acceptance of human frailty, he might go "underground" with his value. He might find volumes of studies which show how pathological and destructive such acts are. He might conduct research which correlates adultery with various forms of mental pathology. He might hold in contempt a client who has had an affair. Without even recognizing it, his judgment about other things is clouded by this fact. He would be more effective in his work if his latent value were made manifest. This would happen if he merely acknowledged that his view about infidelity is a value, and not based on scientific fact. If it is clear to him that it is a value and not a fact, he serves his clients more honestly.

Therapists sometimes claim that some action or cause is best because scientific evidence has proved it to be so. The therapist can convince himself that the opinion is "right," and can find so many quasi-scientific documents which tend to support his view, that he comes to think of it as a verifiable, verified, universal truth, rather than an opinion. His values have acquired the support and respect of others not because they are his values, but because they are allegedly based on science and objectivity.

When therapists recognize their latent values and acknowledge that their treatment goals derive from them rather than from empirically validated fact, they might be more uncomfortable, more uncertain about what is to be done. But at least they are preserving their honesty, their integrity, and facing the reality of the situation.

Values and Expert Opinions

Therapists are more honest about their knowledge today than they were in previous years. They claimed to "know" more than they do now. Many of them were sure that marriages should stay together for the sake of the children, because separations were always harmful to the child's impressionable psyche. They knew that children should stay with their mothers if separations occurred. They were certain that the wives of alcoholics or spouse abusers were masochistic and encouraged the behavior in their mates. It was obvious that women suffered from penis envy and thus were more likely to require therapeutic assistance, usually from men, to help them maximize their limited potentials. Children shouldn't be spanked. Babies should be bottle-fed. Mother should be home with the youngsters. Fathers should be more authoritarian. Men were to be forgiven more than women for infidelity, since it was the natural product of their stronger libidinous impulses. Women were to be given financial support if their husbands left them, because they still needed male protection. One or the other spouse always caused a marriage to break up. Lobotomies helped solve emotional illnesses.

The list of these opinions which once seemed to represent "truth" seems endless. It has only become shorter as therapists have acquired more knowledge; they acknowledge that these universal truths are not so universal and not so true.

To take one example, discussed above, there is the issue of child custody. It was once accepted that children of divorcing parents belonged with their mothers. The view was virtually unchallenged in the United States, and mothers were awarded custody in more than 90 percent of the contested cases (Drinan, 1962). To lose such a case, the mother had to be seen as morally or emotionally unfit. But was this outcome based on scientific fact or on values? Where did such a view originate? Is it natural law, or a decree handed down from God? Or is it really based on the assumption of the child's psychological well-being?

In fact, decisions about child custody are predominately based on the prevailing values of those authorized to make such decisions. There is no scientific proof which demonstrates that children turn out "better" when placed with their mothers or fathers. And it is hard to rely on tradition in the matter, either. Placing custody with mothers is actually of only very recent vintage. It wasn't until the 1920s that mothers started winning custody. For centuries before 1920, it was generally understood that the father would be awarded custody in any dispute (Derdeyn, 1976). This was based on the purely practical notion that since the father owned or managed the family property, he could better support the child.

The change began when the public started to consider more than economic factors, and when women and children achieved greater legal rights. The mental health movement and psychoanalytic insights further contributed to the trend. This resulted in a change of criteria to whatever was deemed in the best interest of the child (Goldstein, Freud and Solnit, 1973). This criterion now appears in the laws of 48 of the 50 states. However, the laws rarely state what or who should decide what "best" is. It was often determined only by trying to prove that one parent was unfit so the custody would be granted to the other. If neither parent was considered unfit, the decision was almost automatically in favor of the mother.

Norms have been changing once again in recent years. Paternal rights are getting more attention; the "mother unless unfit" formula is being challenged. Now the courts often make custody investigations, appoint guardians and call on the "experts" to help in making the decisions. They are defining a new role of "child custody consultant" and looking for the answers in those who supposedly have more knowledge and objectivity for making such decisions (Derdeyn, 1976).

The expertise required to make child custody decisions, or most other decisions about human relationships, is quite illusory. As we have seen, expert opinion cannot be value-free or as objective as desired. It cannot be based on scientific evidence when there are so few universal and lasting truths about human relationships. But since people still want answers, they will seek them from whoever seems to have the knowledge. Marital therapists provide opinions—but not answers. Their opinions are worthwhile, not because of their science or objectiv-

ity, but because the marital therapist is ethically bound to keep the clients interests paramount. It is the ethical code of the therapist which is
the ultimate basis of this credibility.

The Ethics of Marital Therapists

All the helping professions, including marital and family therapy, have
codes of ethics. None of them purport to encompass all the values
which a member might have. They are confined to those which have
achieved general consensus in the profession. A code of ethics is a
framework within which to work, and a prescription of professional
behavior. The profession assures the public that its members will adhere to this code or face the professional organization's sanctions.

However, professional codes of ethics are overendowed with noble
aspirations. At best they provide a modest guide for suggested standards of the profession. They are not definitive enough to automatically make ethical decisions for the marital therapist. Instead, they sen-
sitize the thinking of its members. The code helps the professional to
know the clear ethical boundaries. It helps them avoid impulsive or unethical behavior which exceeds those boundaries. It also attempts to ed-
ucate the professional as to professional responsibilities. Therapists use
the codes for guidance, but typically not for control, vindication, or to
harm the professional (Moore, 1978).

A potential problem is that most marital therapists belong to more
than one professional association, each has its own code. Theoretically
there is the possibility of some conflict between different professions.
But a careful review of the codes of ethics of the American Association
of Marriage and Family Therapists, American Psychological Association, American Family Therapy Association, American Medical Association, American Psychiatric Association, National Association of
Social Workers, American Personnel and Guidance Association,
American Nursing Association, and the American Association of Pastoral Counselors revealed no contradictions or substantive conflicts.

Each professional association has recognized, however, that there
are certain ethical dilemmas facing the individual therapist. There are
sometimes contradictions between what professional codes of ethics say
and what therapists are compelled by law or their own values to do.
Three of the major ethical dilemmas facing marital therapists include
the issues of client self-determination, accountability, and confidentiality.

The Problem of Client Self-Determination

The ethical codes of the marital therapy professions consistently proclaim that it is the client, not the therapist, who ultimately determines goals, treatment methods, and lifestyle. The AAMFT Code, for example, says that the therapist "respects the rights of clients to make their own decisions." Later it states that it is the client's responsibility to decide to divorce or separate. This is, of course, more difficult than it might seem, as was indicated in the discussion in Chapter Four concerning the obstacles to client goal setting.

In many states which license professionals, client self-determination is legally binding through the doctrine of informed consent. Informed consent means that the client must agree to whatever service is being offered and willingly and explicitly must consent to the methods to be employed. To consent, they must be informed about the methods to be used, goals, and possible results. Malpractice verdicts have been consistently awarded against therapists who have not obtained informed consent from their clients before embarking on a procedure which has proved to be harmful to the client.

Informed consent is troublesome for marital therapists because clients may not know enough about the objectives and methods of marital therapy to consent to it. A person might go to a physician or lawyer, and because of the clearly defined expectations of that professional's role, informed consent almost automatically takes place. If the client goes to the marital therapist, however, one cannot assume it exists. The client might believe the sole purpose of the visit is to save the marriage. Some clients expect rapid, positive, low-cost results. Unless the therapist has made it clear when treatment commenced what will happen, what goals and methods will be employed, then the client hasn't given informed consent.

Even then informed consent is complicated. As it is applied in legal or professional ethics disputes, it is seen as a linear process between two, three, or more discrete, rational autonomous parties. It requires the marital therapist to recommend a treatment plan, explain potential benefits, risks, costs, and then obtain permission or refusal to go on with the therapy. The crucial issue is whether or not there was a point at which consent or refusal took place. Informed consent in marital therapy is a process, not a static event, and cannot be abstracted from the total therapy context. The clients consent or refuse to consent as part of this ongoing process (Sider and Clements, 1982). In marital therapy, the husband and wife are not autonomous individuals. They influence one another and invariably will cause one another to accept things which they would not accept if they were really autonomous.

Client self-determination derives from the democratic view that clients have the right to control their own destinies as long as they do not infringe on the rights of others. It logically follows the belief in the client's inherent worth and dignity. To believe otherwise, the therapist would be a paternalistic authority figure. The couple, not the therapist, has the ultimate responsibility for solving or failing to solve the problem. The therapist, as we have seen, not only hasn't the ethical right to do it for the client, but doesn't have all the answers.

However, the principle often contrasts with the expectations some clients ascribe to the therapist. They sometimes want the therapist to make all the decisions, do everything for the client, and remold the client's personality and pattern of relationship with the marital partner. The competent therapist will avoid any such attempts. It not only precludes client self-determination but ultimately defeats the therapy process (Friesen, 1982). Marital therapy is done *with* the couple, and not *to* them. Mistakes and false starts will certainly occur when the clients are responsible for their own selves, but it is worth it.

Self-determination means that the therapist helps the clients become aware of the alternatives available to make informed choices. The marital therapist's expertise lies not in telling clients what to do or knowing what the ultimate outcome of any given course of action will be, but in creating a workable environment in which choices can be made and implemented by the client. This includes providing relevant information, revealing where it can be found, helping the clients to uncover their own potentials and alternatives, and providing emotional support to facilitate their own efforts to implement whatever decisions they have reached.

Client self-determination is not the antithesis of advice giving. It is important for the therapist to share thinking and information, but it should not be presented as an edict from on high: A marital therapist hears a wife's repeated complaint that her husband never listens to her because he is always reading the paper. He might be tempted to advise, "Why don't you read the paper first, and then tell him what you think about some articles you know he will read." This might lead to short-term gains, but is not good therapy. It encourages more dependency, the wish for further advice to deal with the inevitable next problem.

Keeping the client's right of self-determination at the forefront, the marital therapist might say instead: "Have you thought of all the different ways you might get your husband to want to talk with you instead of reading the newspaper?" The wife then considers alternatives, discards some, and experiments with others. She can take credit for her success, and she will feel more confident in her ability to solve problems. If her efforts are not successful, she and the therapist can work together to discover other possibilities. All this, of course, could occur in the presence of the husband just as appropriately as if the wife were alone with the therapist.

The greatest dilemma about this value for the marital therapist is that, since there are at least two people involved, and since they always influence one another, there are limits to self-determination. If they are at odds about a particular course of action, a choice is made to go in one or the other direction. How much self-determination is there for each? There is a fine line between accommodation and self-determination. There is no marriage where self-determination is absolute and accommodation is irrelevant; the married individual must abrogate some self-determination to achieve more enduring goals with the partner.

The Confidentiality Dilemma

Marital therapists and other professionals were once taught unequivocally that it was unethical to divulge information about a client without permission. Not only would breaches of confidentiality violate the client's rights to privacy, but it also would impede the kind of trust and spontaneity considered essential in treatment. Recent social trends have made confidentiality a dilemma rather than an absolute.

Third-party funding was welcomed by therapists and clients alike because it made therapy more accessible—but it came with a string attached. Government and the insurance industry understandably want to know if they got their money's worth. Meanwhile, the various helping professions have wanted assurance that their members were practicing competently. The consumer movement led to the Freedom of Information Act of 1974 which has made it possible in some circumstances for a client to procure the therapist's records if the therapy was conducted in a government-funded organization (Fanning, 1975).

These demands for information may cause ethical problems for marital therapists. In individual therapy where there is a good working relationship, the client can more easily agree to disclose some information. In marital therapy where information about at least two people is on record, it is more complicated. For example, an individual who has later decided upon divorce may want to get the records from a public agency. But the record contains information about the spouse as well. The therapist must then reconcile the rights of the one person to get the information and the rights of the other to preserve confidentiality. Actually, such instances have been rare so far, but the possibility of their occurrence motivates some therapists to keep separate records on each individual. In so doing, they deviate from the essential premise of working with couples rather than with individuals.

Despite outside pressures, confidentiality is important and marital therapists will preserve it whenever possible. Many of the professional associations have already changed the confidentiality provision in their codes of ethics. For example, the AAMFT Code of Ethics now states that confidentiality must exist "to the extent it is permitted by law." The code also states that disclosures are unethical, unless there is a clear and immediate danger to an individual or to society. This provision grows out of the famous Tarasoff decision, which requires therapists in many states to inform potential victims when a client threatens or appears to constitute a danger to that person. The Tarasoff decision involved a young man who told his therapist of his intention to kill a former girlfriend. The therapist notified the police who detained the man. However, after the police released him, he carried out his threat and killed the girl. Her family won a suit against the therapist and his agency for failing to warn them of the girl's peril. The decision was upheld in the California Supreme Court.

Thus some therapists are compelled to warn people they don't know in order to protect them from their own clients. For example, a woman revealed to her husband and therapist that she had been having an affair with another man. The husband was enraged and threatened to beat the other man to death. If the therapist practiced in a state which is subject to the Tarasoff ruling and adheres to the letter of the law, he would have to breach confidentiality and notify the other man. Obviously this would alienate the clients and probably result in their stopping treatment. Then the therapist could do nothing to help the husband assuage his emotions and end the threat.

The Tarasoff ruling applies to California, but many other states use the decision as a partial basis for coming to a similar decision. Some states don't have such requirements. In fact, some have upheld malpractice verdicts against therapists who did warn potential victims about clients' threats, citing deviations from the professional codes of ethics about confidentiality.

Professionals have been advised to deal with this contradiction by discretely retaining the primacy of their confidentiality value (Roth and Meisel, 1977). They say that confidentiality is so important and the interpretation of the law regarding warnings so conjectural that it is usually in the best interests of the couple, the therapist, and society to refrain from most divulgences without permission. The therapist might simply explain the legal limitations of confidentiality to the couple, and indicate the remote circumstances in which such disclosures might have to take place. Then when the therapist is in a position where a confidence might have to be broken, the matter should be thoroughly discussed with the couple. This is by no means a cure-all for a serious dilemma, but only an expedient means by which to deal with a clearly contradictory set of expectations.

The Issue of Accountability

Accountability is demanded of marital therapists by a justifiably cautious public. Professionals are required, through public statute and their codes of ethics, to live up to prescribed standards. They are supposed to do what they claim to do. They are supposed to demonstrate their competence to impartial observers.

This is not so easy to do. Mental health care professionals can demonstrate their adherence to specified standards, but they can't prove satisfactorily that their service is worthwhile or effective. Before there was much stress on accountability, this determination was an individual matter. The client would decide whether the service was worthwhile or not. If it seemed not to be worth it, the client would simply discontinue treatment. If the therapist violated any standards, the client would notify the therapist's professional organization. But in recent years, clients are no longer the primary sources of payment for their own treatment. Clients pay only about 20 percent of the costs of mental health care in the United States at the present time (Barker, 1982). The third parties, i.e., government and insurance companies, which directly pay the rest, want to know if the provider is capable of doing an effective job.

Marital therapists may have more problems in accounting to the public or to third parties than do other helping groups. One reason is because its goals are so diverse. Since the goal of marital therapy is more than to save marriages, the test of its efficacy is dubious. What is to be proved? It will not be possible to show the public that marital therapy is effective without some standard or goal by which to demonstrate the degree to which success or failure was achieved.

Another reason accountability may cause more problems for marital therapists than for other professionals is because of the fragmentation of the field. Marital therapists belong to many different professions; the norms of professional behavior are primarily prescribed for those who practice marital therapy by the other professions to which they belong. These norms are fairly compatible and consistent from one profession to another, but regulation and enforcement of these standards may be difficult in the field of marriage and family therapy.

For a client to seek the services of a marital therapist, therefore, is a somewhat risky procedure. Since the norms for the field are still so ill-defined and not controlled by any single professional entity, the consumer must exercise caution. Potential consumers have been advised by Joanne and Lew Koch (1976) to beware of the many quacks who exploit troubled marriages. Using the services of well-established clinics or professionals who belong to the well-established marital therapy–providing disciplines might be the safest action for most people to take. The Kochs also suggest that the therapist in an established clinic is more likely to be supervised or subject to stringent quality controls.

The Value of Values

The values of the marital therapist are an important determinant of the goals, methods, directions, and merit of the treatment relationship. They are useful as guidelines and frames of reference for both therapist and client. The fact that marital therapy is value-laden does not negate or even detract from its usefulness or importance for the client. The field has a well-defined set of guiding ethical principles which any conscientious marital therapist follows. The ethical considerations call for primacy of the client's interests, maintaining competence to provide service, honesty and integrity, confidentiality to the extent permitted by law, and responsibility to the professional field, to the marriage and family institution, and to society as a whole.

Beyond that, each marital therapist might have unique values which are not within the sanction of the profession. The field is expansive enough to allow its members to have a variety of different values; there is room in the field for those therapists who advocate traditional marriage norms and for those who seek dramatic changes. There are therapists who value the preservation of the marriage more than the well-being of the individuals, while others take the opposite stance. Some therapists may justifiably believe that some behaviors or standards of conduct by either client or therapist are immoral and unconscionable, while others might feel these behaviors are normal and healthy.

The point is that, when values and ethics are concerned, as they inevitably are in this field, there is no single right or wrong ethical resolution to the varied and complex dilemmas marital therapists face. Therapists can only rely to a minor extent on the codified instruments of their professions to guide them as to what is or is not ethical conduct and value-based advocacy. The therapist may facilitate the process of seeking these answers through exploration of the issues with professional colleagues. The therapist would also do well to seek to improve and strengthen the professional ethical codes and their enforcement procedures, and to live up to the highest principles which are espoused for the profession. Above all else, the therapist maintains a therapeutic alliance with the husband and wife so that there is less risk of the imposition of values on them. The couple will be establishing their own goals and maintaining their own integrity when these principles are rigorously observed.

Chapter Fifteen

New Directions for Marital Therapy?

Marital therapy cannot offer a happy resolution to every unhappy marriage; its goals and promises will always be more modest. It cannot ultimately determine the way marriages should be. It can't even determine what should be considered healthy marital functioning—only society can do that. At its best, marital therapy will remain limited to helping some people clarify their expectations of their partners and look at their mates more realistically. It will help some people more effectively adapt and communicate, and become closer to their spouses. It can be only one of several tools couples may use to facilitate workable relationships, or it can help them ease out of their relationships with somewhat less harm to the family members. It might help marital partners understand and cope with the major changes they will face through the life of their relationship. If marital therapy can help achieve these modest objectives, it will be fulfilling its major function.

Yet even with limited goals and modest promises, marital therapy and therapists now face considerable challenges. Incessant debate centers upon who are best suited to do it, and what theories and methods are most appropriate. The field is subjected to closer public scrutiny than ever before. Many question its efficacy, or wonder if it really does immediate or lasting good. The public insists on more protection from unscrupulous or unqualified practitioners. Reputable marital therapists do not obstruct these trends; indeed, they have been at the forefront of public efforts to answer these questions and to regulate and control the practice of marital therapy. The trouble is, as we have already seen, marital therapy cannot be effectively regulated or judged as to efficacy outside the context of goals. The goals will be hard to reach if they keep changing or are contradictory. They will always fluctuate as long as society has changing expectations and standards for marriage itself.

Marriage is in transition. The direction it takes will determine the most appropriate course for marital therapy. When society decides what marriage should be, then marital therapy can be properly evaluated and regulated, and therapists can be judged as to their "success rate." They may then address the recurrent question, "How many couples are you helping to reach the socially accepted view of healthiness in their marriages?"

However, American society seems no closer to consensus about marriage norms than ever. There is great variety of marital styles and greater toleration of deviation from any supposed standard. Marital therapy seems destined to follow the path of marriage itself, possibly toward increased versatility, greater variegation, more disparate values. It seems probable that future marital therapy will serve many different kinds of marriages using different methods and theories; a single type of marital therapy for all types of clients is unlikely.

If more versatility in marriage and marital therapy occurs, many questions must be raised: Should the field of marital therapy even try to influence society toward a "healthy" marital functioning? Should it work toward a uniform national family policy which supposedly fosters this kind of marriage? Should the field itself strive to have uniform philosophies and goals? Should it be one profession or many? Should therapists have uniform methodologies, training, and standards? Should the public have a single standard for the regulation of all marital therapy? What skills and methods of marital therapy are effective toward what ends? Should therapists be limited in their practice, through licensing requirements, to stay with only proven methods, or should they be encouraged to innovate? The direction of marital therapy cannot be predicted until more of these questions are answered.

Should Marital Therapists Seek National Family Goals?

Every culture recognizes the importance of marriage and the family and, in one way or another, tries to keep them healthy and functional.

But there is wide disparity among nations as to what is considered healthy or functional. Marriages based on the economic or psychological dependence of women upon men in asymmetrical relationships, for example, may seem to be the paragon of desirability to some and entirely unsuitable to others. There is disparity among nations as to what family needs will be given priority and what family goals will be sought. Many nations, for example, attempt to influence their populations by imposing tax incentives or penalties on those who would marry and procreate. Some countries pay for marital therapy or couples' enrichment programs. Others simply make it illegal to divorce or permit only men to initiate such action. Some countries pay a parent to remain at home to care for younger children; others subsidize child care services out of the home to encourage both parents to work. Many nations have explicit, uniform policies specifying how they want their families to be, while others prefer to let families decide for themselves how they will conduct their own lives and relationships (Kamerman and Kahn, 1982). The diversity of policies strongly and clearly suggests that there is no single right or wrong decision about the "best" policy. It is a society's predominate value system, traditions, mores, and social objectives, not some natural law, which determine how families and marriages should be.

Compared with most other developed nations of the world, the United States has been laissez-faire in its attitude about marital and family issues. Government involvement has been mostly secondary and residual. There are numerous programs which have a direct or indirect impact on marriages and families, but rarely are they designed as part of a uniform effort to achieve any national objective (Padberg, 1979). There has been little national policy regarding marriages and families. (Policy is defined as a coherent set of principles guiding action.) The traditional arbiter of public involvement with marriage, divorce, child custody, abortion, adoption, child and spouse abuse, and the many other elements of family protection and preservation has been the individual state, and not the federal government. This is consistent with the national ethos which permits an open society and variety of lifestyles.

Movements toward a national family policy are usually very controversial in the United States. For example, one debate occurred in the 1980 White House Conference on Families. An argument centered around whether the nation should do anything to encourage and support marriages and family life. If so, should support go only to one kind of family style or many? If many, which types? Should only traditional families be nurtured and sustained, some delegates asked, or should efforts be also made to serve nonconventional forms of relationships?

Should homosexual unions, communal families, divorced groups, non-marital cohabitation, and other styles be recognized, sanctioned, encouraged, supported? If not, then shouldn't the nation do more to positively encourage the type of family relationship deemed acceptable? The debate ended without resolution; the effect of no resolution is that the laissez-faire policy continues.

Should marital therapists work toward the development of a national family policy? If it existed, the work of the marital therapist would be less confusing; it would make possible the development of uniform standards for practice. Practitioners could be better evaluated as to how well they help fulfill the explicit national goals. The field could impose more accurate quality controls on its practitioners and thus offer better protection to the consumer. But convenience for marital therapists is not the purpose of a national family policy. When marital therapists seek such a policy, they do so because of their conviction that it is good for marriages and families, not good for therapists.

The nation accepts varied lifestyles and demands freedom from government influence. Thus, if family policies ever come, they will be the result of a slowly evolving political and social process. Marital therapists will probably have some small impact on this process. They will be called upon by relevant social institutions to provide their expertise and information about what the goals and policy could be. But, as discussed in the previous chapter, marital therapy is no more value-free or objective than are other institutions. Moreover, those seeking answers from marital therapists will hear conflicting voices—different goals and methods will be advocated. Therapists may become more active as advocates and as organizers to mobilize the public toward one or another family policy, but they have far to go before they could be of one mind about what these goals and methods should be.

Should Marital Therapy Seek a Uniform Methodology?

A diverse methodology has always been a mixed blessing for marital therapy practitioners and consumers. The fact that no one method has yet been established as *the* method for marital therapy has contributed mightily to its creativity and vitality. This diversity has attracted practitioners from different orientations and created a field which is at the heart of interprofessional synergy. On the other hand, serious problems have been the result of the diversity. It has become exceedingly difficult to determine what therapy methods are useful. This diversity obstructs efforts to test efficacy and regulate practitioners, making it hard to protect the public from unqualified marital therapists. Since it is impossible to rationally specify what those qualifications are to be, almost anyone can claim some expertise in marital therapy and justify almost any method or theoretical orientation. If marital therapy methodology consisted of anything one wants to do, then standards or protections for the field would be a hopeless idealization.

Since the nation has not yet defined uniform goals for the marriages of its citizens, there can be no uniform marital therapy goal. Since methodology is only the means of achieving a stated goal, there will not be one methodology practiced by all marital therapists. For the foreseeable future, there are likely to be many methodologies, each designed around a specific goal; the therapy will be designed for a specific clientele. This prediction does not auger well for the hope of a single profession of marital therapy.

Should Marital Therapy Be One Profession?

Primarily because there has been so little uniformity of marital therapy goals or methods, the field has not become a single profession. Its practitioners, if they have any formal training at all, are from most of the helping professions, particularly psychology, social work, psychiatry, the clergy, law, educational counseling, and nursing. A field with practitioners of such disparate backgrounds is naturally going to be in the center of controversy. The professions involved have occasionally had jurisdictional disputes and internecine struggles for predominance in the field. Practitioners have debated ad nauseum about what type of training is best and what theory and practice are most useful. Energies which could have been devoted to treating couples in crisis have sometimes been exhausted trying to resolve issues such as these. There is no question but that the field suffers because it has not been a single profession.

Not being a unified profession has prevented marital therapy from being as influential as its potential would indicate. The vast majority of practicing marital therapists owe their primary allegiance to other professions since they were trained in those professions and usually maintain that licensure. The practitioner has limited time; if he devotes it to his principal profession, he has that much less time for representing the field of marital therapy. If marital therapy were a unified profession, its practitioners would be able to devote their energies to extending its influence. Licensing, educational requirements, continuing education, competency examinations, peer review, and more rigorous standards would result. More important, the consumer of marital therapy would have greater assurance of receiving treatment from a reputable person.

Marital therapy would also lose something if it became a single profession. Because its practitioners come from a variety of other orientations, the field is rich with innovation and the communication of different ideas. It brings together and uses the concepts and practical experiences of many. As such it is less inclined to become caught in dogmatic ideologies or organizational and professional rigidities. It is like a young city located on a major trade route—its opportunities for growth and development are immense.

Whether one sees more advantages or disadvantages to a unified profession for marital therapy may be a matter of personal orientation. But the question posed, "Should it be a unified profession?", is moot. Unification appears unlikely in the foreseeable future, whether or not it is considered desirable. The professions whose members practice marital therapy will not suddenly refrain from doing it; their training and experience are too extensive, and their marital therapy is too valuable. Social agencies, church organizations, and private practitioners who have established reputations for providing competent marital therapy can't be expected to close their doors or fire all employees who belong to professions other than marital therapy. Graduate and professional schools, seminaries and training programs will not end their programs. Professions will not cease their interest in the provision of such important services. So even if a single marital and family therapy profession emerges and becomes widely influential, it will not have exclusive authority for this work. For years to come, the field will be known as "the marital therapy professions."

Should Marital Therapy Have Uniform Standards?

Whether or not the field is a unified profession, the public still has the right to be protected from unqualified or unethical practitioners. To protect that right, consumers need to be informed about what is needed to be a qualified marital therapist, and whether the practitioner meets those qualifications. Generally this is done through legal statute and licensing. The service provider is permitted to practice in the jurisdiction in which he has a license, and must fulfill certain criteria to obtain the license. The requirements usually include specific types and amounts of approved training, passing tests to further demonstrate proficiency, and proof of continuing eduction. Finally, the practitioner's peers periodically review his work to make sure the public is protected.

Inconsistent public regulation makes it difficult for the field to maintain professional standards. Standards for marital therapists have not been uniform nationally or interprofessionally. Marital therapists have not been historically successful in their efforts to correct the problem. Licensing for marital therapy existed in less than half the states until the 1980s; even now, the standards for licenses vary widely among those states which do license (Sporakowski and Staniszewski, 1980). To obtain a license to practice in some states, one needs only to be recommended by other license holders. In other states there are extensive examinations, reexaminations, and rigorously enforced criteria for practice. Most practitioners want such regulation and are the major impetus for a jurisdiction to develop licensing laws; but these are not easy for marital therapy to acquire. As we noted above, marital therapy practitioners have less influence than those of other professions, largely because they may be engaged in efforts in behalf of their original professions. The field must contend with its inability to clearly define its unique expertise. It cannot always clearly distinguish between competent and incompetent practice, but doing so is the most important ingredient in justifying licensing.

The other obstacle to licensing marital therapy results from the variety of professions involved in this practice. Many who work with troubled marriages will do so under the auspices of their original profession and so will not be affected by marital therapy licensing. Furthermore, there is great variability among the professions as to what constitutes enough training, sufficient knowledge, and demonstrable proficiency. It is challenging to find the right standards which would encompass all the professions practicing marital therapy without excluding some competent practitioners or weakening standards.

Thus, even though the field will probably not soon have uniform goals, methods, or a unified profession, it is imperative that its conscientious practitioners work toward standards. It might be necessary to be arbitrary in stating what the requirements for licensed marital therapy practice might be. The American Association of Marital and Family Therapists, the largest multidisciplinary professional organization in the field, is spearheading the movement to adopt standards. The organization has developed model statutes for state licensing of marital therapists, and many of its state affiliates are lobbying legislatures for legal regulation (Hiebert, 1982). Professionally and legally mandated standards will, however, require more than public licensing and someone to enforce conformity to the license. To achieve such conformity, there still needs to be more consensus about what those standards should be as well as the general willingness to conform to them.

Conclusion

Marriage, for better or worse, in sickness and in health, in one form or another, is here to stay. So too, in one form or another, is therapy for troubled marriages. Yet both are on the thresholds of change. Present trends suggest that there will be greater variability of marital styles. If so, further diversity among marital therapists is predictable. Even if American society grows intolerant of divergent marital lifestyles and demands a single standard for all marriages, marital therapy now seems destined to remain diverse. The expanding knowledge base of the field is already leading to more specialization. Some marital therapists will always help couples achieve traditional family and marital goals; others will help couples achieve quite different lifestyles. Marital therapists, in helping couples achieve whatever goals they may have, will need to be more flexible, open minded, and conscientious than ever. When they are, marriage and marital therapy can live together happily ever after.

References

ACKERMAN, N. *The Psychodynamics of Family Life*. New York: Basic Books, 1958.

ACKERMAN, N., AND BEHRANS, N.L. "Family Diagnosis and Clinical Process." In *American Handbook of Psychiatry*, Vol, II, S. Arieti, editor. New York: Basic Books, 1974.

ALLEN, G., AND MARTIN, C.G. *Intimacy: Sensitivity, Sex and the Art of Love*. Chicago: Cowles Books, 1971.

AMERICAN ASSOCIATION OF MARRIAGE AND FAMILY THERAPISTS. "Ethical Principles for Family Therapists." *Family Therapy News*, May 1982.

————. "Task Force Recommends Mandatory CE." *Family Therapy News*, March 1982.

AMERICAN PSYCHIATRIC ASSOCIATION. *Diagnostic and Statistical Manual of Mental Disorders*. Third Edition (DSM-III). Washington: American Psychiatric Association, 1980.

ANDOLFI, M., AND ANGELO, C. "The Therapist as Director of the Family Drama." *Journal of Marital and Family Therapy* 7:3 (July 1981):255–264.

ANNON, J.S. *Behavioral Treatment of Sexual Problems*. New York: Harper & Row, 1976.

APONTE, H.J. "The Person of the Therapist: The Cornerstone of Therapy." *Family Therapy Networker* 6:2 (1982):19–45.

APPLETON, W.S. "The Effect of Retirement on Marriage." *Medical Aspects of Human Sexuality* 15:10 (October 1981):73–87.

BACH, G.R., AND WYDEN, P. *The Intimate Enemy: How to Fight Fair In Love and Marriage.* New York: William Morrow, 1969.

BANE, M.J. "Marital Disruption and the Lives of Children." *Journal of Social Issues* 32 (1976):103–117.

BANDLER, R., AND GRINDER, J. *The Structure of Magic.* Palo Alto, Calif.: Science and Behavior Books, 1975.

BANDURA, A. "The Self System in Reciprocal Determinism." *American Psychologist* 33 (1978):344–358.

BARBARO, F. "The Case Against Family Policy." *Social Work* 24:6 (November 1979):455–458.

BARKER, R.L. *The Business of Psychotherapy.* New York: Columbia University Press, 1982.

BARKER, R.L., AND BRIGGS, T.L. *Using Teams to Deliver Social Services.* Syracuse: Syracuse University Press, 1969.

BART, P.B. "The Myth of a Value-Free Psychotherapy." *Sociology and the Future.* E.W. Bell, editor. New York: Basic Books, 1972.

BATESON, G. *Steps to an Ecology of the Mind.* New York: Ballantine, 1972.

BECK, D.F. "Research Findings on the Outcome of Marital Counseling." *Social Casework* 56 (1975):153–181.

BECK, D.F., AND JONES, M.A. *Progress on Family Problems.* New York: Family Service Association of America, 1973.

BELL, N.W., and VOGEL, E.F., *A Modern Introduction to the Family.* Glencoe, Ill.: The Free Press, 1960.

BENJAMIN, A. *The Helping Interview.* Third Edition. Boston: Houghton Mifflin, 1981.

BENJAMIN, J.E. "Family Consultation Service as a Function of a Family Agency." *Family Life and National Recovery.* New York: Family Welfare Association of America, 1935.

BENT, R.J.; PUTNAM, D.G.; KEISLER, D.J.; AND NOWICKI, J. "Expectancies and Characteristics of Outpatient Clients Applying for Services at a Community Mental Health Facility." *Journal of Consulting and Clinical Psychology* 43 (1975):280–282.

BERARDO, F.M.; VERO, H.; AND BERARDO, D.H. "Age Discrepant Marriages." *Medical Aspects of Human Sexuality* 17:1 (January 1983).

BERMAN, E. "The Individual Interview as a Treatment Technique in Conjoint Therapy." *American Journal of Family Therapy* 10:1 (Spring 1982).

BERMAN, E.M., AND LIEF, H.I. "Marital Therapy from a Psychiatric Perspective: An Overview." *American Journal of Psychiatry* 132 (1975):583–592.

BERNARD, J. *The Future of Marriage*. New York: World Publishing, 1972.

————. "The Good Provider Role: Its Rise and Fall." *American Psychologist* 36:1 (1981):1–12.

BERNSTEIN, B. "Malpractice: An Ogre on the Horizon." *Social Work* 23:2 (March 1978):106–112.

BIRD, C. *The Two-Paycheck Marriage*. New York: Rawson Wade, 1979.

BIRDWHISTELL, R.L. *Kinesics and Context: Essays on Body Motion Communication*. Philadelphia: University of Pennsylvania Press, 1970.

BLANCK, R., AND BLANCK, G. *Marriage and Personal Development*. New York: Columbia University Press, 1968.

BLOCK, S., AND CHODOFF, P. *Psychiatric Ethics*. New York: Oxford University Press, 1981.

BLOOD, R., AND BLOOD, M. *Marriage*. New York: The Free Press, 1972.

BLOOM, B.L. *Changing Patterns of Psychiatric Care*. New York: Human Sciences Press, 1975.

BLOOM, M.L. "Usefulness of the Home Visit for Diagnosis and Treatment." *Social Casework* 54 (1973):67–73.

BOWEN, M. *Family Therapy in Clinical Practice*. New York: Aronson, 1978.

BRENT, D.A., AND MARINE, E. "Developmental Aspects of Cotherapy Relationship." *Journal of Marital and Family Therapy* 8:2 (April 1982):69–77.

BRIDGEMAN, R.P. "Guidance for Marriage and Family Life." *Annals of the American Academy of Political and Social Science*, March 1932.

BRISCOE, C.W., AND SMITH, J.B. "Psychiatric Illness—Marital Units and Divorce." *Journal of Nervous and Mental Disease* 158 (1974):440–445.

BRISSON, N. "A Program to Help Spouse Abusers." *Public Welfare*, Spring 1982:14–16.

BRODY, S. "Simultaneous Psychotherapy of Married Couples." In *Current Psychiatric Therapies*, J. Masserman, editor. New York: Grune & Stratton, 1961.

BUIE, D.H. "Empathy: Its Nature and Limitations." *Journal of the American Psychoanalytic Association* 29 (1981):281–307.

BURGWYN, D. *Marriage Without Children*. New York: Harper & Row, 1981.

CAPLAN, G. "Patterns of Parental Response to the Crisis of Premature Birth." *Psychiatry* 23 (1960):365–374.

CAPLOW, T. *Two Against One: Coalition in Triads*. Englewood Cliffs, N.J.: Prentice–Hall, 1968.

CARTER, R.D., AND GLICK, P.C. *Marriage and Divorce: A Social and Economic Study*. Cambridge, Mass.: Harvard University Press, 1976.

CASHDAN, S. *Interactional Psychotherapy: Stages and Strategies in Behavioral Change*. New York: Grune & Stratton, 1973.

CAVENOR, J.O., AND WERMAN, D.S. "The Sex of the Psychotherapist." *American Journal of Psychiatry* 140:1 (January 1983):85–91.

CHESLER , P. "Patient and Patriarch: Women in the Psychotherapy Relationship." In *Sexist Society*, V. Gornick and B.K. Moran, editors. New York: Basic Books, 1971.

————. *Women and Madness*. Garden City, N.Y.: Doubleday, 1972.

CLATWORTHY, N.M. "Living Together." In *Old Family/New Family: Interpersonal Relationships*. New York: Van Nostrand, 1975.

COLAPINTO, J. "The Relative Value of Empirical Evidence." *Family Process* 18 (1979):427–441.

COMBS, A.W.; AVILA, D.L.; AND PURKEY, W.W. *The Helping Relationship*. Second Edition. Boston: Allyn & Bacon, 1978.

CONSTANTINE, L., AND CONSTANTINE, J. *Group Marriage: A Study of Contemporary Multilateral Marriage*. New York: Macmillan, 1973.

COOGLER, O.J.; WEBER, R.E.; AND McHENRY, P.C. "Divorce Mediation: A Means of Facilitating Divorce and Adjustment." *The Family Coordinator* 28 (1979):255–259.

COOKERLY, J.R. "The Outcome of the Six Major Forms of Marriage Counseling Compared." *Journal of Marriage and the Family* 36 (1973):608–611.

CUBER, J. *Marriage Counseling Practice*. New York: Appleton–Century–Crofts, 1948.

CUMMING, E., AND HENRY, W.E. *Growing Old: The Process of Disengagement*. New York: Bantam Books, 1961.

CURTIS, J.H., AND MILLER, M.E. "An Argument for the Use of Paraprofessional Counselors in Premarital and Marital Counseling." *The Family Coordinator* 25 (1976):47–50.

DAVIS, D.R. "The Therapist as Mediator: Lessons from Plays." *Journal of Family Therapy* 1 (1979):67–73.

DECTER, M. *The New Chastity and Other Arguments Against Women's Liberation*. New York: Coward–McCann & Geoghegan, 1972.

DEPARTMENT OF HEALTH AND HUMAN SERVICES. *Monthly Vital Statistics Reports: Final Divorce Statistics, 1980*. DHHS Publication No. PHS 80–1120. Washington: Government Printing Office, 1980.

DERDEYN, A.P. "Child Custody Contests in a Historical Perspective." *American Journal of Psychiatry* 133:12 (December 1976):1369–76.

DEUTSCH, F.M., AND LEONG, F.T.L. "Male Responses to Female Competence." *Sex Roles: A Journal Of Research* 9:1 (January 1983):79–93.

DICKS, H.V. *Marital Tensions*. Boston: Routledge & Kegan Paul, 1967.

DRINAN, R.F. "The Rights of Children in Modern American Family Law." *Journal of Family Law* 2 (February 1962):101–109.

DUBERMAN, L. *Marriage and Its Alternatives*. New York: Praeger, 1974.

DURANT, W. *Caesar and Christ*. New York: Simon & Schuster, 1944.

————. *Our Oriental Heritage*. New York: Simon & Schuster, 1935.

EDELSON, M. "Psychoanalysis as Science: Its Boundary Problems, Special Status, Relations to Other Sciences and Formalizations." *Journal of Nervous and Mental Disorders* 165 (1977):1–25.

EDINBURG, G.N.; ZINBERG, N.E.; AND KELMAN, W. *Clinical Intervention and Counseling: Principles and Techniques*. New York: Appleton–Century–Crofts, 1975.

EHRENREICH, B. "After the Breadwinner Vanishes." *The Nation*, February 26, 1983.

ELLIS, A.E. "Family Therapy: A Phenomenological and Active Directive Approach." *Journal of Marriage and Family Counseling* 2:4 (October 1976):305–315.

————. "Techniques for Handling Anger in Marriage." *Journal of Marriage and Family Counseling* 2:4 (April 1978):43–50.

ELLZEY, W.C. "Education for the Newly Married." *Pastoral Psychology* 19:184 (1968):21–25.

ENOCH, L., AND SIGEL, G. "Third-Party Reimbursement: Countertherapeutic Considerations." *Psychiatric Opinion* 16:7 (1979):8–16.

EPSTEIN, J. *Divorced in America*. New York: E.P. Dutton, 1974.

ERIKSON, E. *Childhood and Society*. Second Edition. New York: W.W. Norton, 1963.

————. "Psychoanalysis and Ethics—Avowed and Unavowed." *International Review of Psychoanalysis* 3 (1976):409–415.

FAMILY SERVICE ASSOCIATION. *Casebook on Family Diagnosis and Treatment*. New York: Family Service Association of America, 1965.

FANNING, J. "Protection of Privacy and Fair Information Practices." In *Social Welfare Forum 1975*, pp. 115–120. New York: Columbia University Press, 1975.

FARLEY, J.E. "Family Separation-Individuation Tolerance: A Developmental Conceptualization of the Nuclear Family." *Journal of Marital and Family Therapy* 5:1 (January 1979):61–68.

FEFFER, M. "A Developmental Analysis of Interpersonal Behavior." *Psychological Review* 77 (1970):119–129.

FELDMAN, L.B. "Goals of Family Therapy." *Journal of Marital and Family Counseling* 2:2 (April 1976):103–113.

FELDMAN, P.M. "Hidden Expectations of Marriage." *Medical Aspects of Human Sexuality* 16:4 (April 1982):61–64.

FENTON, N. "Foreword." In *Divorce Mediation* by H.H. Irving. New York: Universe Co., 1980.

FIELDS, N.S. "Satisfaction in Long-Term Marriages." *Social Work* 28:1 (January 1983).

FIESTER, A.R., AND RUDESTAM, E. "A Multivariant Analysis of the Early Dropout Process." *Journal of Consulting and Clinical Psychology* 43 (1975):528–535.

FINE, S. "Troubled Families: Parameters for Diagnosis and Strategies for Change." *Comprehensive Psychiatry* 15:1 (January 1974):73–77.

FISHER, B.L.; GIBLIN, P.R.; AND HOOPES, N.H. "Healthy Family Functioning: What Therapists Say and What Families Want." *Journal of Marital and Family Therapy* 8: 3 (July 1982):273–284.

FISHER, B.L., AND SPRENKLE, D. "Therapists' Perception of Healthy Family Functioning." *International Journal of Family Counseling* 6 (1978):1–10.

FISHER, C.E. "A Guide to Divorce Counseling." *The Family Coordinator* 22 (1973):55–61.

FISHER, L. "Dimensions of Family Assessment: A Critical Review." *Journal of Marriage and Family Counseling* 2:4 (October 1976): 376–382.

FLETCHER, B.C. "Marital Relationships as a Cause of Death." *Human Relations* 36:2 (1983).

FOSTER, R.G. "Servicing the Family Through Counseling Agencies." *American Sociological Review*, 2:4 (October 1937):461–464.

FOSTER, S.L., AND HOIER, T.S. "Behavioral and Systems Family Therapies: A Comparison of Theoretical Assumptions." *American Journal of Family Therapy* 10:3 (Fall 1982).

FRANK, E., AND KUPFER, D.J. "In Every Marriage There Are Two Marriages." *Journal of Sex and Marital Therapy* 2 (1976):137–143.

FRANK, E.; ANDERSON, C.; AND RUBENSTEIN, D. "Marital Role Ideals and Perception of Marital Role Behavior in Distressed and Nondistressed Couples." *Journal of Marital and Family Therapy* 6:1 (January 1980):55–64.

FRANK, J. "The Present Outcome of Efficacy Studies." *Journal of Consulting and Counseling Psychology* 47:310 (1979).

FREEMAN, D.R. *Marital Crises and Short-Term Counseling: A Casebook.* New York: The Free Press, 1982.

FRIEDMAN, P.H. "Outline of 26 Techniques of Marital Therapy: A Through Z." *Psychotherapy* 11 (1974):259–264.

FRIESEN, V.I., AND CASELLA, N.T. "The Rescuing Therapist: A Duplication of the Pathogenic Family System. *American Journal of Family Therapy* 10:4 (Winter 1982).

FROMM, E. *The Anatomy of Human Destructiveness.* Greenwich, Ct: Fawcett, 1975.

GARDNER, R.K. *The Parents' Book About Divorce.* New York: Doubleday, 1977.

GARRETT, A. *Interviewing: Its Principles and Methods.* Second Edition. New York: Family Service Association of America, 1972.

_____. "The Worker–Client Relationship." *American Journal of Orthopsychiatry* 19:2 (April 1949).

GELLES, R.J. *The Violent Home: A Study of Physical Aggression Between Husbands and Wives.* Beverly Hills: Sage Publications, 1972.

GILBERT, C. "Women's Place in Man's Life Cycle." *Harvard Educational Review* 49:431 (1979).

GINGRAS-BAKER, S. "Sex-Role Stereotyping and Marriage Counseling." *Journal of Marital and Family Counseling* 2:4 (October 1976):355–365.

GLEASON, J., AND PRESCOTT, M.R. "Group Techniques for Premarital Preparation." *The Family Coordinator* 53 (1977):551–562.

GLICK, I.D., AND KESSLER, D.R. *Marital and Family Therapy.* Second Edition. New York: Grune & Stratton, 1983.

GLICK, P. "A Demographer Looks at American Families." *Journal of Marriage and the Family* 37 (1975):15–26.

GOLDBERG, M. "How to Prevent Marital Sexual Estrangement." *Medical Aspects of Human Sexuality* 17:2 (February 1983).

GOLDMAN, J., AND COANES, J. "Family Therapy After the Divorce: Developing a Strategy." *Family Process* 16 (1977):357–362.

GOLDSTEIN, J.; FREUD, A.; AND SOLNIT, A.L. *Beyond the Best Interests of the Child.* New York: The Free Press, 1973.

GOLDSTEIN, S.E. *Marriage and Family Counseling.* New York: McGraw–Hill, 1945.

GOODSELL, W. *A History of the Family as a Social and Educational Institution.* Revised Edition. New York: Macmillan, 1934.

GOODSTEIN, R.K., AND PAGE, A.W. "Battered Wife Syndrome: Overview of Dynamics and Treatment." *American Journal of Psychiatry* 138:8 (August 1981):1036–1044.

GOTTLEIB, J. "Responses of Married Couples Included in a Group of Single Patients." *International Journal of Group Psychotherapy* 10 (1960):143–159.

GOULD, R.J. "The Phases of Adult Life: A Study in Developmental Psychology." *American Journal of Psychiatry* 129:5 (1972):521–531.

GREEN, R., AND COX, G. "Social Work and Malpractice: A Converging Course." *Social Work* 23:2 (March 1978):100–103.

GREEN, R.G., AND KOLEVZON, M.S. "Three Approaches to Family Therapy: A Study of Convergence and Divergence." *Journal of Marital and Family Therapy* 8:2 (April 1982):39–50.

GREENE, B., AND SOLOMON, A. "Marital Disharmony: Concurrent Psychoanalytic Therapy of Husband and Wife by the Same Psychiatrist." *American Journal of Psychiatry* 17 (1963): 443–450.

GREENE, B.L. "Types of Distress Which Threaten Marriage." *Medical Aspects of Human Sexuality*, January 1980, pp. 149–150.

GREENE, R. *Human Sexuality: A Health Practitioner's Text.* Baltimore: Williams & Wilkins, 1975.

GREENWALD, H. "Marriage as a Non-Legal Voluntary Association." In *The Family in Search of a Future*, H.A. Otto, editor. New York: Appleton–Century–Crofts, 1970.

GROBE, S. "Sunset Laws." *American Journal of Nursing*, July 1981, pp. 1355–1357.

GROUP FOR THE ADVANCEMENT OF PSYCHIATRY. *The Case History Method in the Study of the Family Process.* GAP Report No. 76. New York: Group for the Advancement of Psychiatry, 1970.

GROVER, I., AND OTHERS. "Sex-Role Stereotypes in Clinical Judgements of Mental Health." *Journal of Consulting and Clinical Psychology* 34 (1976).

GUILDNER, C.A. "The Post Marital Followup: An Alternative to Premarital Preparation." *The Family Coordinator* 26 (1977):277–280.

GURMAN, A.S. "Contemporary Marital Therapies: A Critique and Comparative Analysis of Psychodynamic, Behavioral and Systems Theory Approaches." In *Marriage and Marital Therapy*, T.J. Paolino and B.S. McCrady, editors, pp. 445–566. New York: Brunner/Mazel, 1978.

———. "Dimensions of Marital Therapy: A Comparative Analysis." *Journal of Marital and Family Therapy* 5:1 (January 1979):5–18.

GURMAN, A.S., AND KNISKERN, D.P. "Deterioration in Marital and Family Therapy: Empirical, Clinical and Conceptual Issues." *Family Process* 17 (1978):3–20.

———. "Enriching Research on Marital Enrichment Programs." *Journal of Marriage and Family Counseling* 3 (1977):3–11.

HALEY, J. "The Art of Being a Failure as a Therapist." In *The Power Tactics of Jesus Christ and Other Essays.* New York: Grossman, 1969.

———. "Marriage Therapy." *Archives of General Psychiatry* 18 (1968):213–234.

———. *Problem Solving Therapy.* San Francisco: Jossey–Bass, 1977.

———. *Strategies of Psychotherapy.* New York: Grune & Stratton, 1963.

———. "Why a Mental Health Clinic Should Avoid Family Therapy." *Journal of Marriage and Family Counseling* 1:1 (January 1975):3–14.

HALL, E. *The Hidden Dimension.* New York: Doubleday & Co., 1966.

HARRY, J. "Evolving Sources of Happiness for Men Over the Life Cycle: A Structural Analysis." *Journal of Marriage and the Family* 38 (1976):289–296.

HAYNES, J. *Divorce Mediation.* New York: Springer Publishing Co., 1981.

HAYWOOD, R. *The Myth of Rome's Fall.* New York: Thomas Y. Crowell, 1958.

HENTON, J.; RUSSELL, R.; AND KOVAL, J. "Spouse Perception of Midlife Career Change." *American Personnel and Guidance Journal* 61:5 (January 1983): 287–291.

HERTZMAN, M., AND HERTZMAN, R.Z. "Marital Conflicts Caused by Alcoholism." *Medical Aspects of Human Sexuality* 15:7 (July 1981).

HIEBERT, W.J. "Family Therapy Licensure vs. Certification." *Family Therapy News*, March 1982:7–9.

HIRSCHFELD, R.N., AND CROSS, C.K. "Epidemiology of Affective Disorders." *Archives of General Psychiatry* 39 (1982):35–46.

HOFFMAN, L. *Foundations of Family Therapy.* New York: Basic Books, 1981.

HOKANSON, J.E. "Physiological Evaluation of the Catharsis Hypothesis." In *The Dynamics of Aggression*, E.W. Megargee and J.E. Hokanson, editors, pp. 74–86. New York: Harper and Row, 1970.

HOLLIS, F. *Women in Marital Conflict.* New York: Family Service Association, 1949.

_____, AND WOODS, M.E. *Casework: A Psychosocial Therapy.* Third Edition. New York: Random House, 1981.

HOLMES, T.H., AND RAHE, R.H. "The Social Readjustment Rating Scale." *Journal of Psychosomatic Research* 11:216. Reprinted in *Psychiatric Annals* 11:7 (July 1981):34.

HORNEY, K. *Our Inner Conflicts.* New York: Norton, 1945.

HOUGHKIRK, E. "Everything You've Always Wanted Your Clients to Know But Were Afraid to Tell Them." *Journal of Marriage and Family Therapy* 3:2 (April 1977):27–35.

HUMPHREY, F.G. "Changing Roles for Women: Implications for Marriage Counselors." *Journal of Marriage and Family Counseling* 1:3 (1975):219–228.

_____. *Marital Therapy.* Englewood Cliffs, N.J.: Prentice-Hall, 1983.

HUNT, M.M. *The Natural History of Love.* New York: Alfred A. Knopf, 1959.

_____. *Sexual Behavior in the 1970s.* Chicago: Playboy Press, 1974.

_____. *The World of the Formerly Married.* New York: McGraw–Hill, 1966.

IRVING, H.H. *Divorce Mediation.* New York: Universe Books, 1980.

JACKMAN, S. "Anxieties About the Body Which Hinder Sexual Intimacy." *Medical Aspects of Human Sexuality* 14:6 (June 1980).

JACOBS, D., AND WILLIAMS, V. "Clinical Theory and Scientism: Empathy Research as a Case Study." *Journal of Humanistic Psychology* 23:1 (Winter 1983).

Jacobson, G.F. *The Multiple Crises of Marital Separation and Divorce*. New York: Grune & Stratton, 1983.

Jacobson, N.S. "A Review of the Effectiveness of Marital Therapy." In *Marriage and Marital Family*, T.J. Paolino and B.S. McCrady, editors, pp. 395–444. New York: Brunner/Mazel, 1978.

———. "The Effects of Divorce on Fathers." *American Journal of Psychiatry*, 139:2 October 1982.

Jacobson, N.S., and Margolin, G. *Marital Therapy*. New York: Brunner/Mazel, 1979.

Jacques, J.M.; Chason, K.J.; and Saul, D.L. "Premarital Cohabitation Does Not Improve Marital Progress." *Medical Aspects of Human Sexuality* 16:5 (May 1982).

Jager, R. *The Development of Bertrand Russell's Philosophy*. New York: Columbia University Press, 1972.

Jankovich, R., and Miller, P.R. "Responses of Women with Primary Orgasmic Dysfunction to Audio-Visual Education." *Journal of Sex and Marital Therapy* 4 (1978): 16–19.

Johnson, T.F. "Hooking the Involuntary Family into Treatment: Family Therapy in a Juvenile Court Setting." *Family Therapy 1 (1974): 79:82.*

Jourard, S.M., and Jaffe, P.G. "Influence of and Interviewers' Disclosure on the Self-Disclosing Behavior of Interviewees." *Journal of Counseling Psychology* 17 (1970): 252–257.

Jung, C.G. *Man and His Symbols*. New York: Doubleday & Co., 1964.

Kadushin, A. *The Social Work Interview*. Second Edition. New York: Columbia University Press, 1983.

Kamerman, S., and Kahn, A.J. *Helping America's Families*. Philadelphia: Temple University Press, 1982.

Kamerman, S., and Kahn, A.J., editors. *Family Policy: Government and Families in Fourteen Countries*. New York: Columbia University Press, 1978.

Kaplan, H.S. *Disorders of Sexual Desire*. New York: Brunner/Mazel, 1979.

———. *The New Sex Therapy*. New York: Brunner/Mazel, 1974.

Karasu, T.B. "The Ethics of Psychotherapy." *American Journal of Psychiatry* 137:12 (December 1980):1502–1512.

Karson, A., and Karson, M. "Counseling Couples in Their Sixties." *Social Work*, May 1978, pp. 243–244.

Kassel, V. "Polygamy After Sixty." In *The Family in Search of a Future*, H.A. Otto, editor. New York: Appleton–Century–Crofts, 1970.

Kegel, A.H. "Sexual Functions of the Pubococcygeus Muscle." *Western Journal of Surgery, Obstetrics, and Gynecology* 60:2 (1952):521–524.

Kentsmith, D.K.; Crossman, J.A.; Lacy, S.; and Scott, J. "Sex Problems:

When to Treat and When to Refer." *Medical Aspects of Human Sexuality* 15:10 (October 1981). 21–24.

KERCKHOFF, R.K. "Marriage and Middle Age." *Family Coordinator* 25 (January 1976):8–15.

KILGO, R.D. "Can Group Marriage Work?" *Sexual Behavior* 6:2 (February 1972):2–8.

KNAPP, J. "Some Non-Monogamous Marriage Styles and Related Attitudes and Practice of Marriage Counselors." *The Family Coordinator* 24 (1975):505–514.

KNAPP, M.L. *Nonverbal Communication in Human Interaction.* Second Edition. New York: Holt, Rinehart & Winston, 1978.

KOCH, J., AND KOCH, L. *The Marriage Savers.* New York: Coward–McCann & Geoghegan, 1976.

KOTLAR, S.L. "Role Theory in Marriage Counseling." *Sociology and Social Research:* 52 (1967):50–62.

KRANTZLER, M. *Creative Divorce.* New York: Signet, 1975.

KRESSLER, K., AND DEUTSCH, M. "Divorce Therapy: An In-Depth Survey of Therapists' Views." *Family Process* 16 (1977):413–444.

L'ABATE, L., AND McHENRY, S. *Methods of Marital Intervention.* New York: Grune & Stratton, 1983.

LANGS, R. *The Therapeutic Environment.* New York: Jason Aronson, 1979.

LANSKY, M.R., AND DAVENPORT, A.E. "Difficulties in Brief Conjoint Treatment of Sexual Dysfunction." *American Journal of Psychiatry* 132:2 (1975):177–178.

LAZARUS, A.A. Divorce Counseling or Marriage Therapy: A Therapeutic Option." *Journal of Marital and Family Therapy* 7:1 (January 1981):15–22.

LEDERER, W.J., AND JACKSON, D.D. *The Mirages of Marriage.* New York: W.W. Norton, 1968.

LEE, R., AND CASEBEIR, M. *The Spouse Gap.* New York: Abingdon Press, 1971.

LEVANT, R.F. "Developmental Processes in Marriage." *Medical Aspects of Human Sexuality* 16:8 (August 1982):77–92.

LEVINSON, D.J., AND ASSOCIATES. *The Seasons of a Man's Life.* New York: Alfred A. Knopf, 1978.

LIDDLE, H.A., AND HALPIN, R.J. "Family Therapy Training and Supervision: A Comparative Review." *Journal of Marriage and Family Counseling* 4:4 (October 1978):99–108.

LIDZ, T. "The Effects of Children on Marriage." In *The Marriage Relationship,* S. Rosenbaum, editor. New York: Basic Books, 1968.

LIEF, H.I. "Forword." In *Principles and Practice of Sex Therapy,* S.R. Leiblum and L.A. Pervin, editors. New York: Guilford Press, 1980.

————. "The Importance of Marriage in Mental Health." *Psychiatric Annals* 12:7 (July 1982):671–676.

LINDEMANN, E. "Symptomatology and Management of Acute Grief." *American Journal of Psychiatry* 101:9 (September 1944):141–148.

LLOYD, P.A., AND PAULSON, I. "Projective Identification in the Marital Relationship as a Resistance in Psychotherapy." *Archives of General Psychiatry* 27 (1972):410–413.

LONDON, P. *The Modes and Morals of Psychotherapy.* New York: Holt, Rinehart & Winston, 1969.

LUBORSKI, L., AND BACHRACH, H. "Comparative Studies of Psychotherapies." *Archives of General Psychiatry* 32:10 (October 1975):995–1008.

LUBOVE, R. *The Professional Altruist.* Cambridge, Mass.: Harvard University Press, 1968.

LUTHER, G., AND LOEV, I. "Resistance in Marital Therapy." *Journal of Marital and Family Therapy* 7:4 (October 1981):475–480.

MACE, D.R. "Marital Intimacy and the Deadly Love–Anger Cycle." *Journal of Marriage and Family Counseling* 2:4 (October 1976):305–316.

————. *Marriage Counseling.* London: J.A. Churchill, 1948.

————. "Premarital Counseling." In *Marriage Counseling.* London: J.A. Churchill, 1948.

MacKINNON, R.A., AND MICHELS, R. *The Psychiatric Interview in Clinical Practice.* Philadelphia: Saunders & Co., 1971.

MADANES, C. *Strategic Family Therapy.* San Francisco: Jossey–Bass, 1981.

MAHLER, M.S.; PINE, F.; AND BERGMAN, A. *The Psychological Birth of the Human Infant.* New York: Basic Books, 1975.

MALINOWSKY, B. *Magic, Science, and Religion [and Other Essays].* Glencoe, Ill.: The Free Press, 1948.

MANCINI, J.A. "Strengthening Marital Relations of Older Adults." *Medical Aspects of Human Sexuality* 17:1 (January 1983):14–16.

MANUS, G.I. "Marriage Counseling: A Technique in Search of a Theory." *Journal of Marriage and the Family* 28 (1966):449–452.

MARGULIES, A., AND HAVENS, L.L. "The Initial Encounter: What to Do First?" *American Journal of Psychiatry* 138:4 (April 1981):421–429.

MARKS, I.M. "Review of Behavioral Psychotherapy II: Sexual Disorders." *American Journal of Psychiatry* 138:6 (June 1981):750–756.

MASTERS, W.H., AND JOHNSON, V.E. *Human Sexual Inadequacy.* Boston: Little, Brown & Co., 1970.

————. "Sex and the Aging Process." *Journal of the American Geriatric Society* 29:385 (January 1981):385–390.

McDONALD, D. "Coalition Formation in Marital Therapy Triads." *Family Therapy* 2 (1975):141–148.

McMurtry, J. "Monogamy: A Critique." In *Marriage and Alternatives: Exploring Intimate Relationships.* R.W. Libby and R.N. Whitehurst, editors, p. 3–14. Glenview, Ill.: Scott, Foresman, 1977.

Mead, M. "Anomalies in American Post-Divorce Relationships." In *Divorce and After*, P. Bohannan, editor. New York: Doubleday, 1970.

————. "Jealousy: Primitive and Civilized." In *Jealousy*, G. Clanton and L. Smith, editors. Englewood Cliffs, N.J.: Prentice–Hall, 1977.

Mehrabian, A. *Nonverbal Communication.* Chicago: Aldine, 1972.

Meisse, M. "Judgements and the Nonjudgemental Attitude in Therapeutic Relationships." *Social Casework* 41 (1965):27–41.

Meissner, W.W. "The Conceptualization of Marriage and Family Dynamics from a Psychoanalytic Perspective." In *Marriage and Marital Therapy*, T.J. Paolino and B.S. McCrady, editors, pp. 25–88. New York: Brunner/Mazel, 1978.

Merton, R.K. *Social Theory and Social Structure.* New York: The Free Press, 1957.

Messinger, L. "Remarriage Between Divorced People with Children from Previous Marriages: A Proposal for Preparation for Remarriage." *Journal of Marriage and Family Counseling* 2 (1976):193–200.

Meyer, J.K., editor. *Clinical Measurement of Sexual Disorders.* Baltimore: Williams & Wilkins, 1976.

Miller, H., and Geller, D. "Structural Balance in Dyads." *Journal of Personality and Social Psychology* 21 (1972):135–138.

Miller, M. "Beyond 'Mm-Hm': The Importance of Counselor Disclosure." *Counseling and Values* 27: (January 1983):90–99.

Minuchin, S. *Families and Family Therapy.* Cambridge, Mass.: Harvard University Press, 1974.

————. "Interview with Salvador Minuchin." *Family Therapy Practice Network Newsletter* 3 (1980):5–10.

Minuchin, S., and Fishman, H.C. *Family Therapy Techniques.* Cambridge, Mass.: Harvard University Press, 1981.

Mittleman, B. "Concurrent Analysis of Married Couples." *Psychoanalytic Quarterly* 17 (1948):182–197.

Mogul, K. "Overview: The Sex of the Therapist." *American Journal of Psychiatry* 139:1 (January 1982):1–11.

Moore, R.A. "Ethics in the Practice of Psychiatry: Origin, Function, Models and Enforcement." *American Journal of Psychiatry*, January 1978, pp. 157–163.

Moreno, J.L. *Who Shall Survive?* New York: Beacon House, 1953.

Morris, R.J., and Zuckerman, K.R. "Therapist Warmth as a Factor in Automated Systematic Desensitization." *Journal of Consulting and Clinical Psychology* 42 (1974):244–250.

MUNJACK, D.J., AND OZIEL, L.J. "Resistance in the Behavioral Treatment of Sexual Dysfunction." *Journal of Sex and Marital Therapy* 4 (1972):122–138.

NADELSON, C.C. "Marital Therapy from a Psychoanalytic Perspective." In *Marriage and Marital Therapy*, T.J. Paolino and B.S. McGrady, editors, p. 89–164. New York: Brunner/Mazel, 1978.

NATIONAL CENTER FOR HEALTH STATISTICS. *Health U.S. 1981.* Washington, D.C.: Government Printing Office, 1982.

NEUGARTEN, B.L. "Personality and the Aging." In *Human Aging*, S. Crown, editor, pp. 243–255. Baltimore: Penguin Books, 1973.

NEUGARTEN, B.L., AND OTHERS. *Personality in Middle and Late Life.* New York: Atherton, 1964.

NICHOLS, W.C. "Education and Training in Marital Therapy." *Journal of Marital and Family Therapy* 5:3 (July 1979):3–6.

NIERENBERG, G.I., AND CALERO, H.H. *Meta-Talk: Guide to Hidden Meanings in Conversations.* New York: Simon & Schuster, 1973.

NOLL, J. "Needed—A Bill of Rights for Clients." *Professional Psychologist*, May 1974, pp. 3–12.

NOONAN, J.R. "A Follow-Up of Pretherapy Dropouts." *Journal of Community Psychology* 1 (1973):43–45.

NORTON, A., AND GLICK, P.G. "Marital Instability: Past, Present and Future." *Journal of Social Issues*, May 1976: 5–20.

OBERNDORF, C.P. "Psychoanalysis of Married Couples." *Psychoanalytic Review* 25 (1938):453–475.

O'LEARY, K.D., AND TURKEWITZ, H. "A Comparative Outcome Study of Behavioral Marital Therapy and Communication Therapy." *Journal of Marital and Family Therapy* 7:2 (April 1981): 159–169.

OLSON, D.; SPRENKLE, D.; AND RUSSELL, C. "Circumplex Model of Marital and Family Systems." *Family Process* 18 (1979):159–169.

OLSON, D.H. "Marriage of the Future: Revolutionary or Evolutionary Change." *Family Coordinator* 24:1 (1972):411–418.

O'NEILL, N., AND O'NEILL, G. *Open Marriage: A New Life Style for Couples.* New York: J.B. Lippincott, 1972.

OSMOND, H. "Function as a Basis of Psychiatric Ward Design." *Mental Hospital* 8:4 (April 1957):44–49.

OVERTURF, J. "Marital Therapy: Toleration of Differentness." *Journal of Marital and Family Therapy* 2:3 (July 1976):235–241.

PADBERG, W.W. "Complexities of Family Policy: What Can Be Done?" *Social Work* 24:6 (November 1979):451–454.

PAOLINO, T.J., AND MCGRADY, B.S., EDITORS. *Marriage and Marital Therapy.* New York: Brunner/Mazel, 1978.

PAPP, P. "The Greek Chorus and Other Techniques of Family Therapy." *Family Process* 19 (1980):45–58.

PARSONS, T., AND BALES, R.F. *Family: Socialization and Interaction Process.* New York: The Free Press, 1955.

PATTON, B.R., AND GIFFEN, K. Interpersonal Communication. New York: Harper & Row, 1974.

PEARLIN, L.I., AND JOHNSON, J.S. "Marital Status, Life Strains and Depression." *American Sociological Review* 42 (1977):704–715.

PECK, E., AND SENDEROWITZ, J., EDITORS. *The Myth of Mom and Apple Pie.* New York: Thomas Y. Crowell, 1974.

PERLMAN, H.H. "Diagnosis, Anyone?" *Psychiatry and Social Science Review* 3:8 (1970):12–17.

———. "Intake and Some Role Considerations." In *Personna: Social Role and Personality*, H.H. Perlman, editor, pp. 50–62. Chicago: University of Chicago Press, 1968.

———. *Relationship: The Heart of Helping People.* Chicago: University of Chicago Press, 1979.

PERSONS, R.W.; PERSONS, M.K.; AND WOMARK, J. "Perceived Helpful Therapists' Characteristics, Client Improvement and Sex of the Therapist and Client." *Psychotherapy* 11 (1974):63–65.

PIAGET, J. *Play, Dreams, and Imitation in Childhood.* New York: W.W. Norton, 1962.

PIETROPINTO, A., AND SIMENAUER, J. *Husbands and Wives: A Nationwide Survey of Marriage.* New York: Times Books, 1979.

PINE, S. "Troubled Families: Parameters for Diagnosis and Strategies for Change." *Comprehensive Psychiatry* 15 (1947):73–77.

POLANSKY, D., AND NADELSON, C. "Marital Discord and the Wish for Sex Therapy." *Psychiatric Annals* 1:2 (July 1982): 685–696.

POMEROY, W.B.; FLAX, C.C.; AND WHEELER, D.G. *Taking a Sex History: Interviewing and Recording.* New York: The Free Press, 1982.

PROCHASKA, J., AND PROCHASKA, J. "Twentieth Century Trends in Marriage and Marital Therapy." In *Marriage and Marital Therapy*, T.J. Paolino and B.S. McCrady, editors. New York: Brunner/Mazel, 1978.

QUICK, E., AND JACOB, T. "Marital Disturbance in Relation to Role Therapy and Relationship Theory." *Journal of Abnormal Psychology* 82 (1973):309–316.

RABIN, C.; ROSENBERG, H.; AND SENS, M. "Home Based Marital Therapy for Multiproblem Families." *Journal of Marital and Family Therapy* 8:4 (October 1982):451–463.

RAPAPORT, R. "Normal Crises, Family Structure and Mental Health." *Family Process* 2:1 (1963).

Rapoport, L. "The State of Crisis: Some Theoretical Considerations." In *Crisis Intervention: Selection Readings*, H.J. Parad, editor, pp. 222–231. New York: Family Service Association of America, 1964.

Read, D.A. *Healthy Sexuality*. New York: Macmillan, 1979.

Redick, R.W., and Johnson, C. "Marital Status, Living Arrangements, and Family Characteristics of Admission to State and County Medical Hospitals and Outpatient Psychiatric Clinics." Rockville, Md.: National Institute of Mental Health, 1970.

Reik, T. *Listening with the Third Ear*. New York: Ferrar, Straus & Giroux, 1977.

Reiner, B.S., and Edwards, R.L. "Adolescent Marriage—Social or Therapeutic Problem?" *The Family Coordinator* 23 (1974):383–390.

Report of the FSAA Committee on Marriage Counseling. New York: Family Service Association of America, 1943.

Rhodes, S.L. "A Developmental Approach to the Life Cycle of the Family." *Social Casework*, May 1977, pp. 301–311.

Rhodes, S.L., and Wilson, J. *Surviving Family Life*. New York: G.P. Putnam's Sons, 1981.

Rice, J.K., and Rice, D.G. "Status and Sex Role Issues in Co-Therapy." In *Couples in Conflict: New Directions in Marital Therapy*, A. Gurman and D. Rice, editors. New York: Aronson, 1975.

————. "Implications of the Women's Liberation Movement for Psychotherapy." *American Journal of Psychiatry* 130 (1973):191–196.

Ritterman, M. "Paradigmatic Classification of Family Therapy Theories." *Family Process* 16 (1977):29–48.

Roberts, W. "Strengths and Weaknesses of Co-Therapy." In *Family Therapy: Complementary Frameworks for Theory and Practice*, A. Bentovim, G. Gorell-Barnes, and A. Cooklin, editors. New York: Grune & Stratton, 1982.

Rogers, C. *Becoming Partners: Marriage and Its Alternatives*. New York: Dell, 1972.

————. "The Necessary and Sufficient Conditions of Therapeutic Personality Change." *Journal of Consulting Psychology* 21 (1957): 95–103.

————. *On Becoming a Person*. Boston: Houghton Mifflin, 1970.

Rollins, B.G., and Cannon, K.L. "Marital Satisfaction Over the Family Life Cycle." *Journal of Marriage and the Family* 36 (1974):271–283.

Roth, L., and Meisel, A. "Dangerousness, Confidentiality and the Duty to Warn." *American Journal of Psychiatry* 134:5 (1977):508–512.

Russell, A., and Russell, L. "The Uses and Abuses of Co-Therapy." *Journal of Marital and Family Therapy* 5:1 (January 1979):39–47.

Russell, B. *Marriage and Morals*. New York: Liveright, 1929.

RUTAN, J.S., AND ALONSO, A. "Group Therapy, Individual Therapy or Both?" *International Journal of Group Psychotherapy* 32:3 (July 1982): 267–282.

RUTLEDGE, A.L. *Premarital Counseling.* Cambridge, Mass.: Schenkman, 1966.

SAGER, C.J., AND OTHERS. "The Marriage Contract." *Family Process* 10:3 (1971): 311–326.

———. *Marriage Contracts and Couple Therapy.* New York: Brunner/Mazel, 1976.

———. "The Development of Marriage Therapy: A Historical Review." *American Journal of Orthopsychiatry* 36 (1966):458–467.

———. "Transference in Conjoint Treatment of Married Couples." *Archives of General Psychiatry* 16 (1967)185–193.

SALZMAN, L. "Choosing a Spouse." *Medical Aspects of Human Sexuality* 16:1 (January 1982):33–39.

SATIR, V. *Conjoint Family Therapy.* Palo Alto, Calif.: Science and Behavior Books, 1967.

———. "Conjoint Marital Therapy." In *The Psychotherapy of Marital Disharmony*, R.C. Greene, editor. New York: The Free Press, 1965.

———. *Peoplemaking.* Palo Alto, Calif.: Science and Behavior Books, 1972.

SCANZONI, J. *Sexual Bargaining: Power Politics in American Marriage.* Englewood Cliffs, N.J.: Prentice–Hall, 1972.

SCHERZ, F.H. "Motivational Crisis and Parent–Child Interaction." *Social Casework* 60 (June 1971):140–146.

SCHOEN, R. "Measuring the Tightness of a Marriage Squeeze." *Demograph* 20:1 (February 1983).

SCHRAM, R.W. "Marital Satisfaction Over the Family Life Cycle." *Journal of Marriage and the Family* 41 (February 1979): 109–114.

SCHUMM, W.R., AND DENTON, W. "Trends in Premarital Counseling." *Journal of Marital and Family Therapy* 5:4 (October 1979): 27–29.

SCHUTZ, W.C. *Joy: Expanding Human Awareness.* New York: Grove Press, 1967.

SCORESBY, A.L. *The Marriage Dialogue.* Reading, Mass.: Addison–Wesley, 1977.

SCOTT, F.B., AND OTHERS. "Impotence: The Changing Diagnostic Strategy." *Sexual Medicine Today* 7:8 (August 1983):14–19.

SEAGRAVES, R.T. "Marriage and Mental Health." *Journal of Sexual and Marital Therapy* 6 (1980):197–198.

SELVINI-PALAZZOLI, M., AND OTHERS. "The Problem of the Referring Person." *Journal of Marital and Family Therapy* 6:1 (January 1980): 3–10.

SHAHADY, E.J. "Extramarital Sexuality." *Sexual Medicine Today* 6:5 (May 12, 1982):24–29.

SHAW, G.B. *Getting Married and Other Plays.* London: W. Blank Co., 1908.

SHEEHY, G. *Passages.* New York: E.P. Dutton, 1976.

SIDER, R.C., AND CLEMENTS, C. "Psychiatry's Contribution to Medical Ethics Education." *American Journal of Psychiatry* 139:4 (April 1982):498–501.

SIMON, R. "When Family Therapy Was in Flower." *Family Therapy Networker* 5:5 (October 1981):1–6.

SINGER, L.J. *Stages: The Crises That Shape Your Marriage.* New York: Grosset & Dunlap, 1980.

SLUZKI, C.E. "Coalitionary Processes in Initiating Family Therapy." *Family Process* 14 (1975):67–77.

———. "Process of Symptom Production and Patterns of Symptom Maintenance." *Journal of Marital and Family Therapy* 7:3 (July 1981):273–281.

SMITH, G.W. *Couple Therapy (Me and You and Us).* New York: Collier Books/Macmillan, 1973.

SMITH, V.G., AND HAMMOND, D.C. *Relationship Therapy.* San Francisco: Jossey–Bass, 1980.

SOLOMON, M.A. "The Staging of Family Treatment: An Approach to Developing the Therapeutic Alliance." *Journal of Marriage and Family Counseling* 3:2 (April 1977):59–66.

SOMMER, R. "Further Studies in Small Group Ecology." *Sociometry* 24:4 (April 1965):337–348.

SPECK, R.V., AND ATTNEAVE, C.L. "Social Network Intervention." In *Progress in Group and Family Therapy*, C.J. Sager and H.S. Kaplan, editors, pp. 416–439. New York: Brunner/Mazel, 1972.

SPEER, D. "Family Systems: Morphostatis and Morphogenesis, or Is Homeostatis Enough?" *Family Process* 9 (1970):259–279.

SPITZ, R., AND SPITZ, S. "Co-therapy in the Management of Marital Problems." *Psychiatric Annals* 10:4 (December 1980):119–126.

SPORAKOWSKI, M.J., AND STANISZEWSKI, W.P. "The Regulation of Marriage and Family Therapy." *Journal of Marital and Family Therapy* 6:3 (July 1980):335–348.

SPRENKLE, D.H., AND FISHER, B.L. "An Empirical Assessment of the Goals of Family Therapy." *Journal of Marital and Family Therapy* 6:2 (April 1980):131–139.

SPRENKLE, D.H.; KEENEY, B.P.; AND SUTTON, P.M. "Theorists Who Influence Clinical Members of A.A.M.F.T.: A Research Note." *Journal of Marital and Family Therapy* 8:3 (July 1982):367–369.

STANTON, M.D.; STEIR, F.; AND TODD, T.C. "Paying Families for Attending Sessions: Counteracting the Dropout Problem." *Journal of Marital and Family Therapy* 8:3 (July 1982):371–373.

STANTON, M.D., AND TODD, T.C. "Engaging Resistant Families in Treatment." *Family Process* 20 (1981):261–293.

STARTZ, M.R., AND EVANS, C.W. "Developmental Phases of Marriage and Marital Therapy." *Social Casework* 62 (June 1981):343–351.

STEIN, S. "Common-Law Marriage: Its History and Certain Contemporary Problems." *Journal of Family Law* 9 (1969):271–299.

STEINFELD, G.J. "Decentering and Family Process: A Marriage of Cognitive Therapies." *Journal of Marital and Family Therapy* 4:3 (July 1978):61–70.

STONE, H., AND STONE, A. *A Marriage Manual.* New York: Simon & Schuster, 1935.

STRUPP, H. "Some Observations on the Fallacy of a Value-Free Psychotherapy and the Empty Organism." *Journal of Abnormal Psychology* 83 (1974):199–201.

STUART, R.B. *Helping Couples Change: A Social Learning Approach to Marital Therapy.* New York: Guilford, 1980.

SULLIVAN, H.S. *The Interpersonal Theory of Psychiatry.* New York: Norton, 1953.

SUNDLAND, D.M. "Theoretical Orientations of Family Therapists." In *Effective Psychotherapy,* A. Gorman and A. Razir, editors. New York: Pergamon, 1977.

TAMASHIRO, R.T. "Developmental Stages in the Conceptualization of Marriage." *Family Coordinator* 27:237 (1978).

TENNOV, D. *Love and Limerence.* New York: Stein & Day, 1979.

THOMAS, L. "Medicine Without Science." *Atlantic Monthly,* April 1981, pp. 40–44.

THOMPSON, A.P. "Extramarital Sex: A Review of the Literature." *Journal of Sex Research* 19:1 (February 1983):1–23.

THOMPSON, L., AND SPANIER, G. "The End of Marriage and Acceptance of Marital Termination." *Journal of Marriage and the Family* 45:1 (February 1983):103–114.

TITMUSS, R.A. *The Gift Relationship.* New York: Pantheon, 1971.

TOOLEY, M. "The Diagnostic Home Visit: An Aid in Training and Case Consultation." *Journal of Marriage and the Family* 1:4 (October 1975):317–332.

TRAINER, J.B. "Premarital Counseling and Examination." *Journal of Marital and Family Therapy* 5:2 (April 1979):61–78.

TRUAX, C.B., AND MITCHELL, K.M. "Research on Certain Therapist Interpersonal Skills in Relationship to Process and Outcome." In *Handbook of Psychotherapy and Behavioral Counseling,* A.E. Bergin and S.L. Garfield, editors. New York: Wiley, 1971.

TUBBS, S.L., AND MOSS, S. *Human Communication: An Interpersonal Perspective*. New York: Random House, 1974.

TURKEL, A.R. "The Impact of Feminism on the Practice of a Woman Analyst." *American Journal of Psychoanalysis* 36 (1976):119–126.

TURNER, B., AND TROLL, L. "Sex Differences in Psychotherapy with Older People." *Psychotherapy: Theory, Research and Practice* 19:4 (Winter 1982).

TURNER, F.J. *Psychosocial Therapy*. New York: The Free Press, 1978.

UNITED NATIONS. "Marriage Rates." *Monthly Bulletin of Statistics* xxxvii:2 (February 1983).

UNITED STATES BUREAU OF THE CENSUS. *Census of the Population, 1980.* Washington, D.C.: Government Printing Office, 1981.

―――. "Marital Status and Living Arrangements." *Current Population Reports*, June 1982. Washington, D.C.: Government Printing Office.

―――. *Number, Timing and Duration of Marriages and Divorces in the United States*. Washington, D.C.: Government Printing Office, 1979.

―――. "Social and Economic Characteristics of Americans During Midlife." In *Current Population Reports*, June 1981. Washington, D.C.: Government Printing Office.

UNITED STATES CONGRESS, OFFICE OF TECHNOLOGY ASSESSMENT. "The Efficacy and Cost Effectiveness of Psychotherapy." Background Paper No. 3, *Implications of Cost Effectiveness Analysis of Medical Technology*. Washington, D.C.: Government Printing Office, 1980.

UNITED STATES DEPARTMENT OF HEALTH AND HUMAN SERVICES. "Marriage and Divorce Statistics." In *Vital Statistics of the United States*. Washington, D.C.: Government Printing Office, 1981.

VINES, N.R. "Adult Unfolding and Marital Conflict." *Journal of Marital and Family Therapy* 5:2 (April 1979):5–14.

WALKER, P.W. "Premarital Counseling for the Developmentally Disabled." *Social Casework* 58:5 (1977): 281–287.

WALLERSTEIN, J.S. "Children of Divorce: The Psychological Tasks of the Child." *American Journal of Orthopsychiatry* 53:2 (April 1983).

WATSON, R.E.L. "Premarital Cohabitation vs. Traditional Courtship: Their Effects on Subsequent Marital Adjustment." *Family Relations* 33:1 (January 1983):23–29.

WATZLAWICK, P. "Communication Theory and Clinical Change." In *Family Therapy*, P. Guerin, editor. New York: Gardner, 1976.

WATZLAWICK, P.; BEAVIN, J.H.; AND JACKSON, D.D. *Pragmatics of Human Communication: A Study of Interactional Patterns, Pathologies and Paradoxes*. New York: Norton, 1967.

WATZLAWICK, P.; WEAKLAND, J.H.; AND FISCH, R. *Change: Principles of Problem Formation and Problem Resolution*. New York: Norton, 1974.

WEAKLAND, J., AND OTHERS. "Brief Therapy: Focused Problem Resolution." *Family Process* 13 (1974) 141–169.

WELLS, J.G. "A Critical Look at Personal Marriage Contracts." *The Family Coordinator* 25 (1976):33–37.

WELLS, R.A. "Engagement Techniques in Family Therapy." *International Journal of Family Therapy* 2 (1980):75–94.

WHITAKER, C. "The Hindrance of Theory in Clinical Work." In *Family Therapy: Theory and Practice*, P. Guerin, editor. New York: Grune & Stratton, 1976.

WHITEHURST, R.N. "The Monogamous Ideal and Sexual Realities." In *Marriage and Alternatives*, R.W. Libby and R.N. Whitehurst, editors. Glenview, Ill.: Scott, Foresman, 1977.

WHITESIDE, M.F. "Remarriage: A Family Developmental Process." *Journal of Marital and Family Therapy* 8:2 (April 1982):59–69.

WILE, D.B. "An Insight Approach to Marital Therapy." *Journal of Marital and Family Therapy* 5:4 (October 1979):43–52.

_____. "Is a Confrontational Tone Necessary in Conjoint Therapy?" *Journal of Marriage and Family Counseling* 4:3 (July 1978):11–19.

WISER, W.B. "Launching a Program of Premarital Counseling." *Pastoral Psychology* 10:99 (1959):14–17.

WOLBERG, L.R. *The Technique of Psychotherapy*. New York: Grune & Stratton, 1954.

WOODROOFE, K. *From Charity to Social Work*. London: Routledge & Kegan Paul, 1962.

WORLD HEALTH ORGANIZATION. *Manual of the International Statistical Classifications of Diseases, Injuries, and Causes of Death*. Ninth Revision (ICD-9). Geneva: World Health Organization, 1977.

WRIGHT, H.N. "The Church and Premarital Counseling: A Research Study and an Opinion." *Marriage and Family Resource Newsletter* 2 (1976): 10–11.

_____. *Premarital Counseling*. Chicago: Moody Press, 1977.

WYNNE, L.C.; RYCOFF, I.M.; DAY, J.; AND HIRSCH, S.I. "Pseudomutuality in the Family Relations of Schizophrenics." *Psychiatry* 21 (1958):205–220.

ZIMMERMAN, C. "The Future of the Family in America." *Journal of Marriage and the Family* 34 (1972):323–333.

ZUK, G.H. "Family Therapy: Clinical Hodgepodge or Clinical Science." *Journal of Marriage and Family Counseling* 2:4 (October 1976):299–303.

_____. "The Go-Between Process in Family Therapy." *Family Process* 5 (1966):163–178.

_____. *Process and Practice in Family Therapy*. Haverford, Pa.: Psychiatry and Behavior Science Books, 1975.

Author Index

277

Subject Index